Duoethnography in English Language Teaching

NEW PERSPECTIVES ON LANGUAGE AND EDUCATION
Founding Editor: Viv Edwards, *University of Reading, UK*

Series Editors: Phan Le Ha, *University of Hawaii at Manoa, USA* and Joel Windle, *Monash University, Australia.*

Two decades of research and development in language and literacy education have yielded a broad, multidisciplinary focus. Yet education systems face constant economic and technological change, with attendant issues of identity and power, community and culture. This series will feature critical and interpretive, disciplinary and multidisciplinary perspectives on teaching and learning, language and literacy in new times.

All books in this series are externally peer-reviewed.

Full details of all the books in this series and of all our other publications can be found on http://www.multilingual-matters.com, or by writing to Multilingual Matters, St Nicholas House, 31–34 High Street, Bristol BS1 2AW, UK.

NEW PERSPECTIVES ON LANGUAGE AND EDUCATION: 78

Duoethnography in English Language Teaching

Research, Reflection and Classroom Application

Edited by
Robert J. Lowe and Luke Lawrence

MULTILINGUAL MATTERS
Bristol • Blue Ridge Summit

DOI https://doi.org/10.21832/LOWE7185
Library of Congress Cataloging in Publication Data
A catalog record for this book is available from the Library of Congress.
Names: Lowe, Robert J., 1986- editor. | Lawrence, Luke, 1976- editor.
Title: Duoethnography in English Language Teaching: Research, Reflection and Classroom Application/Edited by Robert J. Lowe and Luke Lawrence.
Description: Bristol; Blue Ridge Summit: Multilingual Matters, [2020] | Includes bibliographical references and index. | Summary: "This book sets out duoethnography as a method of research, reflective practice and a pedagogical approach in English Language Teaching (ELT). The chapters are a range of duoethnographies from established and emerging researchers and teachers, which explore the interplay between cultural discourses and life histories with a focus on ELT in Japan"—Provided by publisher.
Identifiers: LCCN 2019037512 (print) | LCCN 2019037513 (ebook) | ISBN 9781788927185 (hardback) | ISBN 9781788927178 (paperback) | ISBN 9781788927192 (pdf) | ISBN 9781788927208 (epub) | ISBN 9781788927215 (kindle edition) Subjects: LCSH: English language—Study and teaching—Japan. | English language—Study and teaching—Foreign speakers. | Culturally relevant pedagogy. | English language—Study and teaching—Research—Methodology. | Narrative inquiry (Research method) | Qualitative research—Methodology. | Ethnology—Methodology.
Classification: LCC PE1068.J3 D86 2020 (print) | LCC PE1068.J3 (ebook) | DDC 428.0071/052—dc23 LC record available at https://lccn.loc.gov/2019037512 LC ebook record available at https://lccn.loc.gov/2019037513

British Library Cataloguing in Publication Data
A catalogue entry for this book is available from the British Library.

ISBN-13: 978-1-78892-718-5 (hbk)
ISBN-13: 978-1-78892-717-8 (pbk)

Multilingual Matters
UK: St Nicholas House, 31–34 High Street, Bristol BS1 2AW, UK.
USA: NBN, Blue Ridge Summit, PA, USA.

Website: www.multilingual-matters.com
Twitter: Multi_Ling_Mat
Facebook: https://www.facebook.com/multilingualmatters
Blog: www.channelviewpublications.wordpress.com

The policy of Multilingual Matters/Channel View Publications is to use papers that are natural, renewable and recyclable products, made from wood grown in sustainable forests. In the manufacturing process of our books, and to further support our policy, preference is given to printers that have FSC and PEFC Chain of Custody certification. The FSC and/or PEFC logos will appear on those books where full certification has been granted to the printer concerned.

Typeset by Nova Techset Private Limited, Bengaluru and Chennai, India.
Printed and bound in the UK by the CPI Books Group Ltd.
Printed and bound in the US by NBN.

Contents

Contributors

Peter Brereton has been teaching English since 2007 and has worked in a wide range of teaching contexts in Spain, Australia, the UK, Ireland, Latvia and France. Peter is currently an English for Liberal Arts instructor at International Christian University in Tokyo as well as a freelance teacher trainer, Delta local tutor and external assessor. He is most passionate about teacher training and development – particularly through reflective practice – as well as teacher creativity, decision making and feedback.

Charles Cook gained his CertTESOL qualification in 2016 and began teaching in Japan in 2017. His interests include learner motivation and the integration of popular culture into language learning. His primary motivation for contributing to this book was to stimulate his professional development at an early stage in his career.

Daniel Hooper has lived and taught in Japan for approximately 12 years and is currently a lecturer in the English Language Institute at Kanda University of International Studies. He worked in the eikaiwa industry for eight years and his varied experiences in that context have deeply influenced both his research interests and approach to pedagogy. In addition to issues related to eikaiwa, his research interests include critical issues in TESOL, learner autonomy and learner/teacher identity.

Chris Hunter has taught English and intercultural education in a wide variety of contexts in Japan and Hawaii since 2004. His research interests include language policy, language ideologies, globalization and language education, as well as the linkages between English language education and economic inequality. He is currently a PhD candidate at the University of Hawaii at Mānoa.

Nick Kasparek has taught English since 2005. He started his career as a US Peace Corps volunteer at a university in China, and since then he has taught primarily Japanese students through online writing courses, conversation classes, private lessons, and university courses. He has an MA in international studies and an MEd in TESOL, and he is currently a PhD student in curriculum studies and teacher education. His research interests include creativity, playfulness, and inclusiveness.

Luke Lawrence has been teaching English in Japan since 2002. He has taught in a wide variety of contexts including eikaiwa, business and university classes. His research interests revolve around teacher identity and social issues in ELT, especially ideas around native-speakerism. As well as teaching full time, he is also currently a PhD candidate at the University of Stirling in the UK.

Robert J. Lowe is a lecturer in the Department of English Communication, Tokyo Kasei University. He holds a PhD in Applied Linguistics and his research focuses on critical issues in ELT. In addition to journal and magazine articles he is the co-author of *Teaching English as a Lingua Franca: The Journey from EFL to ELF* (DELTA Publishing, 2018) and the upcoming monograph *Uncovering Ideology in English Language Teaching: Identifying the 'Native Speaker' Frame* (Springer).

Yuzuko Nagashima is an instructor at the Practical English Center at Yokohama City University. After receiving her MA in Second Language Studies from the University of Hawai'i at Manoa, she has taught ESL and EFL in the United States, Thailand and Japan. Her main research interests are centered on language and identity in relation to gender and sexuality, translanguaging and critical feminist pedagogy.

Momoko Oka teaches at Kanda Institute of Foreign Languages and AGOS Japan. Prior to that, she spent almost six years working in a major English conversation school in Tokyo. She holds a Trinity Certificate in TESOL and is currently working towards Trinity Diploma in TESOL. She has strong interests in native-speakerism and TOEFL and IELTS teaching.

Richard Pinner is an associate professor at Sophia University in Tokyo with over 15 years of experience as a language teacher and teacher trainer. He holds a PhD in ELT and Applied Linguistics and has published several articles on language teaching, most recently in *Language Teaching Research*, *English Today* and *Applied Linguistics Review*. He is the author of three research monographs and is particularly interested in the areas of authenticity and motivation in ELT and Content and Language Integrated Learning.

Matthew Schaefer has taught in France, Italy and Spain and worked as a Director of Studies in the UK and an academic program manager in Japan. His teaching contexts have included public high schools, private language schools and universities. His current research interests are program evaluation, assessment of speaking skills and reflective professional development. He holds a Delta and an MA in TESOL.

Ben Smart has been teaching English to Japanese people in various contexts, including eikaiwa and tertiary education in both England and Japan, since 2004. He has an academic background in linguistics and applied linguistics and has developed a variety of areas of interest for research from this, including using phonetics and phonology, discourse analysis and pragmatics in classroom research.

Matthew W. Turner's English language teaching career began in 2008. Since then, Matthew has taught in a variety of contexts in the UK and Japan, and currently works in a university international tourism faculty. His research interests include reflective practice, continuing professional development and support for learners with special educational needs. As well as teaching full time, Matthew is currently a PhD candidate at the University of Warwick. Matthew is cocreator of The TEFLology Podcast.

Ema Ushioda is a Professor and Director of the Centre for Applied Linguistics, University of Warwick. She has particular research interests in motivation and autonomy in language learning and in qualitative methods of inquiry. Recent books include *International Perspectives on Motivation: Language Learning and Professional Challenges* (Palgrave Macmillan, 2013), *Teaching and Researching Motivation* (co-authored by Dörnyei, Longman, 2011) and *Motivation, Language Identity and the L2 Self* (co-edited by Dörnyei, Multilingual Matters, 2009).

Aya Yamazawa has been teaching English since 2012 and worked in two eikaiwa schools for a total of six years. Now she holds a Trinity TESOL Certificate and is studying for the Trinity TESOL Diploma as she teaches English to international students in a business college in Tokyo. As a Japanese English teacher, her intention is to have a voice in the issue of native-speakerism through research in the Japanese EFL context.

Foreword

In this new book, Robert J. Lowe and Luke Lawrence (along with their co-authors) present, theoretically explore and study duoethnographies related to the cultural and discursive contexts of language. They also discuss the pedagogical implications of duoethnography for language development. In a number of culturally-rich duoethnographies, the authors explore the mutual interplay between cultural discourses and individual/collective life histories in relation to English language teaching in Japan. Similar to a photographer pulling an image from its comforting narrative, they dislodge (with wit and insight) their stories from their popular cultural moorings and surrounding historic discourses, examining, in the process, their own positionality within these cultural constructs. As they tell their own stories in pairs (and a trio) about being non-native English language teachers from Japan or about being native English language teachers from a foreign country, their words are about themselves, but their images are dialogic. Framing and then reframing their stories with those of their inquiry partner, these authors do something remarkable: as they inquire into ELT in Japan, they present a lived form of reflective practice.

Reading their text, I thought about the words of Edward Said. He once famously wrote about the relationship of narrative to colonialism. He said that colonisers who claim the right to narrate other people's stories (and most of them do) – also seek to narrate other people's lives in self-serving ways. Often framed by binaries (e.g. civilised/uncivilised), these stories about the Other echo and reinforce deep genealogies of problematic historical 'truths' and grand narratives. In this book, Lowe, Lawrence and their co-authors deconstruct these grand narratives and narrate their own lives and tell their own stories in a third space of cultural translation (Bhabha, 1990).

Such work is complex and challenging. As many qualitative researchers have experienced first-hand, it is often hard not to tell someone else's story for them. We not only face methodological pressures to tell these stories, but are also encouraged to do so by our own ingrained stances toward research and those we research. And, often raised within the regulatory discourses of colonialism, we are challenged to find an inquiry language not framed by our histories and steeped in the very discourses we seek to disrupt.

When Joe Norris and I began thinking about duoethnography not too many years ago, these were some of the issues we considered. At that time, feeling frustrated and then increasingly stymied by what we saw as the near impossibility of representing the lives and experiences of other people, Joe and I sought a methodology that let people tell their own stories together, building community and collective voice as it emphasized the value of dialogue and difference through inquiry. Going beyond autoethnography (and building on Bill Pinar's notion of *currere*), we sought a way for people to conduct relational inquiry in which difference was a heuristic, dialogue a generative force and stories of difference a lens for critical self-reconceptualization.

After beginning some initial studies and then (usually in cars or trains) discussing meaningful constructs within those studies, we decided that we wanted a fluid but identifiable approach. Eventually, we outlined a non-prescriptive methodology, consisting of a few tenets (which are reviewed beautifully in this book). Soon, we began working with a small group of like-minded theorists. We were all interested in the interplay between life history and critical, regulatory discourses. These colleagues (and friends) include Rick Breault, Francyne Huckaby, Darren Lund, Deidre Le Fevre, Molly Weinburgh, Morna McDermott, Patricia McClellan and Nancy Rankie Shelton. Shortly later other people contributed to our group, including Hillary Brown, Laura Formenti and Pauline Sameshima. Together, we began to explore conceptual boundaries of duoethnography related to equity, voice, subject matter/disciplines, solipsism, epistemology/ontology.

Lowe and Lawrence's text now adds new scholarship to these complex conversations. For me the individual chapters of their book come together to create 'a whole greater than the sum of its individual parts'. In the duoethnographies, for example, each of the authors critically examine how discourses of power, privilege and inequity course through language and our uses of it. Here are a couple of highlights from each chapter that contribute to the evolution of duoethnography as a methodology.

In the first study Daniel Hooper, Momoko Oka and Aya Yamazawa present a witty and critical trioethnography (replete with popular cultural references) in which they deconstruct discourses, both popular and more historic, surrounding views of eikaiwa (private English language schools) and native-speakerism. Demonstrating how stories beget stories, they surface and clarify narratives that run counter to conventional and more academic views of this topic. For example, problematising from her perspective the conventional view of native English-speaking teachers as having a more professional and authoritative stance than local English teachers [LETs], Yamazawa makes the following statement to Hooper:

> Yeah, actually I've always felt that foreigners were like mascots. [....] Recently, I saw an advertisement for a kids' eikaiwa school which said

'practice and rehearse' with LETs before 'the real thing'. For some Japanese people the NEST's presence itself gives students a reason to learn English and motivates them to keep attending lessons. I believe this is also connected to a desire for inclusion in an 'English-speaking imagined community' (Kubota, 2011: 474). NESTs are like the mascots in an exciting theme park filled with special performances and exotic culture and fundamentally removed from reality. Though this may sound quite inappropriate, I think it's the truth here in Japan at some level and this is one of the reasons why eikaiwa schools with only NESTs still sell here. [Chapter 2, p. 39]

Imaginatively, the first duoethnography in the book deconstructs the relationship between surface understandings and deeper epistemologies of knowledge surrounding language and language teaching in Japan.

In their duoethnography in this set, Yuzuko Nagashima and Chris Hunter analyse the layered intersections of personal identity and critical issues in ELT involving power, privilege, gender and sexuality. Exploring the embodied nature of speaking, teaching and writing with academic English in Japan, they isolate their text itself – the chapter they wrote – as a context of these discourses:

Although this political issue of academic writing may not directly affect the outcome of research projects, it is essential to bear in mind the pressure that exists to produce writing that achieves certain standards of English academic writing, which further reflect the hegemony of a certain form of English (Hartse & Kubota, 2014). With that in mind, we refer to this final draft as the 'native-ized version,' in spite of our critically-oriented concerns of representation, authenticity, and legitimacy as teachers, researchers, and authors. [Chapter 3, p. 67]

Lawrence and Lowe, in the first chapter of this book, underscore Nagashima and Hunter's words by referencing a statement from Hammersley and Atkinson (2007) that for some scholars a research report itself creates a reality as much as describes one. Perhaps to disrupt the convention of a 'conclusion' in academic writing, Nagashima and Hunter instead give a 'post-project reflection', highlighting contingent uncertainty in duoethnographies.

In the final duoethnography in the set, this one focused on reflective professional practice and the complexity of authentic identity in doctoral studies, Richard Pinner and Ema Ushioda examine the 'thin blue line' between the personal and professional – the fluidity of boundaries between doctoral supervisor and doctoral student. They describe this process with this compelling phrase: 'relationships which are dynamically constructed through the unfurling context' [Chapter 4, p. 76]. Echoing Bakhtin's (1981) notion of heteroglossia as a generative and multi-voiced text, they mention that theirs was primarily a textual and distance relationship, containing 'many different genres of writing (poetry, stories, formal and informal)' [Chapter 4, p. 81].

Three additional duoethnographies examined reflective practice as well as the use of duoethnography as a methodological context for that study. In their study on the improvement of teaching, Benjamin Smart and Charles Cook demonstrate how to approach a duoethnography with a particular stance towards openness and discovery – perhaps similar to what Maxine Greene described as 'wide awakeness' (1978). This is a step in trying to somehow transcend our patterned and closed ways of being in the world – to deconstruct the clichés with which we see ourselves and others. They selected their topic and their pairing intentionally in order to unpack the expert/novice binary: to turn it inside out, as if viewing it on an old photographic negative. Smart, the experienced and more intuitive teacher, sought to unpack his conditioned beliefs about the classroom through the openness and counter-intuitiveness of Cook, a new teacher; and Cook, still finding his voice as a teacher, sought to gain a dynamic and – through the diffracting process of the duoethnography – a layered craft knowledge from Smart. Their inquiry, set on a human scale, shows how a duoethnography may overlay the known with the unknown, opening new storylines.

In the second duoethnography in the book, Nick Kasparek and Matthew W. Turner explore their own life histories in relation to equitable curriculum for English language learners with special educational needs. This study is noteworthy for the human scale of Kasparek and Turner's writing and thinking as juxtaposed against the setting, that of students and educators framed by institutional language and structures. In their study they examine their own perceptions about how to support and validate students with special needs and special assets. Slowly, they unpack the rhetoric – and their lived relationship to that rhetoric – surrounding a technical medical model of education for students with special needs.

The final contribution was a duoethnography with an explicit 'meta' focus, in which Peter Brereton and Matthew Schaefer created a reflective space for the discussion and exploration of reflection in professional practice. Initially in the foreground were questions about how they worked in supervision with ESL instructors. They asked about how they followed and applied formal supervision models to their own practice. But then, entering a more engaged dialogic space, they turned the intuitive in their work to the counterintuitive as Peter asked Matt the following question:

> Are we more reflective about bad lessons than we are about good lessons? If you came out of a lesson thinking the lesson had gone really well and the students had responded well to everything, would the same level of reflection be evident if you came out of class dejected because the lesson hadn't gone so well? [...] I still feel it's the case now that I'll reflect more on the negatives; I don't know if there's necessarily as much reflection involved when you're happy with a lesson. [Chapter 7, p. 137]

This question is fertile ground for a duoethnography. As they contrasted their different approaches, they begin to disrupt the taken-for-granted in their practice (reinforced within seemingly successful lessons) or, as Matt put it, 'to stave off staleness'. For me, their inquiry became especially generative when they became transtemporal and begin to investigate their patterns of engaging in reflection in their early teaching days. It was with these transtemporal reflections that their use of language changed and transcended the textbook definitions and models of professional reflection. As they began their inquiry, perhaps, they first discussed the practice of others and explore the topic with a certain distance. But through their transtemporal and personal connections, their language centered back to themselves, destabilizing their thinking and putting it in a new light. Their awareness of their language within their duoethnography (in a study about language teaching) itself formed a counterpoint to their more academic analysis. Their inquiry shows how researchers can use language in dialogic and relational research to spark the imagination.

As someone with a degree in curriculum studies and theory, I was especially interested in the last section of Lowe and Lawrence's book. In the initial chapter of the last section they first provide a rationale and guide for using duoethnography projects as a form of project-based learning in language courses. Drawing from Sociocultural Theory, they show a parallel between the methodological framework in duoethnography and a curricular framework in the classroom. Describing the curricular framework, they are precise and clear with different learning approaches (e.g. students interviewing each other in the classroom, reflecting at home with prompts, writing their fictional dialogue). But what I especially appreciated is that – contrasting their approach to explicit or more didactic lecture-based teaching – they describe an emergent and lived curriculum. They discuss how creating a duoethnography and learning a language may be mutual scaffolds for students. I personally found this discussion one of the clearest – and, perhaps more importantly – most promising frameworks for a pedagogical use of duoethnography in the classroom that I have seen.

The last two chapters, written separately by Lawrence and Lowe, situate these pedagogical uses of duoethnography into theoretical frameworks in support of additional inquiry. Closely examining language related episodes among their students, they use their curricular spaces as a laboratory of practice (and theory).

This book is about uses of duoethnography for ELT in Japan, but it goes beyond that purpose. I would suggest that the book itself is a pedagogical text, asking the reader to put the different pieces of the book together in imaginative ways to start thinking about language and language teaching in a new key. It contributes greatly to the ongoing, complicated conversations around the evolution of duoethnography as a relational and developmental methodology.

Richard D. Sawyer

References

Bakhtin, M.M. (1981) *The Dialogic Imagination: Four Essays*. Austin: University of Texas Press.

Bhabha, H. (1990) The third space. In J. Rutherford (ed.) *Identity. Community, Culture, Difference* (pp. 207–221). London: Lawrence & Wishart.

Greene, M. (1978) *Landscapes of Learning*. New York: Teachers College Press.

Hammersley, M. and Atkinson, P. (2007) *Ethnography: Principles in Practice* (3rd edn). London: Routledge.

1 An Introduction to Duoethnography

Luke Lawrence and Robert J. Lowe

Luke: *I'm trying to think how the idea for this book came about.*

Rob: *I think it all began when we both found ourselves engaging in research projects which were in search of a method. My first forays into duoethnography came when a fellow teacher and I realised that an examination of the differences in our career trajectories could be valuable, but we had no idea of how to express that academically. Duoethnography seemed the natural way forward.*

Luke: *Yeah, I think that's a good way of putting it. I was just starting to plan a project with a colleague and I can't remember if I had seen the duoethnography you had published or not. Either way, I hadn't quite connected the two, or if I had I wasn't sure if it was something that I would be able to do, and secondly, I wasn't sure if it was something that would be publishable. After we chatted about it at a conference, talking to you gave me the confidence to turn the research I had done with a colleague into a full duoethnographic research paper (thank you!) and I think we both realised that there were probably a lot of people like us, in similar situations.*

Rob: *That led us to work on a research project together using the method, and during the discussions we had at that time, I think we gained a greater appreciation of the ways duoethnography might be useful for teachers and researchers in our field. We also began to experiment with the method in our classrooms.*

Luke: *And I think that made us realise the diverse potential of duoethnography, I mean, how it could be used in different ways. I remember thinking: 'why isn't everybody doing this?!'*

> Some may think that to affirm dialogue – the encounter of women and men in the world in order to transform the world – is naively and subjectively idealistic. There is nothing, however, more real and concrete than people in the world and with the world, than humans with other humans. (Freire, 1970: 102)

Introduction

We begin this book with a dialogue and a quote from Freire to make the point clear from the start that dialogue and conversation are at the heart of what this book, and the duoethnographic method, is about. Through dialogue with others we can gain deeper insights and understandings of ourselves and the world around us. When we engage in dialogue, we are not only communicating with our conversation partner, we are also communicating with ourselves and with the wider world. It is only through dialogue that we can come to understand who we are, what we do and why we do what we do.

Duoethnography is a qualitative research methodology in which two researchers utilise dialogue to juxtapose their individual life histories in order to come to new understandings of the world. Our main purpose with this book is to introduce duoethnography as a method of research, reflective practice and as a pedagogical approach in the field of English language teaching. In this chapter we will define what duoethnography is and give an introduction to the history of duoethnography and its theoretical underpinnings, as well as situating it within the historical development of qualitative enquiry. We then go on to give a descriptive guide as to how to conduct a duoethnographic research project and provide some examples of how duoethnography has been used in the fields of ELT and applied linguistics to date. Finally, we discuss some of the ways that the duoethnographic approach to research, reflection and pedagogy could be adapted or employed for future use in ELT.

Following this introductory chapter, the book goes on to explore each of these themes by providing a selection of duoethnographies from both established and emerging researchers and teachers. The chapters in Part 1 of the book focus on duoethnography as a research methodology in ELT and applied linguistics, exploring critical and personal issues among English language teachers. Part 2 of the book provides examples of reflective practice conducted through duoethnography. Each chapter demonstrates how duoethnography can benefit teachers in learning to understand themselves, their colleagues, or their context through the exploration of personal and jointly-constructed narratives. Finally, Part 3 of the book explores the ways in which duoethnography can be adapted for use as a pedagogical tool in English language learning and teaching which provides opportunities for practice of the four skills, for language development, and for experiences of positive group interaction.

Duoethnography is principally a method of research which, while gaining some traction in various areas of social science, has yet to make a substantial impact in the fields of ELT and applied linguistics. However, within applied linguistics, in recent years there has been a move towards more qualitative approaches to research, particularly sociocultural viewpoints and issues concerning identity (Lei & Liu, 2018), and this has involved experimental forays into subjective methods of enquiry, such as autoethnography (see Canagarajah, 2012, for example). Narrative inquiry has also been developed by a number of researchers, and forms a strong strand in the language teaching and learning literature (Barkhuizen *et al.*, 2014). Against this backdrop, duoethnography with its innovative and inclusive approach to ethnographic enquiry and qualitative research, seems perfectly poised to assume a place in the current landscape of ELT and applied linguistics research. Over the previous two or three years, beginning with a paper by Lowe and Kiczkowiak (2016) a steady trickle of duoethnographies have begun to appear in the ELT literature (see Gagné *et al.*, 2018; Lawrence & Nagashima, 2019; Rose & Montakantiwong, 2018, for example). This book represents the first attempt to introduce this methodology to the field of ELT and to establish duoethnography as a credible and effective way to engage in qualitative research for novice teachers, teacher educators and experienced researchers alike.

Duoethnography is a relatively new method of research that has so far mainly focused on fields such as education, health and social science. While it can be classed as an 'emerging' rather than as an 'established' methodology, duoethnography's growing influence has recently been recognised through the publication of a special issue of the *International Review of Qualitative Research* in 2015, featuring a retrospective article from the method's progenitors (Sawyer & Norris, 2015), as well as a variety of studies demonstrating the diverse ways in which it is being used. However, because of its emergent status, some explanation may be required of what duoethnography is, where it came from, and how it is generally used by researchers. To this end, this chapter will focus on introducing duoethnography, situating it within broader trends in qualitative research and examining how it developed from previous approaches to research such as autoethnography and narrative enquiry. An explanation will also be given for how duoethnography has traditionally been conducted by scholars in the fields of social, health and educational research, before describing the tentative steps that have been taken by researchers working in applied linguistics and ELT.

As well as its more traditional use as a research approach, duoethnography has also been employed as a form of reflective practice for educators, taking advantage of its dialogic format to contrast views and perspectives in order to help teachers develop as critically engaged practitioners. This aspect of duoethnography will also be discussed in this chapter, again situated within the literature on teacher reflection, and with a specific focus on ELT. Finally, this chapter will briefly address the most recent use of duoethnography: as a form of project-based learning within the field of English language teaching.

The Emergence of Duoethnography

Duoethnography was initially conceived of as a method of qualitative research in which two researchers contrast and juxtapose their life histories in order to provide multiple understandings of a topic or a phenomenon. The method was first conceptualised by Norris and Sawyer (2004), and has since developed in a number of directions, both theoretical and methodological. Our aim here is to situate duoethnography within its historical context, both in terms of social theory and approaches to qualitative research.

Theoretical background

Qualitative approaches to research are well established in social science and related areas such as education and healthcare. In particular, ethnography formed a basis of much early work in anthropology and other fields which sought to understand the functions and behaviours of societies and social groups. Early ethnographic work, as with other approaches to social scientific research from the late 19th century to the first half of the 20th century was strongly influenced by the natural sciences, and was focused on efforts to establish a 'science of society' (Halsey, 2004). As a result of this influence, much sociological research was carried out using quantitative approaches such as surveys, and a great deal of effort was expended in attempting to make precise and robust measurements of phenomena and populations in society. Qualitative researchers, including ethnographers, followed this natural science model by advocating a 'naturalistic' approach based more on observational branches of the natural sciences such as biology (Hammersley & Atkinson, 2007). Understanding that the subjectivity and the influence of the researcher is perhaps more problematic in the social than natural sciences, over time qualitative researchers developed procedures which could be used to make their data more reliable and minimise their subjective biases. One influential procedure of this type was grounded theory, an approach to data analysis developed by Glaser and Strauss (1967) in which, through a rigorous and comprehensive process of coding, confidence in the conclusion of the researcher's analysis may be increased and justified. Another longstanding procedure developed with this goal in mind is bracketing, in which researchers seek to acknowledge and set aside their assumptions and suppositions in order to analyse their data with a more objective eye. While these researchers conceded that it was not possible for their research to reflect reality with complete accuracy and objectivity, they did nevertheless assume that there was an objective social reality that was discoverable, observable and describable with some degree of confidence. This theoretical orientation is generally known as postpositivism, as it assumes some of the ontological principles associated with positivist research, but without the belief that true objective certainty in investigation or description was possible.

While postpositivism is still a popular research paradigm in qualitative inquiry in general, its realist assumptions (that is, assumptions based on the belief that social science can get close to describing an objective existent reality, if not to describe it entirely) have been strongly questioned. This is true both in general sociology (in which the influence of critical sociology led to what Halsey (2004: 119) describes as 'the onslaught of anti-positivism'), and in the specific case of ethnography. Influenced by poststructuralist and postmodernist critiques of social research, ethnographers have been compelled to consider foundational questions about the ways in which they conduct their research. One example of this is the nature of ethnographic writing and the objectivity of research reports. Whereas such writing was intended to be objectively descriptive, researchers influenced by Derrida's concept of deconstruction (see Stocker, 2006) have argued that the research report is itself a construct which serves, through various rhetorical strategies, to create a reality as much as it is a means of describing one (Hammersley & Atkinson, 2007). Likewise, the influence of the philosopher Michel Foucault's work has led researchers to evaluate ethnographic accounts as one element through which 'regimes of truth' are constructed, and how therefore power, and power relations, in society are upheld (see Gutting, 2001 for a more thorough discussion).

Another criticism levelled at the nature of ethnographic writing has been the tendency for ethnographers to adopt the present tense in their writings. This 'ethnographic present' implies a timeless, unchanging, state without past or future, within which all there is to know about a given group or society has been captured by the researcher (Davies, 2008). In addition, Fabian (1983) argues that when combined with the third person voice of the researcher this serves to address the analysis directly to other researchers only, marking the objects of the research as Other, excluded from the discussion.

While these attacks on realism have been influential, they have not led to an abandonment of this perspective. Indeed, influential qualitative theorists such as Hammersley (1995) have gone to great lengths to defend realist epistemologies in their writing, and there are convincing reasons for doing so. Despite this, ethnographers and other researchers influenced by this anti-realist strand of thought have sought to develop approaches to research which challenge the objectivity of written research accounts, which question established societal regimes of truth, and which consider one aim of research to be the promotion of social justice and the elevation of marginalised voices. Some of these approaches to research include critical ethnography, narrative enquiry, life histories and autoethnography. It is these approaches to qualitative research on which duoethnography is built.

Life histories and autoethnography

As positivism gave way to postpositivism and there was less pressure to produce empirical generalisations in data, life histories and autoethnographies began to emerge in ethnographic studies.

Life histories (or biographies) have been used for many years to capture the lives of one or a small number of people within an identified population under study. Through unstructured interviewing, life histories allow for a greater depth of reflection on the part of the participants and a richer data set for the researcher. However, it should be noted that the purpose of life histories is not simply to collect individual stories, 'but in order to improve understanding and knowledge of social and cultural processes more generally' (Davies, 2008: 207). The idea (and justification) behind this was that in contrast to empirical generalisabilities, the social and cultural processes identified by the individual story can also be relevant in other contexts, and therefore have value in terms of research.

In relation to the future impact that it would have on the development of duoethnography the biggest theoretical contribution that the emergence of life histories had was the logical outcome of this lower priority on generalisations and representativeness. As Davies (2008: 207) states: 'It can be argued that the more effective use of life histories is not to make generalizations but to challenge them … or to provide material about the processes behind established generalizations'.

Related to this, the increasing recognition of the ways in which ethnographic accounts are influenced by the beliefs and subjectivity of the researchers led to a reevaluation of the possibility of objective ethnographic accounts. This can be reflected in the work of writers such as Goldschmidt (1977), who argued that all ethnography is 'self-ethnography', because it 'reveals personal investments, interpretations and analysis' (Adams *et al.*, 2015: 16). The term 'auto-ethnography' also began to emerge at around this time, in reference to ethnographies written by members of the community under study. However, as Adams *et al.* (2015: 16) note, in this early work 'the move to include personal experience is implied, rather than explicitly stated', and as such cannot be said to be true autoethnography in the modern sense.

Autoethnography as a genre began to be developed by scholars in the social sciences during the 1980s, particularly in the fields of sociology, communication and gender studies. At this time, researchers in these fields began to abandon the dominant commitment to objectivity, instead recognising that the inclusion of their own subjective experience as a researcher would in fact add more validity to their reports, rather than less. By removing the pretense of objectivity, these researchers were able to acknowledge and critically reflect on the ways in which their accounts were influenced by their positioning as researchers and as members of society.

Autoethnographies are research accounts featuring 'stories of/about the self told through the lens of culture' (Adams *et al.,* 2015: 1). Autoethnographers use the personal experiences of the researcher as a viewpoint through which they can explore cultural practices and beliefs, critically reflecting on their own subjective understanding of the practice, rather than pretending to produce an objective account. There is no fixed method for doing autoethnography; rather, it can be more accurately viewed as a set of principles. These principles include acknowledging the positionality of the researcher, and the relationship of the researcher to the subject(s) under investigation. Following these principles may lead to small changes, such as acknowledging these relationships, to more radical approaches such as engaging in collaborative research projects with the subject, or even to focusing on the self as subject entirely. Written accounts of autoethnographies can range from rather traditional reports through to semi-fictionalised, novelistic accounts. What all of these have in common however is the focus on personal experience, critical reflexivity and subjective interpretation both in how the research is conducted and in the production of written accounts. This can be broadly seen as a post-modern approach to social research, as it rejects the possibility of uncovering objective truth in matters of social life and embraces subjectivity as an inevitable component of this kind of research.

Narrative inquiry and positioning theory

Narrative theory in general starts from the position that 'self and society are storied productions' (Denzin, 2000: xi) and it is within these narrative (re)tellings that identities are constructed. Narrative research incorporates sociolinguistics, psychology and anthropology, adopts a constructionist concept of narrative as constitutive of reality, and attempts to make links between personal stories and wider societal narratives (Benwell & Stokoe, 2006). In narrative inquiry, the task of the researcher is to analyse the underlying reasonings behind the aspects of self that the narrator chooses to reveal and the performance they present to the listener, which is then placed within wider narratives of culture and society.

Narrative theory is often combined with positioning theory (Davies & Harré, 1990), in which 'poststructuralism shades into narratology' (Davies & Harré, 1990: 46). Positioning theory rejects static notions of fixed, pre-existing roles located in a space/time grid and replaces them with the alternative ontological referential grid of persons/conversations (van Langenhove & Harré, 1999). This places conversations, as discursive practice, as the basic substance that makes up the social world and posits that it 'is within conversations that the social world is created' (van Langenhove & Harre, 1999: 15). In this conceptual framework speakers in a conversation can 'position' themselves (and others) to comply with or resist dominant narratives of identity and selfhood in order to retain their individual agency (Benwell & Stokoe, 2006). As with general narrative theory, in final analyses, positioning theory focuses on the link between individual identity positioning and the wider social context – micro and macro – with the view that discursively constructed identity positioning can effectively counter master narratives (Bamberg, 2004).

The collaborative turn

This allowance of personal experience in forming part of the research process has led to new avenues for researchers to explore, particularly in terms of art-based approaches, and working with other researchers. Gershon (2009) has called this 'the collaborative turn' in qualitative research, and this can be seen reflected in the development of approaches such as collaborative autoethnography (Chang *et al.*, 2013), ethnodramatic playwriting (Conrad *et al.*, 2009) and duoethnography.

The first example of a duoethnography was published in 2004 by Joe Norris and Richard Sawyer, the two researchers who would go on to define and develop the method. Although not bearing the name duoethnography, this research paper contained many elements which would become significant features of the methodology, including a focus on personal experience, dialogue and a playscript-style presentation.

What is Duoethnography?

Duoethnography can be defined as 'a collaborative research methodology in which two or more researchers of difference juxtapose their life histories to provide multiple understandings of the world' (Norris & Sawyer, 2012: 9). The conceptual framework which underlies duoethnography is built on social justice, narrative and autoethnographic work, and curriculum theory (Sawyer & Norris, 2013). Adams *et al.* (2015) note that autoethnography was developed in tandem with the rise in identity politics, reflected in the belief that members of communities should be free to tell their own stories, rather than have their stories told by outsiders who may project their own beliefs and backgrounds onto the community in question. This preoccupation with social justice survives in duoethnography and is evident in its genesis. The first paper that can be described as a duoethnography, mentioned above, was a dialogic exploration by Norris and Sawyer (2004) of sexual orientation and experiences of schooling, using vignettes to highlight feelings of shame or fear that they experienced, with the goal of calling for social justice in schools. Duoethnography can perhaps best be understood by examining some of the underlying tenets on which it is based. We discuss below five key tenets of duoethnography, though others have been suggested (see Sawyer & Norris, 2013: 23–34).

A focus on *currere*

Currere is a concept developed by William Pinar (1974), which focuses on the ways in which each person's current skills, abilities and beliefs are a result of a life history which has served as a form of 'curriculum' during their development. Originally conceived of in regards to education, *currere* is a framework for autobiographical reflection which has four steps, described by Beierling *et al.* (2014), as regressive (with a focus on past experiences), progressive (with a focus on the future), analytical (with a focus on the present) and synthetical (with the aim of integrating the previous three stages). Through analysing their life histories in these four stages, educators are able to come to a self-understanding regarding their beliefs and their place in society.

While *currere* was initially conceptualised in terms of reworking curriculum studies, it has been adapted by researchers and writers to fit a range of contexts, one of which is duoethnography. By examining life histories, duoethnographers are able to understand how different events and experiences acted as a curriculum which influenced their current state. Within duoethnography, *currere* is interpreted as 'one's process of engagement within the contingent and temporal cultural webs of one's life' (Sawyer & Norris, 2013: 12), in order to make new meanings on the basis of previous experience. Duoethnographers explore how life history interacts with cultural constructs such as beauty, writing and sexual orientation to influence beliefs, understandings and identities in the present, with the goal of moving towards positive social change. For example, Norris and Sawyer's 2004 duoethnography highlighted negative experiences of school systems in relation to homosexuality and thus aimed to 'expose the curriculum of the past, in the hope it can positively change the curriculum of the future' (2004: 140). By exploring life histories in this way, duoethnographers can give voice to otherwise unheard stories, and thus demonstrate where, why, and how change needs to be made.

The self as research site

In a duoethnographic research project the self should not be seen as the topic of the research, but as 'research site in relation to lived cultural worlds' (Sawyer & Norris, 2013: 16). This distinction is key. The purpose of duoethnographic research is to explore social phenomena and examine commonly held beliefs about the social world. In order to achieve this, researchers construct and reconstruct their own narratives of experience as they relate to the topic being explored. In this way, the researchers use the self as the research site within which the topic under scrutiny can be interrogated.

The poststructuralist approach that duoethnography requires does not see the self-as-research-site as a fixed entity, rather it recognises the fluidity of identities and the discursive construction of identities in the process of dialogue and communication. In this sense, although broad categories such as gender, race, sexuality or class may be alluded to and used as the basis for inquiry in duoethnographic research, they should not be seen as unproblematic, essentialised markers of identity, but as contested constructions that are apt to change over time and according to context. They should also be seen with regard to hierarchies of power, not only between researchers, but also in relation to the institutional and social context to the lived experiences described in duoethnographic data.

Polyvocal and dialogic

In most multi-author research papers, the voices are blended together so that the individual voice of each researcher is unified into one nameless, faceless singularity. In duoethnography, reports are polyvocal with the individual voice of each researcher/author made explicit. The benefit of 'fracturing the notion of a solitary whole' (Sawyer & Norris, 2013: 76) is that the reader is privy to the differences and tensions that are the inevitable result when researchers of difference explore complex social phenomena. This is in line with Bourdieu's (1999: 3) statement that 'we must relinquish the single, central, dominant, in a word, quasi-divine, point of view that is all too easily adopted by observers … we must work instead with the multiple perspectives that correspond to the multiplicity of coexisting, and sometimes directly competing point of view'. In duoethnography this allows the reader to take the elements from each duoethnographer's story that they find the most relatable and relevant to their own beliefs and experiences.

The dialogic presentation of the data in a reconstructed 'playscript' format also marks out duoethnography as distinct from other research methodologies. Methods such as Conversation Analysis (CA) and Critical Discourse Analysis (CDA) use representations of dialogues as data sets in order to investigate the social order. However, the focus on '*naturally occurring* data' (Benwell & Stokoe, 2006: 58, italics in original) rather than interviews or observations mean that most conversations in CA research focus on the here and now, rather than on past experiences. In addition, a key feature of these methodologies are technical transcripts, which contain a complex system of signs and symbols. Although these are very useful for conveying the nuance and complexities of speech acts, they may present difficulties for the lay reader if they are unfamiliar with transcript conventions. The result of this is that there may be a tendency for CA and similar methodologies to stay within an academic bubble, which can be seen to have the detrimental effect of excluding the practitioners that may have the most potential to benefit from reading the research.

The reconstructed 'playscript' of duoethnography, free from the constraints of transcription conventions, avoids these potentially exclusionary and elitist practices and makes the data more accessible to a wider population of readers. Another advantage of using a reconstructed version of the original verbatim conversation is that it allows duoethnographers to present a large amount of diverse data in a linear fashion. As with traditional ethnography, duoethnographic data can be collected at a number of different times in different formats. For example, in a duoethnography by Lawrence and Nagashima (2019), conversations occurred mainly face to face, but also included e-mail exchanges, classroom observations and personal journals. The final data set, although mainly based on the face to face conversations, was a synthesis of all of the information gathered, but presented as a simple, readable, accessible conversation.

Requires trust

Due to the fact that duoethnographies often require researchers to dig deep into their personal histories and reveal often long-forgotten, or hitherto unrecognised experiences, feelings and emotions, it is essential that research partners trust and respect each other. As Bourdieu states: 'A research presentation ... is a discourse in which you *expose yourself*, you take risks ... The more you expose yourself, the greater your chances of benefiting from the discussion' (Bourdieu & Wacquant, 1992: 219, *italics in original*). This vulnerability is central to collaborative research such as duoethnography. As Chang *et al.* (2013: 30) note, the 'quality of the data deteriorates if participants are not willing to be honest with each other', for two main reasons: firstly, participants may hold back from sharing their true thoughts and experiences if they do not feel open with their research partner, and secondly participants who do not have a sufficient level of trust may be reluctant to challenge or question each other, again leading to incomplete data with only a surface level of interpretation. However, these challenges may be overcome by the fact that duoethnographers tend to share research interests with each other, and those drawn to duoethnography may be people who are more willing to be open and vulnerable in the first place.

Disrupts metanarratives

As mentioned earlier, autoethnography and related methods of research can be considered postmodern in nature, and this is reflected in one of the key tenets of duoethnography; disrupting metanarratives. Metanarratives can be defined as 'a global or totalizing cultural narrative schema which orders and explains knowledge and experience' (Stephens & McCallum, 1998: 6). Although many definitions of postmodernism exist, Lyotard's (1984) notion that postmodern research requires 'skepticism towards grand narratives' at the cultural level is instructive for work on duoethnography. Through dialogic enquiry, duoethnographers can consider alternative ways of thinking that escape dominant rhetorical framing, and thus this form of research can lead to the 'insurrection of subjugated knowledge' (Foucault, 1980: 81), which may take the form of 'local and subcultural discourses' (Sawyer & Norris, 2013: 42). By focusing on individual experience, duoethnographers may provide idiosyncratic counternarratives which disrupt dominant discourses. The dialogic format of duoethnography is particularly suited to this disruption. While autoethnography provides contextualised accounts which do not claim universality, they nevertheless only present one side of the story. Duoethnographies, by including two or more voices in the text, provide multiple perspectives on an issue and thus act more effectively to question cultural grand narratives. It is here that the notion of 'difference' between the participants becomes important, as this difference helps to dispel the notion that there can be only one framing of an issue.

How Do We Do Duoethnography?

With an understanding of what duoethnography is in place, it is time to discuss how duoethnography can be carried out by researchers. As with other forms of research there are several basic steps; data collection, interpretation of data and production of a research report. However, the ways in which these steps are carried out vary from other forms of research in some key areas.

Data collection

As duoethnography is based on dialogue, it is unsurprising that dialogue itself forms part of the data collection method. Duoethnographers typically gather their primary data through dialogue, both with their research partner, and also with various texts such as artifacts which feature in their discussion, and the emerging account of the discussion itself. This dialogue is itself inspired by research questions, as is usual in all types of research. However, the highly reflexive nature of duoethnography means that initial research questions may change over the course of the project, as new meanings arise and new avenues of dialogue open themselves up on the basis of dialogue (see Nagashima & Hunter, this volume for an example of this). As is to be expected with a data collection method focused on life history and autobiography, storytelling forms a large part of duoethnographic data collection, drawing on personal experience and the ways these experiences interact with cultural constructs in order to form present beliefs and understandings. These stories are 'shared around specific themes that provide dialogic framing' (Sawyer & Norris, 2013: 43) and thus new insights are generated through the ongoing dialogue between co-researchers.

In practical terms, the dialogue between researchers can take place either face-to-face, or at a distance. These discussions should be recorded in some way for later reference. Duoethnographers may also choose to include other forms of data such as documentary artifacts. These may include photographs, school report cards and other elements of the life history under discussion. The purpose of including these artefacts is often for illustrative purposes, or to promote further discussion and remembrance. However, some recent work (see Lowe & Lawrence, 2018b) has suggested that documentary evidence could be used as a more active element of duoethnographic work for the purposes of triangulation and validation of memory, taking a more critical realist approach to the research (see Epilogue).

Analysis

Analysis within duoethnography takes the form of discussion. Discussion allows researchers to question each other, to explore issues raised in more depth, and to collaboratively construct narratives and counter-narratives through and between their personal stories. Through discussion, and further dialogue based on that discussion, duoethnographers can identify emerging themes in their interaction, which leads them to focus and refine their data into clear narratives.

Data analysis within duoethnographic writing often overlaps with data collection. The process of data collection focuses more on storytelling, while the analysis focuses on discussion, however these two processes are inseparable. Inasmuch as duoethnography is a collaborative form of meaning-making, the element of restorying that arises from interaction means that storytelling and discussion cannot be neatly disentangled. Duoethnography must therefore be seen as a process whereby researchers engage in storytelling and dialogue, and through their ongoing discussion are able to bring themes to the fore, with personal narratives exemplifying these themes and with individual researchers' personal narratives in a productively tense relationship with one another.

Writing

Duoethnography is most commonly written in a way which directly reflects its dialogic nature, and also the theatrical influences of its creators; as a playscript. After a general introduction to the subject matter, duoethnographies are generally organised into sections, each of which addresses themes which were uncovered through the process of analysis. In the majority of cases, each themed section begins with a short introduction contextualising the theme, which is then followed by a fictionalised dialogue making use of the data collected in earlier stages of the process. The advantage of presenting data in this way is that it allows for greater audience accessibility (as mentioned earlier), and also provides a way for data to be drawn together into neat and readable forms, rather than through verbatim quotations. Each dialogue is generally followed by a concluding paragraph, and the research report itself ends with a standard academic conclusion.

It is important to note here that this is simply a description of how the majority of duoethnographies are written – a 'natural fact', rather than a prescription. There is in fact great variety in both the general and the specific aspects of duoethnographic writing. In terms of the specifics, some authors choose to provide traditional literature reviews at the beginning of the paper, while some opt to sprinkle references throughout the dialogues as needed. Some authors choose to write extremely naturalistic dialogues, while others prefer to present them in a more standard academic tone. In some cases, authors will provide full and verbatim sections of discussion from their data, while others may choose to present entirely fictionalised dialogues. On a grander scale, some duoethnographers may present their research reports as complete dialogues, with few aspects of traditional academic writing retained (see Norris & Greenlaw, 2012 for an example). Other duoethnographers, on the other hand, choose to take a more traditional or conservative style, presenting their papers in standard academic prose, with the data reproduced as the topic of discussion (see Rose & Montakantiwong, 2018; Pinner & Ushioda, this volume).

Duoethnography as Reflective Practice

Although duoethnography has primarily been used as a research method, it has also recently been adapted as a tool for reflective practice. Reflective practice (RP) as an educational discipline can be traced back to Dewey's (1933: 3) call for teachers to engage in 'reflective thinking: the kind of thinking that consists of turning a subject over in the mind and giving it serious and consecutive consideration'. The original model of RP put forward by Dewey focused on conscious, systematic thought, as opposed to routinised everyday thinking, which is often guided by external or institutional authority (Zeichner & Liston, 1996). As mentioned previously, one of the core tenets of duoethnography is to challenge grand narratives and to question received wisdom, which fits well with Dewey's original intentions. Dewey also outlined open-mindedness, whole-heartedness, and responsibility as essential character traits for carrying out RP, which are all values which are also key to the duoethnographic method. Open-mindedness entails a willingness to listen without prejudice and to engage with all sides of an issue, which the dialogic nature of duoethnography demands and ensures. Whole-heartedness is to thoroughly immerse yourself in the process of intellectual development and to 'throw yourself into' the task at hand. This immersion can be seen in the often revealing and intimate nature of duoethnographic data, in which the mutual trust instilled by personal narratives may allow research participants to give more of themselves than they perhaps would as a solo researcher. Responsibility in this context aligns with duoethnography's focus on social justice and refers to an ability to commit ourselves to the consequences of our beliefs. As Dewey puts it: 'Intellectual responsibility secures integrity' (Dewey, 1933: 32), which is very much in line with what duoethnographers are attempting to achieve.

Schön (1983, 1987) picked up from Dewey and introduced the idea of 'reflective practitioners' engaging in 'reflection-in-action' and 'reflection-on-action', which was later expanded to include 'reflection-for-action' by Killion and Todnem (1991). Reflection-in-action is reflecting in real time on an incident when there is still the opportunity to change the circumstances. In this way new approaches can be constructed in the moment to meet the needs of the unique situation that you are in. Reflection-on-action is done after the event and involves reflecting on how our past knowledge and experiences led to the incident being reflected on. Reflection-for-action attends to 'the desired outcome of both previous types of reflection' (Killion & Todnem, 1991: 15), that is it draws on previous and past actions and experiences in order to inform future actions. The inclusion of this third type of reflection helped to systematise RP and turn it into a more formalised research methodology (Mann & Walsh, 2017). It is these latter two types of reflection (reflection-on-action and reflection-for-action) that duoethnographic enquiry focuses on in order to provide an empirically-based, but deeply personal form of RP.

Duoethnography distinguishes itself from alternative reflective practice methodologies by the addition of a collaborator into the normally closed world of self-study. This allows duoethnographers to examine their practices in their own context, 'but through the eyes of one distant to it – to provide a new and destabilising lens' (Sawyer & Norris, 2016: 3). So far, the duoethnographic destabilising lens has been applied to studies on professionalism (Sebok & Woods, 2016), the power dynamics of the student/professor relationship (Schultz & Paisley, 2016; Pinner & Ushioda, this volume) as a tool for encouraging understanding of diversity and mental health in pre-service teachers (Brown & Barrett, 2017), and investigation of the links between teacher identity and professional trajectories (Lawrence & Nagashima, 2019).

Duoethnography in ELT: Research, Reflection and Classroom Application

The preceding sections served to situate duoethnography within traditions of qualitative research, explain the ways in which researchers can go about engaging in duoethnographies, and outlined the ways in which duoethnographies have been adapted for the purpose of engaging in reflective practice. In the final section of this chapter, we will turn our attention to the fields of applied linguistics and ELT, discussing some of the ways that duoethnography could be used for purposes of research and teacher reflection in these fields, before finally briefly outlining a new ELT-specific use of duoethnography as a form of project-based English language learning.

Duoethnography for ELT research

The first use of duoethnography in ELT that we would like to explore is as a research methodology, which is fitting as this is how duoethnography was first conceived of by its creators. As already mentioned earlier in this chapter, duoethnography may be used to research any number of issues, as long as such research will benefit from the dialogic interaction of two or more participants. However, it is a method which has social justice concerns at its core, reflecting its development from strands of research such as autoethnography. Within applied linguistics and ELT, the same is true; duoethnography may be used to explore any number of issues, but seems particularly well-placed to tackle those which concern social justice and questions of identity.

Research in ELT includes not only explorations related to language acquisition and pedagogy, but also into what can be broadly termed 'critical issues'; that is, those issues which sit at the intersection of language, power and ideology. There are several such areas that could be attended to within ELT. One example is gender, which has been addressed by an increasing number of scholars in recent years, with research focusing on issues such as the ways in which the identities of male and female teachers are constructed and constrained (see Appleby, 2014; Nagatomo, 2016). A second critical area in ELT is the strand of research into what has been called 'native-speakerism'; a term referring to the ideological belief that the Western 'native speaker' is the most desirable speaker and teacher of English, and that by extension the educational technology they are thought to embody is more suitable than local methods (see Holliday, 2005, 2006).

Duoethnography, with its focus on challenging grand narratives and promoting social justice, is uniquely placed to question these issues in ELT. Through the contrasting of experiences, duoethnographers may show that binary groupings (such as 'native speaker' and 'non-native speaker'), with their attendant supposed characteristics, do not ring true for individual teachers, and may therefore not ring true for others. Indeed, the first piece of duoethnographic work in ELT – or at least the first named as such – was an exploration of the ways in which two teachers experienced native-speakerism (Lowe & Kiczkowiak, 2016), finding that not only did the supposed fixed characteristics not fully apply to the authors, but that in some cases their experiences were directly at odds with general beliefs about 'native' and 'non-native' speakers in the profession. Questions of teacher identity have also been explored by Oda and Toh (2018), and Gagné *et al.* (2018), while Lowe and Lawrence (2018b) investigated the social reproduction of native-speakerism through ELT teacher training. Also, Gagné *et al.* (2015) and Corcoran *et al.* (2017) used trioethnographies to discuss the need for systems capable of responding to diverse identities of teachers and graduate students in educational settings.

There are, of course, many other critical issues in applied linguistics, such as social class (Block, 2014), linguistic imperialism (Phillipson, 1992), and the power dynamic between teachers and students. All of these issues are open to duoethnographic inquiry, and much could be learned from this form of dialogic engagement. Duoethnography is a research method which has great potential for investigating critical issues as well as promoting social justice through the deconstruction of limiting discourses and narratives. However, duoethnographic research need not be limited to critical issues, and could also be used to explore personal relationships which have a broad impact on the field. For example, Pinner and Ushioda (this volume) use duoethnography to explore how they managed their relationship as PhD student and supervisor (see also Schmidt & Gagné, 2014 for an exploration of collaborations between supervisor and former PhD student). Additionally, duoethnography has been used to contrast accounts of teaching success, with Rose and Montakantiwong (2018) using a duoethnographic approach to examine the authors' experiences of teaching using pedagogy influenced by theory surrounding English as an International Language. It appears, considering the diverse range of topics currently being explored using duoethnography in ELT, that the method has a great scope for application in ELT and applied linguistics research.

As mentioned above, one of the aims of using duoethnography for research purposes is to use the personal to disrupt metanarratives around a particular issue, thus contributing to wider theoretical and empirical insights in the field. However, as we will outline in the following section, when employed as a means of carrying out reflective practice, the intention is often to provide practical solutions to concrete, local issues. At first glance, the tension between these differing approaches to the use and purpose of duoethnography may appear distant. However, as we hope the chapters in this volume show, rather than acting as a divide between more theory-based research and practical professional development-oriented research, duoethnography can act as a bridge between the two.

By placing the individual lived experience at the heart of theoretical research, duoethnography allows the reader to become 'participants, not consumers' who 'do not apply findings so much as engage the study as a catalyst for their own understanding and reflexivity' (Sawyer & Norris, 2013: 46). In this way, wider theoretical insights generated by duoethnography can also be used as a form of reflexivity and personal development. At the same time, even when acting as a facilitator for reflective practice and professional development, by examining and critiquing the underlying structures at the heart of various issues, duoethnography can provide useful insights for the ELT field.

Duoethnography for reflective practice in ELT

In the field of ELT, Thomas Farrell (2015) has been credited with providing a comprehensive framework for teachers to become 'reflective practitioners'. By drawing on Dewey (1933) and Schön (1983), Farrell offers a five-stage framework of reflection: Philosophy, Principles, Theory of Practice, Practice and Beyond Practice (Farrell, 2015). The Philosophy and Principles stages ask teachers to examine their own background and beliefs and assess the influence that they have on their teaching practice. In the Theory of Practice stage teachers are asked to dig deeper into the often-unmarked theoretical beliefs that underpin their teaching approaches and to reflect on critical incidents that may highlight these theories. The Practice level of the framework focuses on using classroom observations and audio and video recordings to engage in action research to reflect on what actually happens inside our own classrooms. The final stage is Beyond Practice, which broadens the scope of isolated reflective practice to take account of wider society and culture. This can be done by critically reflecting with other teachers through dialogue or the formation of RP groups (Farrell, 2015).

Since Dewey's original conception and Schön's refinement, RP has become an extremely popular and established form of professional development and as Farrell (2015) notes has become virtually mandatory for both pre- and in-service teachers worldwide. However, as Mann and Walsh (2013, 2017) argue, in the field of TESOL and applied linguistics RP 'has achieved a status of orthodoxy without a corresponding evidence-led description of its value, processes and outcomes' (Mann & Walsh, 2013: 291). They also point out that the (inevitably positive) results of RP are often presented without showing the audience exactly how it was done, which means that the 'practice' of reflective practice remains opaque and abstract. In order to counter this, they propose that 'RP needs to be rebalanced, away from a reliance on written forms and taking more account of spoken, collaborative forms of reflection; in sum, we argue for a more dialogic, data-led and collaborative approach to reflective practice' (Mann & Walsh, 2013: 291).

Mann and Walsh list four criticisms of RP in the applied linguistics field in its current form: lack of data-led accounts, a focus on the individual, the dominance of written (as opposed to spoken) reflection, and the failure for RP to utilise the appropriate reflective tools to fit the context (Mann & Walsh, 2013). As the chapters in this book attest, the duoethnographic method used as a form of reflective practice goes some way towards mitigating against these criticisms. The ethnographic approach of duoethnography puts data, in whatever form this may be – recordings, transcripts, as well as 'cultural artifacts' such as photos, school reports, song lyrics, diaries etc. (Sawyer & Norris, 2013) at the centre of the reflexive process. Mann and Walsh's second and third criticisms are attended to directly by the fundamental basis of the duoethnographic method that defines a duoethnography as research involving 'two or more researchers of difference' (Norris *et al.*, 2012: 9). Similarly, their assertion that: 'Dialogue allows meanings to be co-constructed, new understandings to emerge and professional learning to develop' (Mann & Walsh, 2017: 189) reflects the view of duoethnography as being distinct from solo self-reflection in that it is a means 'for the generation of new insights and understandings' that emphasises 'difference of perspective about a topic to generate new perspectives about a topic… and in doing so attempt(s) to disrupt the metanarrative' (Brown & Sawyer, 2016: 5).

Both pre- and in-service teacher education are the most common sites for the use of RP in ELT. In the past this has often been a didactic, checklist exercise (Walsh & Mann, 2015) that served to ensure that teachers were not deviating from the prescribed methodology laid down by the institution or training body (Lowe & Lawrence, 2018b). For pre-service teachers, what is presented as reflective practice can often be an intimidating experience, with the pressure to conform to expectations taking precedence over genuine reflection and growth. Or, it is also the case that much of the time, novice teachers simply do not yet have the language available with which to self-evaluate and reflect. For trainers and educators, time pressures and institutional requirements produce 'contrived and ritualistic' (Mann & Walsh, 2017: 47) models of reflective practice that fail to take advantage of the knowledge and experience that trainers have accumulated.

In the case of in-service teachers, the approach to RP, either as INSET or one of the various models of Continuous Professional Development (CPD), is usually carried out on an ad hoc basis, with little systematic planning and a common failure to link theory with practice (Mann & Walsh, 2017) as well as being tangled up with uneven power dynamics. For teachers, this can lead to them coming away from an INSET or RP session with a feeling of not being listened to and not having their specific situation and needs attended to.

Again, duoethnography can provide an effective methodology to address these criticisms. The use of dialogue allows for a more collaborative, two-way form of reflection, which also recognises that one participant may be more knowledgeable and better able to offer advice. This dialogic angle avoids the potential for the one-way transmission of expertise from trainer to trainee that often makes up INSETs and reflective practice in teacher education. Instead, duoethnography engenders a Vygotskian (1978) sociocultural theory approach, with the trainer/educator providing scaffolding and support in order to aid the development of trainees. This produces a more egalitarian and effective reflective practice process in which individual teacher needs can be attended to, while at the same time offering an opportunity for new insights and ideas to be transmitted to the more experienced interlocutor. This can help to tackle complacency and ennui that may be prevalent amongst long-term teachers that have become set in their ways or feel that there is nothing new to learn (see Smart & Cook, this volume).

Also, in regard to novice teachers lacking the language of reflection, Sawyer and Norris (2016: 2) state that, 'part of the difficulty in acknowledging the complexity of practice may stem from the lack of an enquiry language to access the relationship between self and practice'. Duoethnography offers an intuitive and accessible enquiry language that novice and expert teachers alike can easily relate to. By using conversational dialogue as the primary method of enquiry, novice teachers, especially those without academic training, are able to instantly carry out a deep and intensive form of reflective practice. Although, as Mann and Walsh (2017) point out, there is often too much focus on producing a report or publishable material from RP, if practitioners, even novice ones, do want to do so, the playscript style of duoethnography provides an avenue to do so without the need for technical transcription knowledge. It is also less labour intensive than formal transcription, which may be an essential asset for many busy, working teachers that do not have the time or funding available to tenured professors and other members of the academic community.

Duoethnography in language learning

Finally, we turn to perhaps the most unorthodox use of duoethnography in ELT: as a form of project-based language learning. This idea had its genesis in a recent theoretical article which put forward the idea of adapting the duoethnographic research process into a student project (Lowe, 2018), and Part 3 of this book provides both an extended and developed account of this early theoretical work, as well as two reports of ongoing research studies which focused on the use of duoethnographic projects in the classroom. Lowe's 2018 article suggested that by engaging in the dialogic collection of data, and through the writing of a duoethnographic report, students would be able to take advantage of the linguistic benefits of peer interaction (Philp *et al.*, 2014) and collaborative writing (Storch, 2013), as well as developing positive group dynamics and practising the four skills of speaking, listening, reading and writing. These points will be addressed in Part 3 in detail, so we will not spend too much time covering them here. It is suffice to say that when adapted as a form of project-based learning, the duoethnographic research process has the potential to be an effective technique in ELT.

The Genesis of this Project

With a methodology such as duoethnography, which is focused on the lives and stories of individuals, we feel it is important to explain how this book came about, and how the editors and contributors came to be involved in using the method. As hinted at in the introductory dialogue of this chapter, the two editors of the book were initially searching for an academic frame in which to explore our personal experiences. In particular, we were both independently engaged in projects in which we sought to contrast our experiences with those of a partner whose experiences were very different from our own. An exploration of the literature led us to the concept of duoethnography, which was first used in a paper by Lowe and Kiczkowiak (2016). This paper sparked the interest of several researchers and colleagues with whom we had personal contact, and soon a small community of researchers and teachers began to develop, all of whom were interested in using duoethnography both for research purposes and as a tool of reflective practice. Further interest in the method was kindled through presentations at local conferences in Japan (Lowe, 2017; Lowe & Lawrence, 2017, 2018a) and this has led to a slim but growing output of both research papers (Hooper & Iijima, 2019; Lawrence & Nagashima, 2019; Lowe & Lawrence, 2018b; Nagashima & Lawrence, 2019), and presentations (Brereton & Kita, 2019; Lawrence & Nagashima, 2018; Nagashima & Lawrence, 2018a, 2018b).

We approached a number of researchers who had expressed an interest in the methodology to gauge their willingness and ability to contribute to the volume. In some instances, the individuals approached had a clear sense of the kind of duoethnographic study that they intended to carry out and had already chosen co-researchers. In others, individual researchers that had expressed an interest, but did not have a co-researcher, were introduced to other like-minded researchers by the editors. Once we had received proposals detailing the planned chapters, we classified them as research-based or reflective practice-based and sent out guidelines for the contributors. Due to the fact that duoethnography is an emerging research methodology, we provided all contributors with a short reading list of recommended titles and gave a brief overview of the method. The guidelines given to researchers wishing to contribute a research-based chapter (Part 1) were to keep to a traditional academic style and include: a literature review, research questions, data collection method, dialogues and analysis (data), conclusion and references, with the caveat that contributors were free to deviate from this in any way they wanted, as long as such deviation could be justified. For contributors to Part 2 we recommended that they adopt a more personal narrative style and that the chapters include: inspiration for the project, a literature review, data collection method, dialogues and analysis (data), conclusion and references. Again, we made it clear that these were suggestions only and that the contributors were free to interpret the duoethnographic method in whatever way they saw fit.

For many of those involved, duoethnography seems to have offered a personal, reflective and dialogic approach to research and development that engaged and motivated them, eventually leading to teachers also experimenting with using duoethnography in the classroom (Lowe, 2017, 2018). This book is an attempt to capture some of the energy generated by this community; to show the creative and original ways in which duoethnography can be used to both explore issues in the field, as well as help teachers to develop professionally and engage in new classroom practices. By necessity these pictures are incomplete, showcasing the experiences of only a handful of individuals. However, we believe that one of the chief strengths of the book is in highlighting the diverse potential of duoethnography, especially when it is used by a group of committed and creative practitioners.

Conclusion

As has been shown in this chapter, duoethnography is a method of research which has developed and been adapted for use in not only research, but also in reflective practice and, most recently, in language pedagogy. As a method of research, it allows us to challenge grand narratives by exploring the complexity of personal stories and experiences, in juxtaposition with those of other people. As a way of conducting reflective practice, it gives teachers the tools to deeply examine their own beliefs, practices and experiences in dialogue with another. Finally, as a form of project-based learning it gives students the space to experiment and develop both their spoken and written language, and to develop their interpersonal relationships with other members of the class. With this understanding in place, the rest of this book goes on to explore each of these themes by providing a selection of duoethnographies from both established and emerging researchers and teachers. The chapters in the Part 1 of the book focus on duoethnography as a research methodology in ELT and applied linguistics, exploring critical and personal issues among English language teachers. Part 2 of the book provides examples of reflective practice conducted through duoethnography, with each chapter demonstrating how duoethnography can benefit teachers in learning to understand themselves, their colleagues, or their context through the exploration of personal and jointly-constructed narratives. Finally, Part 3 of the book explores the ways in which duoethnography can be adapted for use as a pedagogical tool in English language learning and teaching. In order to retain the voice of the authors, the chosen spelling conventions of the individual contributors has been retained through the editing process. This has resulted in a mix of US and UK spelling conventions across chapters, with consistency maintained within individual chapters.

References

Adams, T.E., Holman Jones, S.L. and Ellis, C. (2015) *Autoethnography*. Oxford; New York: Oxford University Press.

Appleby, R. (2014) *Men and Masculinities in Global English Language Teaching.* New York, NY: Palgrave Macmillan.

Bamberg, M. (2004) Positioning with Davie Hogan: Stories, tellings and identities. In C. Daiute and C.G. Lightfoot (eds) *Narrative Analysis: Studying the Development of Individuals in Society.* London: Sage.

Barkhuizen, G.P., Benson, P. and Chik, A. (eds) (2014) *Narrative Inquiry in Language Teaching and Learning Research.* New York; London: Routledge, Taylor & Francis Group.

Beierling, S., Buitenhuis, E., Grant, K. and Hanson, A. (2014) 'Course' work: Pinar's Currere as an initiation into curriculum studies. *Canadian Journal for New Scholars in Education* 5 (2), 1–9.

Benwell, B. and Stokoe, E. (2006) *Discourse and Identity.* Edinburgh: Edinburgh University Press.

Block, D. (2014) *Social Class in Applied Linguistics.* London; New York: Routledge.

Bourdieu, P. (1999) *The Weight of the World: Social Suffering in Contemporary Society.* Stanford, California: Stanford University Press.

Bourdieu, P. and Wacquant, L.J.D. (1992) *An Invitation to Reflexive Sociology.* Chicago: University of Chicago Press.

Brereton, P. and Kita, S. (2019, May) A creative look at creativity: Discussion and duoethnography. Paper presented at excitELT 2019.

Brown, H. and Barrett, J. (2017) Duoethnography as a pedagogical tool that encourages deep reflection. In J. Norris and R.D. Sawyer (eds) *Theorizing Curriculum Studies, Teacher Education, and Research through Duoethnographic Pedagogy* (pp. 85–110). New York: Palgrave Macmillan US. https://doi.org/10.1057/978-1-137-51745-6_5

Brown, H. and Sawyer, R.D. (2016) Dialogic reflection: An exploration of its embodied, imaginative, and reflexive dynamic. In H. Brown, R.D. Sawyer and J. Norris (eds) *Forms of Practitioner Reflexivity: Critical, Conversational, and Arts-based Approaches.* New York: Palgrave Macmillan US.

Canagarajah, A.S. (2012) Teacher development in a global profession: An autoethnography. *TESOL Quarterly* 46 (2), 258–279. https://doi.org/10.1002/tesq.18

Chang, H., Ngunjiri, F.W. and Hernandez, K.-A.C. (2013) *Collaborative Autoethnography.* Walnut Creek, CA: Left Coast Press.

Conrad, D., McCaw, K. and Gusul, M. (2009) Ethnodramatic playwriting as collaborative work. In W.S. Gershon (ed.) *The Collaborative Turn: Working Together in Qualitative Research* (pp. 165–184). Rotterdam: Sense Publishers.

Corcoran, J., Gagné, A. and McIntosh, M. (2017) A conversation about 'editing' plurilingual scholars' thesis writing. *Canadian Journal for Studies in Discourse and Writing* 27, 114–138.

Davies, B. and Harré, R. (1990) Positioning: The discursive production of selves. *Journal for the Theory of Social Behaviour* 20 (1), 43–63.

Davies, C.A. (2008) *Reflexive Ethnography: A Guide to Researching Selves and Others* (2nd edn). Abingdon: Routledge.

Denzin, N.K. (2000) Foreword: Narrative's moment. In M. Andrews, S.D. Sclater, C. Squire and A. Treacher (eds) *Lines of Narrative: Psychosocial Perspectives* (pp. xi–xiii). Abingdon, Oxon: Routledge.

Dewey, J. (1933) *How we Think: A Restatement of the Relation of Reflective Thinking to the Educative Process.* Boston, MA: D. C. Heath.

Fabian, J. (1983) *Time and the Other: How Anthropology Makes its Object.* New York: Columbia University Press.

Farrell, T.S.C. (2015) *Promoting Teacher Reflection in Second Language Education: A Framework for TESOL Professionals* (1st edn). London: Routledge.

Foucault, M. (1980) *Power/Knowledge: Selected Interviews and Other Writings, 1972–1977.* (C. Gordon, ed.) (1st American Ed edition). New York: Vintage.

Freire, P. (1970) *Pedagogy of the Oppressed*. New York: Continuum Press.
Gagné, A., Chassels, C. and McIntosh, M. (2015) Plurilingual teachers and their experiences navigating the academy: Lessons and strategies for equity. *Australian Review of Applied Linguistics* 38 (3), 106–122.
Gagné, A., Herath, S. and Valencia, M. (2018) Exploring privilege and marginalization in ELT: A trioethnography of three diverse educators. In B. Yazan and N. Rudolph (eds) *Criticality, Teacher Identity, and (In)equity in English Language Teaching: Issues and Implications* (pp. 237–273). Cham, Switzerland: Springer.
Gershon, W.S. (2009) *The Collaborative Turn: Working Together in Qualitative Research*. Rotterdam: Sense Publishers.
Glaser, B.G. and Strauss, A.L. (1967) *The Discovery of Grounded Theory: Strategies for Qualitative Research*. New Brunswick: Aldine.
Goldschmidt, W. (1977) Anthropology and the coming crisis: An autoethnographic appraisal. *American Anthropologist* 79 (2), 293–308.
Gutting, G. (2001) *French Philosophy in the Twentieth Century*. Cambridge; New York: Cambridge University Press.
Halsey, A.H. (2004) *A History of Sociology in Britain: Science, Literature, and Society*. Oxford; New York: Oxford University Press.
Hammersley, M. (1995) *The Politics of Social Research*. London; Thousand Oaks, CA: Sage Publications.
Hammersley, M. and Atkinson, P. (2007) *Ethnography: Principles in Practice* (3rd edn). London; New York: Routledge.
Holliday, A. (2005) *The Struggle to Teach English as an International Language*. Oxford: Oxford University Press.
Holliday, A. (2006) Native-speakerism. *ELT Journal* 60 (4), 385–387. https://doi.org/10.1093/elt/ccl030
Hooper, D. and Iijima, A. (2019) Examining the 'invisible wall' of native-speakerism in Japanese ELT: A duoethnography of teacher experience. *Asian Journal of English Language Teaching* 28, 1–27.
Killion, J.P. and Todnem, G.R. (1991) A process for personal theory building. *Educational Leadership* 48 (6), 14–16.
Lawrence, L. and Nagashima, Y. (2018, June) Teacher journeys in context: Identity, intersectionality, and collaborative reflection. Paper presented at Teacher Journeys 2018.
Lawrence, L. and Nagashima, Y. (2019) The intersectionality of gender, sexuality, race and native-speakerness: Investigating ELT teacher identity through duoethnography. *Journal of Language, Identity & Education*.
Lei, L. and Liu, D. (2018) Research trends in applied linguistics from 2005 to 2016: A bibliometric analysis and its implications. *Applied Linguistics*. https://doi.org/10.1093/applin/amy003
Lowe, R.J. (2017, June) Duoethnography: From research method to pedagogical approach. Paper presented at the EFL Teacher Journeys Conference 2017.
Lowe, R.J. (2018) Duoethnographic projects in the language class. *Modern English Teacher* 27 (1), 74–77.
Lowe, R.J. and Kiczkowiak, M. (2016) Native-speakerism and the complexity of personal experience: A duoethnographic study. *Cogent Education* 3 (1), 1264171.
Lowe, R.J. and Lawrence, L. (2017, June) Research and reflection through duoethnography. Paper presented at exciteELT 2017.
Lowe, R.J. and Lawrence, L. (2018a, June) Duoethnographic research in applied linguistics and language teaching. Presented at The Fifth Annual Conference on Global Higher Education.
Lowe, R.J. and Lawrence, L. (2018b) Native-speakerism and 'hidden curricula' in ELT training: A duoethnography. *Journal of Language and Discrimination* 2 (2), 167–187.

Lyotard, J.-F. (1984) *The Postmodern Condition: A Report on Knowledge.* Minneapolis: University of Minnesota Press.

Mann, S. and Walsh, S. (2013) RP or 'RIP': A critical perspective on reflective practice. *Applied Linguistics Review* 3 (2), 291–315.

Mann, S. and Walsh, S. (2017) *Reflective Practice in English Language Teaching: Research-based Principles and Practices.* New York: Routledge.

Nagashima, Y. and Lawrence, L. (2018a, May) Reflective practice through duoethnography. Paper presented at JALT PanSig 2018.

Nagashima, Y. and Lawrence, L. (2018b, November) Intersectionality and language teacher identity. Paper presented at JALT 2018.

Nagashima, Y. and Lawrence, L. (2019) Reflective practice through duoethnography. *PanSIG Journal 2018*, 167–173.

Nagatomo, D. (2016) *Identity, Gender and Teaching English in Japan.* Bristol: Multilingual Matters.

Norris, J. and Greenlaw, J. (2012) Responding to our muses: A duoethnography on becoming writers. In J. Norris, R. Sawyer and D. E. Lund (eds) *Duoethnography: Dialogic Methods for Social, Health, and Educational Research.* (pp. 89–114). Walnut Creek, CA: Left Coast Press.

Norris, J. and Sawyer, R. (2004) Null and hidden curricula of sexual orientation: A dialogue on the Curreres of the absent presence and the present absence. In L. Coia, M. Birch, N. Brooks, E. Heilman, S. Mayer, A. Mountain, and P. Pritchard (eds) *Democratic Responses in An Era of Standardization* (pp. 139–159). Troy, NY: Educators' International Press.

Norris, J. and Sawyer, R. (2012) Toward a dialogic methodology. In J. Norris, R. Sawyer and D.E. Lund (eds) *Duoethnography: Dialogic Methods for Social, Health, and Educational Research* (pp. 9–40). Walnut Creek, CA: Left Coast Press.

Norris, J., Sawyer, R. and Lund, D.E. (2012) *Duoethnography: Dialogic Methods for Social, Health, and Educational Research.* Walnut Creek, CA: Left Coast Press.

Oda, M. and Toh, G. (2018) Significant encounters and consequential eventualities: A joint narrative of collegiality marked by struggles against reductionism, essentialism and exclusion in ELT. In B. Yazan and N. Rudolph (eds) *Criticality, Teacher Identity, and (In)equity in English Language Teaching* (Vol. 35, pp. 219–236). Cham: Springer International Publishing. https://doi.org/10.1007/978-3-319-72920-6_12

Phillipson, R. (1992) *Linguistic Imperialism.* Oxford: Oxford University Press.

Philp, J., Adams, R.J. and Iwashita, N. (2014) *Peer Interaction and Second Language Learning.* New York, NY: Routledge.

Pinar, W. (1974) Currere: Toward reconceptualization. In J. Jelinek (ed.) *Basic Problems in Modern Education* (pp. 147–171). Tempe, AZ: Arizona State University.

Rose, H. and Montakantiwong, A. (2018) A tale of two teachers: A duoethnography of the realistic and idealistic successes and failures of teaching English as an international language. *RELC Journal* 49 (1), 88–101. https://doi.org/10.1177/0033688217746206

Sawyer, R.D. and Norris, J. (2013) *Duoethnography.* New York: Oxford University Press.

Sawyer, R.D. and Norris, J. (2015) Duoethnography: A retrospective 10 years after. *International Review of Qualitative Research* 8 (1), 1–4. DOI: 10.1525/irqr.2015.8.1.1

Sawyer, R.D. and Norris, J. (2016) Dialogic interdisciplinary self-study through the practice of duoethnography. In R.D. Sawyer and J. Norris (eds) *Interdisciplinary Reflective Practice through Duoethnography* (pp. 1–13). New York: Palgrave Macmillan US. https://doi.org/10.1057/978-1-137-51739-5_1

Schön, D.A. (1983) *The Reflective Practitioner: How Professionals Think in Action.* New York: Basic Books.

Schön, D.A. (1987) *Educating the Reflective Practitioner: Toward a New Design for Teaching and Learning in the Professions* (1st edn). San Francisco, CA: Jossey-Bass.

Schultz, C.S. and Paisley, K. (2016) Social and institutional power structures meet duoethnography: The pedagogy of negotiating roles, dismantling Santa, and 'tilting' bitch. In R.D. Sawyer and J. Norris (eds) *Interdisciplinary Reflective Practice through Duoethnography* (pp. 141–161). New York: Palgrave Macmillan US. https://doi.org/10.1057/978-1-137-51739-5_7

Sebok, S. and Woods, J. (2016) Using duoethnography to cultivate an understanding of professionalism: Developing insights into theory, practice, and self through interdisciplinary conversations. In R. Sawyer and J. Norris (eds) *Interdisciplinary Reflective Practice through Duoethnography: Examples for Educators* (pp. 165–182). London: Palgrave Macmillan.

Schmidt, C. and Gagné, A. (2014) Diversity and equity in an educational research partnership: A duoethnographic inquiry. *International Journal of Education for Diversities* 3, 1–19.

Stephens, J. and McCallum, R. (1998) *Retelling Stories, Framing Culture: Traditional story and Metanarratives in Children's Literature.* New York and London: Garland Publishing.

Stocker, B. (2006) *Routledge Philosophy Guidebook to Derrida on Deconstruction.* London; New York: Routledge.

Storch, N. (2013) *Collaborative Writing in L2 Classrooms.* Bristol: Multilingual Matters.

van Langenhove, L. and Harré, R. (1999) Introducing positioning theory. In R. Harré and L. van Langenhove (eds) *Positioning Theory: Moral Contexts of Intentional Action* (pp. 14–31). Oxford: Blackwell.

Vygotsky, L.S. (1978) *Mind in Society: The Development of Higher Psychological Processes* (Nachdr.). Cambridge, MA: Harvard University Press.

Walsh, S. and Mann, S. (2015) Doing reflective practice: A data-led way forward. *ELT Journal* 69 (4), 351–362.

Zeichner, K.M. and Liston, D.P. (1996) *Reflective Teaching: An Introduction.* Mahwah, NJ: L. Erlbaum Associates.

Part 1

Duoethnography for ELT Research

Part 1: Duoethnography for ELT Research

In the first part of this book, we will explore the use of duoethnography in ELT research. As mentioned in Chapter 1, duoethnography may be used in numerous areas of ELT research, particularly in critical work focused on social justice and questions of identity. However, it may be used to examine other questions too, such as relationships between colleagues, and teacher and student classroom experiences and perceptions. The following chapters aim to provide a balance and variety of approaches to duoethnographic research, both in terms of form (how the duoethnographies are presented) and content (the focus of the research); ranging from critically focused projects written in a dialogic format, to more traditionally-presented reports focused on personal relationships.

In Chapter 2, Daniel Hooper, Momoko Oka and Aya Yamazawa explore the intersections and complexities of race, gender and speakerhood on their experiences within the Japanese conversation school, or *eikaiwa*, industry. The authors take advantage of the dialogic nature of duoethnography (or trioethnography in this case) to contrast their different experiences and perspectives on these schools, allowing for a highly complex and nuanced picture to emerge, which stands in contrast to popular descriptions of eikaiwa (and eikaiwa teachers) as some kind of monolith.

Chapter 3 focuses on critical issues in ELT, and the authors, Yuzuko Nagashima and Chris Hunter take advantage of the differences and contrasts in their personal and professional backgrounds to provide contrasting views and understandings of criticality. Starting with their own stories, the authors discuss how they came to a critical orientation in their teaching and in their lives, and how this is expressed in their particular teaching contexts. Expanding on this, the authors emphasise the importance of self-reflexivity among teachers who wish to engage in critical teaching in a sensitive and legitimate manner.

Finally, Chapter 4 moves in a slightly different direction as Richard Pinner and Ema Ushioda engage in duoethnographic reflection about their relationship as PhD supervisor and student. Using artefacts of their working relationship such as emails to spark their recollections, the authors provide an examination of the ways in which their relationship developed and changed over time and how the personal and professional aspects of their relationship intermingled and overlapped at different times. The chapter explores not only the PhD process, but also the changing nature of their relationship beyond this, including their work as co-authors on this chapter.

The chapters in this part of the book provide a varied look at the ways in which duoethnography can be used in ELT and applied linguistics research. As well as exploring a variety of topics, each chapter also takes a unique approach in how the project both was conducted and is presented. The chapters included here should give readers a sense of the diverse potential of duoethnography for conducting research in the field of English language teaching.

2 Not all *Eikaiwas* (or Instructors) are Created Equal: A Trioethnography of 'Native Speaker' and 'Non-native Speaker' Perspectives on English Conversation Schools in Japan

Daniel Hooper, Momoko Oka and Aya Yamazawa

Introduction – *Eikaiwa* within Japanese ELT

Eikaiwa schools are private English conversation schools that can be found in almost every town and city across Japan (Bailey, 2007). People attend these schools to enhance their professional capital, to learn a language for travel, to prepare for standardized tests or simply as a sociable pastime. At their peak in the mid-2000s, approximately 9 million Japanese people were attending eikaiwa classes (METI, 2005) and although in recent years that figure has significantly decreased, the industry still employs around 10,000 full-time and part-time teachers (Nagatomo, 2016).

However, despite their ubiquitous position in Japanese society, this presence has not been represented in academia (Lowe, 2015; Nagatomo, 2013). There continues to be a paucity of scholarly research into eikaiwa schools, perhaps due to issues such as schools restricting access to researchers (Kubota, 2011), a lack of teachers working in the sector willing or able to conduct research (Bueno & Caesar, 2003), and stigmatization in the field (Appleby, 2013). In this trioethnography, three former and current eikaiwa teachers (two Japanese and one British teacher) aim to offer a rare insider or *emic* perspective on the eikaiwa industry and how native-speakerism manifests itself in this context.

Review of Literature

Profit vs education

Tensions emerging from the simultaneous demands of business and education are a common theme in eikaiwa research. Bossaer (2003) conducted interviews with Japanese school managers and foreign teaching staff from five different eikaiwa schools and highlighted the disparity in the two groups' views on professionalism. Bossaer discovered that school managers felt that 'real teachers ... were hard to handle' and that foreign staff 'didn't understand Japanese business practices' (Bossaer, 2003: 3). On the other hand, foreign teachers viewed eikaiwa as a part of the service industry rather than an educational institution and stated that they were sent the message that friendliness was more important than pedagogy. Similar tensions were revealed in a study by Nuske (2014) where both Japanese and foreign participants spoke of their discontentment with the commercial pressure put on them by school managers. Staff pushed students to enter classes that did not match their proficiency level in order to meet financial quotas and were often forced to sell supplementary materials even though they felt that students would not benefit from them. One participant claimed that the management 'focused on increasing the amount of revenue they could get from a student instead of satisfying the student's needs as an English pupil' (Nuske, 2014: 116–7).

These accounts lend weight to comparisons drawn between eikaiwa schools and the fast food industry (Currie-Robson, 2015; McNeill, 2004; Seargeant, 2009). In a Japan Times article, McNeill (2004) uses the term 'McEnglish', highlighting parallels between George Ritzer's (2000) notion of McDonaldization and the characteristics of the eikaiwa industry. Factory-style working conditions, low wages, standardized lessons, high staff turnover and a 'convenient but low-nutrition product' (McNeill, 2004: 2) are cited as evidence for this comparison. Currie-Robson (2015: 25) echoes these claims while discussing lax hiring practices in eikaiwa, stating: 'Just as in fast food, where all customer service positions are entry level, all foreigners in eikaiwa have the same value'.

Most existing research tends to portray eikaiwa schools as 'sociocultural curiosities rather than educational institutions' (Makino, 2016: 4) that share consistent overarching traits. Makino (2016) attempted to dispel this image by calling for greater research on this sector of Japanese ELT while also setting out distinct categories of eikaiwa school. He argued that eikaiwa schools may differ significantly in hiring practices, standardization, teaching practices, target students, advertising and scheduling. Makino argues that recognizing the diversity in these factors needs to be considered in future research on eikaiwa teaching.

Eigo vs eikaiwa

Skepticism about the educational value of eikaiwa classes is also linked, in part, to a dichotomy of language learning approaches said to exist within English education in Japan. A number of researchers (Hiramoto, 2013; McVeigh, 2004; Nagatomo, 2016) claim English language learning in Japan includes two distinct categories: *eigo* – an academic discipline where grammatical comprehension is emphasized for the purpose of passing standardized tests and *eikaiwa* – English for communicative purposes that may be studied as an extracurricular skill or hobby. Furthermore, it has been claimed that these categories are tied to nationality or race with *eigo* described as 'Japan-oriented English' and *eikaiwa* dubbed 'non-Japan oriented English' (McVeigh, 2004: 215). These two discourses within English education are at times at odds with each other as can be seen in Nagatomo's (2016) book where one participant, an eikaiwa school owner, describes how a nearby Japanese chain school attacked her school's reputation. According to the participant, the Japanese chain school was utilizing prevalent beliefs related to the differences between eigo/eikaiwa by claiming that 'We (the other school) don't play' and that 'Gaijin (foreigners) don't know grammar' (Nagatomo, 2016: 151).

Race and speakerhood in eikaiwa

Also inseparable from issues of race and nationality is the arguably unavoidable issue of native-speakerism in eikaiwa. Discriminatory practices related to speakerhood are common in the industry with some schools offering higher salaries based on 'native speaker' status (Cater, 2017) and hiring practices being biased in favor of 'native speakers' – a title defined often by factors such as ethnic background (Caucasian), nationality, or physical appearance – regardless of qualifications or experience (Appleby, 2013). This corresponds closely with Holliday's (2006) original conception of the term 'native-speakerism' which claims the existence of a socially-constructed dichotomy where 'native speakers' are in a dominant position within the ELT industry over 'non-native speakers', consigned to a deficient status. Houghton and Rivers (2013) have more recently questioned Holliday's original conceptualization of the term by offering examples of ways in which 'native speakers' are also marginalized in certain contexts. Lowe and Kiczkowiak (2016) examine both perspectives on the issue and, through a duoethnographic approach, show that personal experience and individual context can problematize generalized 'truths' in this area. In this paper, we have chosen to use the terminology of NEST (Native English-Speaking Teacher) and LET (Local English Teacher) (Copland *et al.*, 2016) as the term LET does not restrict Japanese teachers to a position of deficiency in the same way that the label 'non-native speaker' might. However, despite using these terms for the purposes of this study, we also recognize that these distinctions within the field are ideological constructions rather than objective realities (Holliday, 2006) and should therefore be challenged wherever possible.

Escapism and 'akogare'

Profit, consumption and tensions stemming from race, sexuality and gender are shown to merge within the world of eikaiwa in a commonly cited study by Kubota (2011). Her research examines the enjoyment and informality attributed to eikaiwa schools and posits that attendance in eikaiwa schools represents a form of casual leisure – an 'intrinsically rewarding, relatively short-lived pleasurable core activity' (Stebbins, 2007: 38). Rather than a means of language learning, Kubota argued that enjoyment is often the primary motivation for attending eikaiwa classes and that this was reflected in her study by minimal use of the target language and a reluctance to study outside of class. She also claims that eikaiwa offers students opportunities for inclusion in an imagined community – 'a captivating space removed from learners' daily life filled with exotic sounds, words, culture and a person with different facial features and skin color' (Kubota, 2011: 486). In the eikaiwa industry, Caucasian NESTs, Kubota argues, are commodities marketed by schools and consumed by a sizeable customer base attracted by the exoticism and escapism their presence offers.

One key theme that appears in Kubota's 2011 study, as well as in other eikaiwa-based research, is the influence of *akogare*. *Akogare* is a Japanese word that describes a sense of desire or longing and is often used in eikaiwa research to refer to Japanese women's romantic desire towards Caucasian men (Appleby, 2014; Bailey, 2006, 2007; Kelsky, 2001; Takahashi, 2013). The idea of romantic *akogare* linked to eikaiwa is pervasive in Japan, with it being often used as an advertising strategy by schools where posters depict young, attractive Caucasian men alongside Japanese women (Bailey, 2006; Takahashi, 2013). According to Bailey, this practice 'valorizes and celebrates female erotic subjectivity and positions the white male as an object of consumption for sophisticated, cosmopolitan female consumers' (Bailey, 2006: 106). *Akogare* has also become a source of comedy among the foreign community in Japan through the stereotype of the 'Charisma Man' (Rodney & Garscadden, 2002) – the geeky white man who, when he arrives in Japan, transforms into an Adonis who is adored by Japanese women (Appleby, 2014; Bailey, 2007). More recently, the theme of eikaiwa-situated *akogare* has permeated into mainstream entertainment in the 2018 Japanese movie 'Oh Lucy!' The movie depicts a lonely, isolated female office worker whose life takes a series of dramatic turns when she begins taking eikaiwa classes with a young, handsome American teacher (Brooks, 2017).

However, while it has been claimed in a number of research studies (Appleby, 2014; Bailey, 2007; Takahashi, 2013) that *akogare* and a desire for an exotic imagined community may be common among eikaiwa students, Kubota (2011) is careful not to make broad claims about their motivations for attending these schools. She states that, despite the way in which these ideas are promoted in advertisements and mainstream culture, 'not every learner is affected by these discourses in the same way' (Kubota, 2011: 486) and that learners coming to eikaiwa may be motivated by a wide range of different individual aims.

Research Design

Participants

Aya is a Japanese English teacher who has worked in the eikaiwa industry for almost six years. During that time, she has worked in both the teaching and sales departments in two different eikaiwa schools. She holds a Trinity CertTESOL and is now teaching English to international students in a business college while studying towards a Trinity DipTESOL. Momoko is a Japanese English teacher who has previously lived in the UK working as a Japanese cookery teacher. Upon returning to Japan, she worked at a large chain eikaiwa for approximately five years before starting a new job at a specialist language school affiliated with a private university in March 2018. She has become interested in research in the areas of EAP and native-speakerism. Dan is an English teacher from the UK who moved to Japan in 2006 at the age of 22 and has remained there since. Although he currently teaches in university, until the spring of 2017, he worked for eight years in eikaiwa schools. He continues to research and write on the eikaiwa context and aims to draw attention to its role in ELT in Japan. Aya and Momoko had previously been co-workers for three years at a large chain eikaiwa where Momoko was still working at the time the study began. Dan had never met Aya or Momoko before this study but due to our shared passion for eikaiwa teaching and our interest in critical issues such as native-speakerism, we quickly became comfortable with each other and found ourselves highly invested in the topics we were discussing.

Data collection and analysis

The data for this study was gathered via audio recordings made during two face-to-face meetings all three of us arranged over a two-month period. During these meetings we discussed our individual experiences in eikaiwa schools and our points of view on a wide range of topics related to these experiences including native-speakerism, the relationship between business and education, and our own confidence as teachers. These topics arose from an initial Skype conversation between Momoko and Daniel where they discussed issues that they felt strongly about and that they felt would highlight their different positionalities within the study. Thorough notes were taken by Daniel as he listened to the original three and a half hours of recorded audio (which was listened to several times by all three of us separately) and these were supplemented by exchanging messages via Facebook where we continued to share ideas on the conversations. The notes and messages were compiled on a shared online document and allowed us to meet up and discuss our data together during face-to-face meetings we had in local restaurants and the school where Momoko worked. Based on this written data, we carried out thematic analysis together to identify what we thought were important emerging themes from our conversations. Based on this process we highlighted three areas of focus that we felt were central to our conversations: perception of eikaiwa as an institution, teacher role and confidence/respect as teachers. We then met on an additional two occasions to further discuss these three areas and any points of disagreement that we came across through our evolving analysis of the data. We then created another shared document that we used to construct semi-fictional dialogues based on our original data and subsequent joint analysis, incorporating the literature we had already looked at around the topics. Finally, we started each themed section with broad explanatory introductions and concluded each section with a joint analysis of the preceding dialogue.

Dialogues

Perception of eikaiwa as an institution

In the first section of our dialogue we attempt to address several prevalent assumptions about the nature of the eikaiwa industry that contribute to the common perception of it as purely profit-focused and the bottom rung of English language teaching in Japan (Nagatomo, 2016). Along with the widely held belief that eikaiwa schools are analogous to fast food restaurants due to accusations of standardization and an unskilled labor force (Currie-Robson, 2015; McNeill, 2004), we felt that these grand narratives obscured the diverse range of schools and educators that the 'eikaiwa' tag encompasses.

Dan: I don't think we can discuss eikaiwa without addressing whether or not business interests can really co-exist with an honest desire to provide quality education. From my experiences in eikaiwa schools, I didn't really feel the business concerns enhanced the quality of the instruction provided. Conversely, I found there were many times where the drive for profits negatively affected the quality of teaching. I feel this underlies why eikaiwa hiring practices are generally so flawed, with minimal educational requirements and usually no teaching experience necessary (Bossaer, 2003).

Teacher salaries are also usually rather low with few opportunities for professional development or mobility. All of these factors contribute to extremely high staff turnover and low-quality instruction.

Then, on a classroom level, I also experienced what I perceived as a push for short-term financial gain further lowering opportunities for effective language learning. The first of these was the attitude of the Japanese staff and management regarding class administration. I was often in a situation where Japanese staff would attempt to shoehorn in a student whose level was completely inappropriate for a class just to boost their average student/class ratio. Despite my protests that this would negatively affect the quality of the lesson for all students involved, I was told that I should relax more. The second major issue was scheduling. In a large chain eikaiwa, I was required to teach 8 classes per day with a 5–10-minute break between classes. Obviously, we weren't able to do any real preparation due to these time constraints and just pure exhaustion. This was where the in-house textbook came in. We were encouraged to simply follow a script that I believe was designed to allow anyone with a pulse to teach a class no matter how tired they were. Gradually all of these things eroded my belief that business and education could effectively co-exist in eikaiwa.

Momoko: I feel the same as you regarding the workload in eikaiwa. Even those 10-minute breaks are packed with level checks and mini tests with students and we can't really rest. But I am surprised that you didn't get any preparation time. There is enough at my school as the limit of teaching hours is 30 out of 40 working hours. Moreover, it is sad to hear that teachers at your school didn't have any say over student levels in the classroom. If that happened in my school, other teachers would check the student's level to make sure that was the case and then we teachers (both LETs and NESTs) would raise the issue to the counsellors asking if they could do something about it. Otherwise, other students in the class might be bothered by that one particular student and the teacher might have difficulties teaching a mixed-level class.

Aya: Yeah, one of the biggest chain eikaiwa schools I worked at with Momoko did actually have great original textbooks and manuals. Even on days where I had seven classes, I could still provide roughly the same quality of instruction just by following the script. The company was very proud of the system because no matter the teacher, what was taught in each classroom was basically the same. On the other hand, this is exactly what McEnglish (McNeill, 2004) is all about. Like you said, teachers are basically discouraged to be creative with the heavy workload and almost no break or preparation time between lessons. This repetition of teaching eventually killed me both in terms of fatigue and my motivation as a teacher.

Dan: Aya, that's interesting that you emphasize your motivation as a *teacher.* In my experiences, because most of the business-related demands came from Japanese staff members, there was definitely a sense among the foreign staff of 'us' and 'them' – we cared about teaching and they cared about making money. As I became more interested in improving the pedagogy where I worked and grew more hostile towards the industry, I'm sorry to say that I embraced the prevalent stereotype of the Japanese staff as 'company people' with little regard for students' language development.

Momoko: I see what you mean but my experience is quite different. It is true that my company has a profit-driven system as the head office decides the sales target every month and every staff member is aware that we need to constantly reach those targets. The pressure on the Japanese manager is especially high. I remember one manager told me that whenever she sees a student, she could automatically recall their individual contract (which course the student signed up for or how much he/she paid). The first two years in the company, I felt really uncomfortable when I had to recommend extra materials and courses to the students in order to meet the school's sales targets. On top of that, every head teacher (most full-time LETs were in this position) has to attend a big meeting every month or so where we can learn how to make more money as well as how to improve our lessons. But as I got more serious about teaching and helping students improve their English skills, recommending something extra become more natural to me. I decided to recommend something to my students only if I was convinced that the student needed it. Of course I felt pressure from head office when it came to increasing student numbers, preventing students from quitting, and basically, making more money. However, I didn't want to pass that pressure onto other teachers, so I let them focus on providing good-quality lessons in a comfortable environment without pressuring them about the financial side. I only missed my quarterly sales target once in five years, so I think I made the right decision on not stressing out other teachers about making more money for the company. Since I started working with Aya, I haven't felt the division of 'them' (foreign staff) and 'us' (Japanese staff) that you described.

Dan: Yeah, it was partly through talking with you guys that I started rejecting the negative stereotype that I had embraced as I realized that it stemmed partly from privilege (foreign teachers didn't have to really worry about the bottom line) and partly from pure generalization. Aya, I found through the description of your eikaiwa career that you actually shared a lot of the same frustrations that I did. We both had issues with the way teachers' individual creativity and agency were stifled due to 'McDonaldization' via inflexible methodology and production line-style scheduling.

Also, Momoko, I thought that it was admirable that you, despite being under pressure from head office in your role as head teacher, made a firm commitment to creating a buffer between business concerns and your colleagues' classroom practice. On the other hand, however, you guys mentioned before that you believed the business side of the industry actually could enhance the quality of instruction. What did you mean by that?

Aya: When I was a head teacher, I often felt I was a moderator in my school, understanding the needs of both sides – business and education. For me, the business pressure from the head office was so overwhelming that I decided to share the sales targets with all the staff. At the same time, I strongly believed that providing quality lessons where students can improve their English and accomplish their goals would have the best outcome. So I often discussed with the manager how important it was to let the teachers do their best in classrooms. I was responsible for training them and sharing ideas to create a better environment for our students to learn. My manager and I had a good relationship so there was less of an 'us' and 'them' situation. In this sense, we all had the same belief that educational quality enhanced business practice.

On the other hand, in the corporate sales department in a previous job, it was totally 'us' and 'them.' The sales reps ('us') attracted the clients with unrealistic expectations and the teachers ('them') did their job poorly. The company never spent enough money on training those teachers, so it was a vicious cycle of business prioritised over educational quality. I was extremely frustrated by the fact that my job was to sell defective products/lessons, so to speak.

Momoko: I remember clearly my first day of training at the company. There were only four LET trainees but the company president paid a visit to greet us and made a short speech. He made his point very clear that it is our job as LETs to be responsible for teaching English to Japanese learners. That was so vivid for me that it encouraged me to take this job seriously. He never talked about the financial side and encouraged us to provide good-quality lessons and to be actively involved in students' progress. His overall message is to focus on teaching first and money later. Also in the training, we learned how much each lesson costs for a student, so we are very aware of the lesson fees our students are actually paying, which are rather expensive. That pushed me to improve the lesson quality.

In our conversations, we were able to problematize several stereotypes of, and within, eikaiwa schools. Dan was presented with counter-examples to the conception of the 'other' that he had created from his eikaiwa experiences – the solely profit-focused Japanese staff as a foil to foreign teachers striving to increase the quality of education (Bossaer, 2003).

Momoko and Aya as passionate teachers, albeit constrained in part by the business demands of their job, presented the notion of a healthy compromise between business and education being possible. This allowed Dan to reevaluate his previous predominantly condemnatory view of the industry and recognize Japanese teachers' agency in negotiating institutional obstacles. Conversely, Momoko recognized that, despite being able to work around these demands in her school, many of the business practices prevalent in certain eikaiwa schools may shortchange students by reducing teachers' ability to provide well-planned and level-appropriate lessons. In Aya's case, whereas she too had been able to act as a moderating influence in one school, the purely profit-focused mentality of her second job foregrounded the idea that compromise may not always be possible. She also became aware of ways in which the ubiquitous standardization of the fast food chain (McNeill, 2004) had taken root in some eikaiwa schools and of the damaging effects this could have on her professional identity.

Our significantly different experiences highlight the interplay between structure and agency in terms of negotiating identity within an organization. To varying degrees of success, we attempted to exercise our personal agency in order to negotiate a compromise in terms of identity that we as teachers were willing to accept (Barkhuizen, 2017). Momoko was able to use her agency as a teacher to create a buffer between profit and teaching due to the authority that she had within the institution in which she worked. Aya was able to find compromise at first, but later the institutional demand to sell 'defective products' created growing resentment and a sense of frustration. As Dan's passion for teaching grew, he found the structural constraints of his job increasingly irreconcilable with his professional beliefs and this caused him to reject the eikaiwa business model. Our exchange also problematizes the idea of 'eikaiwa' being viewed as one entity. Each school we taught at presented us with a unique range of constraints and affordances that generalizations in society and the research literature may overlook. This conversation makes a case for looking at eikaiwa as a taxonomy (Makino, 2016) or, better still, on a case by case basis rather than assigning essentialized characteristics to an industry comprising hundreds of unique schools.

Teacher role

In this section we move on to discuss claims of NESTs and LETs in eikaiwa often inhabiting distinct and contrasting roles (Nuske, 2014). Through our individual experiences, however, we find that while these assumptions about the roles of NESTs and LETs are prevalent in Japan, accepting these categorizations as unassailable truths can be limiting to classroom practice.

Dan: Over the last six months we've been debating these issues, I've noticed that the socially ascribed roles of NESTs and LETs in Japan have run through almost all of our discussions. Rather than an authoritative teacher, I often felt as if I was merely assigned the role of entertainer, curiosity, or 'professional foreigner' (Houghton & Rivers, 2013; Nuske, 2014). No-one in my company really cared that I was doing my MA as it didn't really factor into what they were selling. This is another area in which Kubota's (2011) research resonated with me – students often weren't paying for language learning, they were paying for an experience, an hour of escapism with an 'exotic icon to be consumed' (Kubota, 2011: 486).

Aya: Yeah, actually I've always felt that foreigners were like mascots.

Dan: Mascots?

Aya: Yeah, sorry! It sounds kind of negative! However, on the other hand, I have always felt that I could never compete with NESTs regardless of my teaching competence. To some, NESTs' presence in the classroom has great value (Árva & Medgyes, 2000). Recently, I saw an advertisement for a kids eikaiwa school which said 'practice and rehearse' with LETs before 'the real thing'. For some Japanese people, just as was described in Árva and Medgyes (2000), the NEST's presence itself gives students a reason to learn English and motivates them to keep attending lessons. I believe this is also connected to a desire for inclusion in an 'English-speaking imagined community' (Kubota, 2011: 474). NESTs are like the mascots in an exciting theme park filled with special performances and exotic culture and fundamentally removed from reality. Though this may sound quite inappropriate, I think it's the truth here in Japan at some level and this is one of the reasons why eikaiwa schools with only NESTs still sell here. Momoko, what do you think?

Momoko: I understand that, even in my company, there is a dichotomy between NESTs and LETs even though we both teach the same lessons most of the time. However, I don't like this idea. I'd like to believe we are all just teachers. People often say that NESTs' lessons are more fun and entertaining and LETs' lessons are more educational and serious, but I have seen NESTs teaching very serious and informative lessons or sometimes deadly boring lessons and vice versa. I try to make my lessons entertaining as well as educational, so whenever I hear, 'LETs' lessons are more boring', I feel it's unjustified. Why do we have to put ourselves into two different boxes of NESTs or LETs? We automatically limit ourselves and it's a dangerous thing to do as a teacher.

Dan: Actually, this links up with one point from our previous conversations that I wanted to bring up. One of you guys said that you didn't know if NESTs actually knew how to be strict and that was why they had this playful presence in class. To be honest, this made me feel quite uncomfortable and highlighted to me how deeply the *eigo/eikaiwa* ideology or native-speakerist beliefs are embedded in teachers' consciousness in Japan (Nagatomo, 2016). This statement bothered me because it assumes that NESTs lack professional authority because of an inherent deficiency rather than because of tensions stemming from institutional or social demands. During my time in eikaiwa, I witnessed many times where teachers were reprimanded or even fired for 'being too serious', 'not smiling enough' or because their classes weren't 'fun'. These were not lax backpackers, but rather experienced and passionate teachers who were pressured by the school to conform to a stereotype of what NESTs should be (Houghton & Rivers, 2013). By the same logic, I could reasonably make the statement that Japanese high school teachers teach grammar from textbooks because they are uncreative and lazy. This belief, while unfortunately existing in Japan, is unfair and inaccurate.

Aya: Some people have the stereotype that Western education supports praise and encouragement for students' motivation whereas Japanese/Eastern education has the idealization of discipline, cramming and being strict with less freedom. Therefore, NESTs are expected to be the opposite in Japan, hence, laidback and fun. We can also see this in the idea of *eigo* and *eikaiwa* where foreigners teach *eikaiwa* (fun and communicative English) whereas Japanese teach *eigo* (grammar or test-focused lessons) (Hiramoto, 2013; Nagatomo, 2016). Basically, we like to generalize teachers and perhaps assign each group a role. This is why ALTs in public schools 'have to be' NESTs, I suppose. So I wondered how those NESTs feel about their students. In eikaiwa schools, do they aim to educate students or entertain them?

Dan: That's a very important question and actually ties in with another distinction we talked about. Do we have *customers* or *students*?

Aya: My perception is it changes depending what I do, since I have experienced both in eikaiwa. As I have been a teacher as well as working in the sales side, I see them as students in classrooms but definitely customers/clients when talking about money. I think it's interchangeable.

Momoko: Students to teachers and customers to counsellors, maybe? Do we have to put them into those two boxes? I don't know at the moment ... Pass!

Dan: I don't know either. I guess because I was questioning my professional role in eikaiwa, I tended to regard it as a service industry rather than a school per se (Bossaer, 2003). Especially in private classes, the customer really does call the shots and can request things like free conversation that may have little sound pedagogy behind them (Bueno, 2003). I also experienced 'students' wandering into class late or laughing off homework I had set them. There was certainly a sense of entitlement there as a paying customer. I actually felt like I was almost always in a position of weakness in relation to my students as I knew they had a great deal of power over my reputation in the company and, from that, even my livelihood (Bueno, 2003; Currie-Robson, 2015). What do you guys think about this?

Momoko: My experience is completely different from yours, Dan. My school provides loads of homework to students, both adults and young learners. We are entitled to check their homework every week and can be demanding if they haven't done it. Otherwise we believe they are not getting what they have paid for and that is not a good service. It is our job to encourage them to study outside of the classroom. More importantly, students at my school like those demanding teachers and we get a lot of positive feedback from students. To be honest, we never get negative comments such as 'This teacher is too strict' from adult students.

Aya: I completely agree with Momoko's points since I was kind of 'raised' as a teacher by a company who believes every minute of our teaching should be used for students' improvement. I was told and still believe that every student wants to get better and it may be part of our jobs as educators to evoke that feeling of accomplishment. I'm sure those students in Momoko's school feel it's rewarding to study outside of the classroom and have demanding teachers.

Our conversation highlights the categorization of teachers by what roles they are assigned not only within the eikaiwa industry but also in Japanese society. Dan felt that NESTs are often expected to be service providers or entertainers, or as Aya described them, 'mascots', and he felt that his students were sometimes there for escapism rather than language learning (Kubota, 2011). Because of this exoticism that NESTs are believed to possess, Aya recognized the value of NESTs in classrooms (Árva & Medgyes, 2000). Although Momoko agreed with the generalization, she strongly rejected the dichotomy between NESTs and LETs, claiming that both can provide the same quality lessons. In our discussion, we all agreed that there are stereotypical views of how NESTs/LETs should be. For example, the generalization of NESTs being fun and entertaining and LETs teaching serious grammar and test-prep. However,

Dan problematized this idealization of NESTs to be 'always smiling', which links to a socially-constructed eigo/eikaiwa dichotomy in Japan (Nagatomo, 2016). Momoko recognizes NESTs' capability of being strict and demanding as she experienced what she saw as a more egalitarian workplace. It became clear from our conversation that such roles and categorization often stem from contextual demands.

Having worked for various institutions and been assigned distinct roles, we all have different views toward learners. Dan has the firm belief that eikaiwa is fundamentally a service industry and therefore sees learners as customers who have a dominant influence on his position as a teacher. On the other hand, Momoko resists categorizing them into distinct customer/student groups, whereas Aya sees these categories as interchangeable depending on the context, as money can often be a defining factor in student/teacher relations. What Momoko and Aya agreed is that they believe every student deep down is eager to be a better English speaker to some degree despite the differences in roles and expectations of NESTs and LETs.

It could be argued that this section underscores socially constructed ways in which NESTs' and LETs' roles are distinctly framed within eikaiwa (Nagatomo, 2016; Nuske, 2014). Furthermore, these perceived roles are reinforced by the institutions they work in and are shown to have a significant impact on teachers' language teacher identity. Aya and Momoko were 'raised' by their school to push for students' improvement and often displayed a sense of pride in their role as 'demanding teachers'. Conversely, Dan experienced instances where schools would demand NESTs to conform to the stereotypical entertainer (Amundrud, 2008) role, thus casting them as 'professional foreigners' (Houghton & Rivers, 2013) rather than educators.

Confidence/respect as teachers

In this final section, we discuss factors that foster or threaten our confidence or perceived respect as teachers in eikaiwa schools. We will aim to show that the dominance of the NEST is still present, but not always clear cut in eikaiwa and that the industry may have evolved somewhat from its 'host club' past. Furthermore, we intend to highlight the important role of teaching communities in teacher identity and resolving institutional tensions.

Momoko: Actually, I have not really faced any discrimination at my school. My company advertises that we have both NESTs and LETs. When a student comes to enroll, they are informed that we have Japanese teachers who have English language qualifications (Eiken and TOEIC) as well as NESTs. In line with the stereotype, some people prefer NESTs' lessons, but not always. Also, even when a student initially prefers taking a NEST's lesson, there are some cases where they change their mind after taking LET's lessons. Through my experience, I now believe that students just want quality lessons and they can tell if it is a good lesson or not and whether their teacher is passionate about teaching English.

On top of that, in my company, mostly LETs have the title of 'Head Teacher' which gives us (LETs) more important responsibilities and much more respect from other teachers, counsellors, students and student's parents. Even though LETs receive lower salaries than NESTs, I haven't felt frustrated as I get more respect and I don't teach as many lessons as NESTs. There is a nice balance, so we don't look at things too negatively.

Aya: I felt the same when I was working with Momoko, but where I work now, I have a new perspective on the dichotomy. There definitely exists the belief that NESTs are better than LETs even though all the serious teaching, such as Eiken and TOEIC test prep, is expected to be taught by LETs and, in my opinion, the demands are much higher than they used to be. Japanese parents have realized that their children's success in English education is crucial to their future. No one in my company expects NESTs to show their language proficiency level but for LETs, it's set high and is very rigid. And yet, LETs are still looked down upon by some, especially those who have worked there for a long time.

Dan: How do you feel about your position as eikaiwa teachers in Japanese society or in the field of education?

Aya: One time when I was back in my hometown, talking to my grandfather, a former elementary school principal, about my job, I mentioned that I'd consider getting a Japanese teaching license just because there seemed to be more possibilities for me in the future if I got one. His eyes lit up and he told me that that would be the decent thing to do as a teacher. What he basically meant was that eikaiwa teachers are beneath school teachers in the hierarchy. Despite the fact that I have high English proficiency and teach a wide range of students, there is a huge gap regarding social respect between Japanese licensed teachers and teachers working in other contexts like eikaiwa and *juku* (cram schools). To me this seems like if you are a LET with no license or post-graduate qualification, there is nothing to do but stay in eikaiwa.

Momoko: Now I'm looking for a job and when I respond to an ad that says they need Japanese teachers of English they always get back to me but if I see ads for NESTs or 'native-level English teachers', I don't hear anything from them. This makes me feel that while things might seem to be changing on the surface, basically things are very much the same as before. It's like these schools are trying to get away with native-speakerism by just rewording it as 'native-level teachers'.

Dan: Yes, unfortunately, I have had the same concerns about job postings I've seen online. On the other hand, however, I perceived a gap in the respect that LETs and NESTs are afforded through my experiences in eikaiwa. Parents and some adult students would often defer to Japanese staff despite them knowing I was upper-intermediate in Japanese and more highly qualified. This reinforced the idea that we were not seen as authoritative teachers (Lowe & Kiczkowiak, 2016; Nuske, 2014). It was also around this time that I discovered the idea of eikaiwa as 'casual leisure' being partially based on *akogare* for Western men (Bailey, 2007; Kubota, 2011; Takahashi, 2013). This led me to question my role in these schools and whether it was more 'host' or 'novelty' than 'teacher'.

Momoko: I remember how shocked I was the first time I heard about Kubota's (2011) notion of NESTs as hosts and Bailey's (2007) claims about *akogare* for western men because I hadn't seen or experienced that at my school. Foreign male teachers are never seen as some sort of 'host', they are seen as 'teachers'. To be honest, Kubota's article seemed outdated and made me realize the world of eikaiwa is changing rapidly. If students want to meet up with foreign guys or girls, they have other options such as using online dating sites or going to international parties. They don't have to spend loads of money on eikaiwa schools. I think that change makes my company, and possibly other eikaiwa schools, focus on the educational side because the students were generally keen to learn English, not keen to find 'pretty faces'.

Aya: I felt the same way, Momoko. I have to admit, though, when I just started learning English in Junior High School, I had a crush on one American movie actor, a blond haired, blue-eyed Caucasian man. This was the beginning of everything I am. If it were not for him, I wouldn't be teaching nor writing this paper. But I had never thought people would be looking for partners in eikaiwa although I know many teachers who got married to their students and are now living happily in Japan. Speaking of the changes in eikaiwa, I know a lot of business people looking for professional teachers who can teach English for career-related purposes. This challenges the 'casual leisure' and '*akogare*' claims in Kubota's study (2011). There are now more specialized needs and demands for English learning in Japan, I think.

Dan: Although students coming to eikaiwa purely because of *akogare* might be uncommon, I can't agree that it doesn't exist at all in the industry. Young blond-haired, blue-eyed Caucasian men were plastered all over the advertising for one of the schools I worked at with no mention of qualifications or experience those teachers might have. I told you guys about the 'dating profiles' (our name for them) that were stuck in the lobby of my school. One teacher had an MA TESOL but this was ignored in favor of stating how *oshare* (stylish) he was. Wouldn't you consider that as appealing to something other than purely language learning? I think for me the point here is that the umbrella term eikaiwa can be misleading and can represent a disparate range of schools with very different qualities (Makino, 2016). In this way, I agree that perhaps some of the research unintentionally paints a misleading picture of eikaiwa that may obscure some of the solid language teaching that goes on in certain schools. This stereotype made me feel like I had to prove myself by getting an MA, publishing research and developing my teaching skill so as to prove my worth as a real teacher and escape the 'Charisma Man' image (Appleby, 2014; Bailey, 2007). You both said that you have to prove yourselves too. In what way?

Aya: I'm sure you've had the same experience many times, Momoko, but I can't help but feel that the students are always testing me, to see if I'm as good as NESTs. The first thing they look at would probably be my language skill, whether I make mistakes or whether my pronunciation is acceptable. I remember back in my previous school my manager told me that she could easily sell my lessons as she could prove their quality because I sounded 'like native.' The students may eventually realize that LETs can be great teachers or even better than NESTs if they really want to improve and see results.

Momoko: Yes, I completely agree. As you mentioned, we LETs are 'tested' in the first few lessons by students, especially those who prefer NESTs. To be accepted by students as a LET, we have to show two things: language ability and teaching skills. I was also surprised that Aya showed her frustration when she could feel the students were testing her. I always thought Aya's English is perfect and her pronunciation is beautiful even though I think mine is not too bad as a LET. I always felt my English needed to be improved even after becoming a teacher, and luckily, that helped to push me further.

Dan: Actually, I feel another important issue that links to respect and confidence is community. Aya, you mentioned that you were sometimes frustrated with the Japanese teachers you work with because of their attitude towards the image of the NEST. Why was that again?

Aya: In my current company, LETs are considered to be secondary. Despite having high English proficiency and usually being successful in helping students to achieve test goals, they are basically part-time and limited to teaching children and English grammar to adults. This department stays small despite profit growth and the overall number of teachers increasing. What frustrates me most is that school counselors and teachers themselves accept that NESTs are superior, and what's worse, they are all Japanese teachers undermining their own worth. This is the opposite of Momoko's company president's remark about LETs' influence and responsibility in Japanese English education. Teachers are no better or worse because of their first language.

Dan: Yeah, I thought that was interesting as I feel that we share similar frustrations but from different sides of the NEST/LET divide. You were annoyed at a lack of critical awareness among your Japanese co-workers regarding the dominance of NESTs in your company. For me, I got annoyed with my NEST co-workers for the same lack of criticality in terms of both recognizing our deprofessionalization and the privilege that many of us were abusing as unqualified native speakers. Essentially, we are highlighting irritation with the unquestioning acceptance of native-speakerism from both sides of the issue.

Momoko: I understand your frustration, Dan. I've heard of the 'backpacker teachers' so many times, but I have seen many LETs who left school after 1 or 2 years and changed their jobs completely. Deprofessionalization and unqualified teachers exist among both NESTs and LETs, especially in major eikaiwa chains, who often let me down and made me think that I should leave the company because I want to be surrounded by more experienced and passionate teachers.

In this conversation, we can see how our experiences in eikaiwa being labelled as NESTs and LETs impacted us in different ways. For Dan, despite his L2 ability and MA TESOL, he felt he lacked authority as a teacher. Conversely, Momoko and Aya often felt that they were expected to pass two kinds of tests as 'non-native' teachers in the eyes of students related to both their language ability and their teaching skills whereas NESTs did not.

Although both having high English proficiency, Aya and Momoko went through varying experiences at two different eikaiwa companies. Momoko believed that she was treated fairly as a LET at her school whereas Aya strongly perceived the existence of a NEST/LET dichotomy and felt restricted by the prevailing native-speakerism in her current company. They also raised claims of hidden native-speakerism still influencing hiring practices and the existence of a hierarchy of English teachers in Japanese society.

There were different levels of doubt among us about the impact of akogare in eikaiwa and this difference in view might have been partly due to how we viewed the current state of the industry and our professional identity as NESTs and LETs. Aya and Momoko felt that, due to changes in the industry, eikaiwa has become more focused on producing educational results. Conversely, while admitting past research may have slightly overplayed the issue, Dan noted some examples where he felt akogare still influenced eikaiwa advertising. Our different perceptions might also stem from our nationality or ascribed speakerhood. Most literature in this area describes male NESTs as the target of akogare (Kelsky, 2001; Kubota, 2011; Takahashi, 2013), therefore it is possible to say that Dan felt it more keenly as it challenged his professional identity. It must also be stated, however, that despite the tensions in identity perceived by Dan related to his racialized and gendered status in eikaiwa, many studies highlight a wide range of professional and societal benefits in Japan that stem from being a male 'native speaker' (Appleby, 2014; Hicks, 2013).

All of us talked about different frustrations we had with the communities we worked with at different eikaiwa schools as they clashed with our teacher identities. However, that frustration stemmed from our strong desire to work with non 'casual' teachers, whatever their nationalities were, and that was one mutual feeling we all shared.

Conclusion

In this trioethnography, we identified and analyzed several distinct areas where our individual experiences within eikaiwa were markedly different due to issues of race, speakerhood, gender, as well as our respective personalities. By juxtaposing our often-opposing perspectives on eikaiwa as an institution, the role of eikaiwa teachers and the way in which eikaiwa shaped our confidence as teaching professionals, we were able to problematize established narratives that we had encountered through our professional and academic lives. One point we felt was particularly significant to both our personal view on eikaiwa and the place of this educational sector within the larger field of Japanese ELT was the realization that eikaiwa cannot be defined as one single entity. Our diverse experiences and tensions instead lend weight to the framing of eikaiwa schools as highly individualized contexts each with different characteristics relating to native-speakerism, pedagogic rigor and professional identity.

Rather than reinforcing the unconstructive and stigmatized image of eikaiwa as mere 'McEnglish' or the realm of the 'Charisma Man', we hope that further qualitative enquiry can shed light on the complexities of teaching and learning in this industry. Duoethnographic research in particular provides opportunities for deconstructing essentialized images of eikaiwa and eikaiwa teachers as it focuses on the notion of identity as fluid, layered and often contradictory (Sawyer & Norris, 2013). We strongly believe that providing eikaiwa teachers with more of a voice in the field and recognizing their contributions to English education in Japan will lead to tangible improvements in the industry as a whole and therefore better-quality learning for millions of students.

References

Amundrud, T. (2008) Talking about the roles of non-Japanese teachers of English. In K. Bradford Watts, T. Muller and M. Swanson (eds) *JALT2007 Conference Proceedings*. Tokyo: JALT.

Appleby, R. (2013) Desire in translation: White masculinity and TESOL. *TESOL Quarterly* 47 (1), 122–147.

Appleby, R. (2014) *Men and Masculinities in Global English Language Teaching*. Basingstoke: Palgrave Macmillan.

Árva, V. and Medgyes, P. (2000) Native and non-native teachers in the classroom. *System* 28 (3), 355–372.

Bailey, K. (2006) Marketing the eikaiwa wonderland: Ideology, akogare, and gender alterity in English conversation school advertising in Japan. *Environment and Planning D: Society and Space* 24 (1), 105–130.

Bailey, K. (2007) Akogare, ideology, and 'Charisma Man' mythology: Reflections on ethnographic research in English language schools in Japan. *Gender, Place and Culture* 14 (5), 585–608.

Barkhuizen, G. (2017). Language teacher identity research: An introduction. In G. Barkhuizen (ed.) *Reflections on Teacher Identity Research*. London and New York: Routledge.

Bossaer, A. (2003) The power of perceptions: A look at professionalism in private language schools in Japan. *JALT Hokkaido Journal* 7, 13–23.

Brooks, X. (2017) Oh Lucy! review: Japanese tale of office worker in love with her teacher is a little wonky. The Guardian May 22 2017 (accessed April 21 2018). See https://www.theguardian.com/film/2017/may/22/oh-lucy-review-japanese-office-worker-josh-hartnett-cannes-2017

Bueno, E.P. (2003) A leading language school. In E.P. Bueno and T. Caesar (eds) (2003) *I Wouldn't Want Anybody to Know: Native English Teaching in Japan* (pp. 98–114). Tokyo: JPGS Press.

Bueno, E.P. and Caesar, T. (2003) *I Wouldn't Want Anybody to Know: Native English Teaching in Japan*. Tokyo: JPGS Press.

Cater, M. (2017) Learner native-speakerism at the eikaiwa gakkou. In P. Clements, A. Krause and H. Brown (eds) *Transformation in Language Education*. Tokyo: JALT.

Copland, F., Garton, S. and Mann, S. (eds) (2016) *LETs and NESTs: Voices, Views and Vignettes*. London: British Council.

Currie-Robson, C. (2015) *English to Go: Inside Japan's English Teaching Sweatshops*. CreateSpace Independent Publishing Platform.

Hicks, S.K. (2013). On the (out)skirts of TESOL networks of homophily: Substantive citizenship in Japan. In S. Houghton and D. Rivers (eds) *Native-speakerism in Japan: Intergroup Dynamics in Foreign Language Education* (pp. 147–158). Bristol: Multilingual Matters.

Hiramoto, M. (2013) English vs English conversation: Language teaching in modern Japan. In L. Wee, R.B.H. Goh and L. Lim (eds) *The Politics of English: South Asia, Southeast Asia and the Asia Pacific* (pp. 228–248). Amsterdam: John Benjamins.

Holliday, A. (2006) Native-speakerism. *ELT Journal* 60 (4), 385–387.

Houghton, S.A. and Rivers, D.J. (2013). Introduction: Redefining native-speakerism. In S.A. Houghton and D.J. Rivers (eds) *Native-Speakerism in Japan: Intergroup Dynamics in Foreign Language Education*. Bristol: Multilingual Matters.

Kelsky, K. (2001) *Women on the Verge: Japanese Women, Western Dreams*. Durham, NC: Duke University Press.

Kubota, R. (2011) Learning a foreign language as leisure and consumption: Enjoyment, desire, and the business of eikaiwa. *International Journal of Bilingual Education and Bilingualism* 14 (4), 473–488.

Lowe, R.J. (2015) Cram schools in Japan: The need for research. *The Language Teacher* 39 (1), 26–31.
Lowe, R.J. and Kiczkowiak, M. (2016) Native-speakerism and the complexity of personal experience: A duoethnographic study. *Cogent Education* 3, 1264171.
Makino, M. (2016) A taxonomy of eikaiwa schools. *JALT School Owners SIG Newsletter* 3, 4–11.
McNeill, D. (2004) McEnglish for the masses. *The Japan Times* February 24, 2004 (accessed October 15 2017). See https://www.japantimes.co.jp/community/2004/02/24/issues/mcenglish-for-the-masses/#.Wtr4XIhubIU
McVeigh, B. (2004) Foreign language instruction in Japanese higher education: The humanistic vision or nationalistic utilitarianism? *Arts and Humanities in Higher Education* 3 (2), 211–227.
METI (Ministry of Economy, Trade, and Industry) (Japan) (2005) 2005 Survey on Selected Service Industries (accessed November 2, 2017). See http://www.meti.go.jp/english/statistics/tyo/tokusabizi/result/pdf/2005k-e/h17-gai-20.pdf
Nagatomo, D.H. (2013) The advantages and disadvantages faced by housewife English teachers in the cottage industry Eikaiwa business. *The Language Teacher* 37 (1), 3–7.
Nagatomo, D.H. (2016) *Identity, Gender and Teaching English in Japan*. Bristol: Multilingual Matters.
Nuske, K. (2014) 'It is very hard for teachers to make changes to policies that have become so solidified': Teacher resistance at corporate eikaiwa franchises in Japan. *The Asian EFL Journal* 16 (2), 283–312.
Ritzer, G. (2000) *The McDonaldization of Society: New Century Edition*. Thousand Oaks, California: Pine Forge Press.
Rodney, L. and Garscadden, N. (2002) *Charisma Man: The Complete Collection*. Tokyo: AKNG Press.
Sawyer, R.D. and Norris, J. (2013) *Duoethnography*. New York, NY: Oxford University Press.
Seargeant, P. (2009) *The Idea of English in Japan: Ideology and the Evolution of a Global Language*. Bristol: Multilingual Matters.
Stebbins, R.A. (2007) *Serious Leisure: A Perspective of Our Time*. New Brunswick, NJ: Transaction Publishers.
Takahashi, K. (2013) *Language Learning, Gender and Desire: Japanese Women on the Move*. Bristol: Multilingual Matters.

3 Critical ELT in Japan: A Duoethnographic Exploration of Origins, Identities, Obstacles and Concerns

Yuzuko Nagashima and Chris Hunter

Introduction

Critical ELT is an approach to language teaching and learning that seeks to foreground issues of power and inequality, both within the classroom and in society at large, with the goals of heightening students' awareness, encouraging self-reflection about their place in the world, and ultimately, pushing for positive social transformation. From the point of view of critical English language teachers, there is no such thing as an 'apolitical' classroom, no matter how politically neutral the teacher may be or how politically benign the course content may seem, since teachers and students bring with them into the classroom their diverse personal histories, complex identities and multitude of roles. These varied histories, identities and roles are interwoven into an existing set of broader social relations and hierarchies that empower some and disadvantage others. Critical ELT teachers aim to make explicit these issues of power, privilege and inequality within their classrooms through a wide variety of approaches, from something as simple as fostering student agency through the act of negotiating a course syllabus with students (Breen & Littlejohn, 2000; Crookes, 2013) to something as complex and multifaceted as facilitating the development of critical consciousness and political participation among underrepresented communities (Freire, 1970; Giroux, 1983).

Critical ELT practice is as diverse as its practitioners and their varied motivations for adopting this approach to teaching. As the authors of this project, we were previously acquainted and had briefly discussed our shared critical orientation to teaching, as well as our successes, failures, hopes and concerns as teachers. What was also notable, however, was just how different we were from each other in most other ways: from our national, ethnic and linguistic backgrounds to our genders and sexualities to our initial motivations for adopting a critical approach to teaching. Although this research could have been explored from a number of methodological approaches, duoethnography seemed particularly well suited for our purposes. First and foremost, the concept of social justice rests at the center of duoethnographic inquiry (Sawyer & Norris, 2013). With its foundation in the pursuit of social justice and positive social transformation and its emphasis on the intersubjective process of meaning sharing, meaning making and meaning transformation between co-equals, rather than a one-way investigation *by* a 'researcher' *of* a 'subject,' duoethnography offered the right methodological tools for tracing our unique histories and critical awakenings, comparing our respective understandings of the meaning of *critical ELT* and exploring our experiences, successes, concerns and obstacles as critical teachers. In addition to enhancing our awareness of our own journeys, it is our hope that the varied paths and experiences described in this project demonstrate the diversity of motivations and possible manifestations of critical ELT, while also offering food for thought for other critically minded teachers.

Notes on Terminology

Before proceeding further, we would like to clarify our usage of two key terms/phrases: (1) 'context' and (2) 'native' versus 'non-native' English speakers. For our purposes, we refer to teaching 'contexts' as complex ecologies that encompass not only classrooms and the teachers and students within them, but also the programs, departments and institutional environments in which teachers operate on a daily basis. These complex contextual factors interact with one another and the unique identities and practices of teachers to produce different opportunities and restrictions for language teachers, something that becomes apparent in the dialogues below. Another key phrase that often appeared in our dialogues, 'native/non-native English speakers/teachers,' is mediated in this chapter by putting them in scare-quotes to signify its problematic nature (e.g. Holliday, 2015). It should be borne in mind that the term is used to critique its material power that affects our daily lives as teachers throughout the paper.

Review of the Literature

While not a new area of focus in English language teaching and learning (e.g. Canagarajah, 1999; Fairclough, 1989; Pennycook, 2001), the concept of *critical* ELT remains confusing and confounding, not only for those who have limited knowledge of the area, but also for those of us who describe ourselves as critically oriented language teachers. As a multifaceted field with a wide variety of context-specific goals and instantiations of practice, critical ELT derives inspiration from an array of theoretical orientations and forms of practice. While a thorough exploration of the influences undergirding critical ELT lies well beyond the scope of this chapter, we will briefly touch on some of the influences in the field, as well as review the limited amount of literature that exists on critical ELT in Japan. In terms of social theory, one of the most influential intellectual movements includes the work of the Frankfurt School, a loose, multi-generational collection of European neo-Marxists (e.g. Habermas, 1987; Horkheimer, 1972) who sought to better explain the socio-political upheavals of the 20th century. Similarly, theorists associated with a series of 'posts' – postmodernism (e.g. Baudrillard, 1994); poststructuralism (e.g. Derrida, 2016; Foucault, 1977, both of whom have also been labeled postmodernists); and postcolonialism (e.g. Fanon, 1963; Said, 1978) – all sought to move away from structuralist views of people and societies that often emphasized static, discrete and essentialized categories of human existence in favor of views that explicitly questioned 'objective' reality, dominant ideologies and essentialized views of identity. The work of Pierre Bourdieu critically examined the interplay between language, politics and power relations (e.g. 1991) in a way that remains highly influential to critical language scholars and practitioners. Finally, feminist social theories (e.g. Beauvoir, 1953; hooks, 1994) and Queer Theory (e.g. Nelson, 2009) and the educational practices they helped to inspire, have helped to further highlight issues of power and representation, not least of which within the field of English language education (e.g. Benesch, 1993; Vandrick, 2009). In terms of practice, critical ELT derives further inspiration from critical pedagogy and the concept of praxis, defined by Freire (1970: 126) as 'reflection and action directed at the structures to be transformed.' Freire's work, and the work of those inspired by him, continues to impact the practice of critical language educators (e.g. Häusler *et al.*, 2018).

Critical ELT occupies a minor position in contemporary English language teaching in Japan. Nevertheless, there are some instructive examples in the existing literature. In terms of critical language education policy, Tsuda (1998), building on the critiques of Phillipson (1992), has long argued against English hegemony in Japanese education, while Hashimoto (2013) has written about the mixed messages and contradictions within Japanese English language education policy. Kubota (2011) has questioned the role of neoliberalism in Japanese ELT policy and practice. McMahill (1997) wrote on the challenges and successes of implementing feminist-inspired pedagogy within English teaching contexts in Japan, while Hammond (2006) discussed the use of critical discourse analysis within a Japanese university classroom to raise awareness through a simulated racial inequality activity.

To the best of our knowledge, however, there has not been a duoethnographic exploration of the beliefs and practices of two critically minded English language teachers in Japan. We hope that this chapter begins to address that gap in the research, and stimulates further analysis and action among critical teachers in Japan and beyond.

Research Design

Research participants

While we share very similar values in relation to critical ELT and its possibilities, we also recognize that we have very few areas in common when it comes to our respective identity markers. Yuzuko was born and raised in Japan, while Chris was raised in the United States. Chris identifies, rather uncritically, as a heterosexual male, while Yuzuko identifies as bisexual and possesses a more fluid sense of gender. Within the Japanese ELT world, despite many years of living and studying in the United States, Yuzuko is generally characterized as a 'non-native English speaker,' while Chris is awarded the status of 'native English speaker.' Finally, nine years older than Yuzuko, Chris has a longer history of working in ELT, although most of those years were not spent teaching from a critical perspective. Thus, though philosophically aligned, we acknowledge our vast differences in terms of language backgrounds, nationality, race, gender, age and sexuality, differences which are viewed as a strength when examined via duoethnography (Sawyer & Norris, 2013). These culturally recognized differences, indeed, launched us onto very different life paths that, nevertheless, have led us to an ideologically similar position as ELT teachers in Japan. Finally, it is worth noting that we had a previously existing friendship that did not overlap with our professional lives. Because we got to know each other outside of the realm of academia, the nature of our relationship differs from that of coworkers, colleagues, or research-related acquaintances, and instead reflects a more genuine and personal friendship. We believe the friendship that we had already built played a significant role in creating a solid foundation of trust, another key tenet of duoethnography (Sawyer & Norris, 2013). The nature of our relationship allowed for collaborative and critical dialogues where we could freely and honestly express ourselves, ask for clarification or further explanation, negotiate meaning and suggest alternative interpretations without concern for jeopardizing a professional relationship. We believe that the genuine friendship that we had previously developed played a positive and productive role in this research endeavor.

Research questions

When Yuzuko first took up this project, her initial aim was to learn and expand her practical knowledge of how to incorporate critical issues related to gender and sexuality into her language classes. She approached Chris about this project because she knew that he had some experience with critical teaching and researching. Through this project, she was hoping to gain more practical insights on the matter to utilize in her own teaching context through the sharing of our lived experiences and reflecting on our teaching practices (Farrell, 2015). However, as is typical of duoethnography (Sawyer & Norris, 2013), the trajectory of our project took various turns as we juxtaposed our life stories and lived experiences, and the salience and relevance of teacher identities in our professional practice emerged. In the end, we realized that the concepts of criticality and identity (or, more accurately, *identities*) are effectively inseparable, since a critical approach to language teaching must take into account the power dynamics within and beyond the classroom (including workplace contexts and their opportunities and constraints), as well as the multiple identities and roles claimed by and assigned to teachers and students. Therefore, our research questions emerged as we collected and analyzed the data as follows:

(1) How does one's unique personal history and set of identities impact one's understanding and approach to critical English language education?
(2) What opportunities or restrictions exist in each individual's work environment and how are they related to our individual identities?

These research questions will be addressed through our critical reflection and collaborative dialogues that follow below.

Data collection methods

After we had an initial meeting for brainstorming in November 2017, we met for a series of five face-to-face interviews over a six-month period, resulting in over seven hours of audio-recorded conversations. Each session was loosely structured around a specific theme, and due to time constraints, four of the five sessions focused primarily on one individual's story. Each meeting lasted from one to two hours, and during the conversations we also utilized a variety of cultural artifacts, such as pictures, music and websites, to better contextualize and give more concrete illustration to our stories. In each meeting, notes were taken so that we would be able to reflect on the dialogues afterward. After all the data collection sessions were finished, we met again in person twice to conduct thematic analysis by carefully and repeatedly listening to the audio data in order to look for emerging and recurrent themes (Creswell, 2007). Based on this process, we found three themes that emerged: (1) our personal histories and experiences that have led to the formation of our critical language teacher identities and our current teaching practices (both actual and ideal versions), (2) our idiosyncratic struggles and issues related to our differential positioning as critical language teachers within our respective workplaces and

(3) our self-reflections as critical language teachers. At the writing stage, in addition to email and online correspondence on a regular basis, we held three mutual writing sessions, as we found this style to be a more reliable, effective and truly collaborative method of writing that better reflects the tenets of duoethnography. Following the advice of Sawyer and Norris (2013), the transcripts were deconstructed and reconstructed to a certain extent in the writing stage in order to create a more coherent narrative.

Dialogues

Theme 1: Origin stories – tracing unique paths to criticality

Although we already had a developing friendship, at the time we began this project we didn't know much about our respective personal histories. Given the vast differences in our individual and social identities, we felt that a sensible place to begin was with personal narratives of our pasts, and how we explain our journeys to adopting critical views of society.

Yuzuko's path and definition of criticality

Yuzuko: My mom is naturally a very hardworking, driven, passionate person who always knows what she is doing and where she wants to go. So, in a way, she was my first role model and has had a strong impact on my perception of self. But while she was so fierce and protective, I was a very shy, spoiled, awkward kid, so it was challenging for me to socialize, especially with girls at school. Now I think about it, that social isolation may have helped me gain a critical gaze toward the society. And as I grew up, I started to subconsciously notice that being a woman was very restricting in Japan. There were many gendered rules that I had to follow just because I was a girl, which I didn't really do and got scolded all the time at school. So, I guess I kind of knew that it was related to me being a girl. So anyway, I was one of those girls who just wanted to get out and try something challenging in a brand-new place, in a language that I really enjoyed learning.

Chris: I see what you mean. How do you think your experience studying abroad affected your identity?

Yuzuko: I think one of my major incidents was my encounter with intersectional feminism (e.g. Collins & Bilge, 2016). I met this person that I became a close friend with, and she taught me really diverse women's issues. She showed me how to be critical and just… be true to the authentic self. She was particularly critical in whitewashing and how prevalent it is in our mundane daily life (Hill, 2008). She really opened my eyes about how brainwashed I had been, like pretty much everything I believed in was basically centered around whiteness as a norm and sign of prestige. Anyway, I started to take some women's studies courses to cultivate my own sense of criticality by deconstructing what I had believed about myself, about my value, and everything. And it's a learning process, you know, I think part of me is still so deeply whitewashed especially when it comes to English language teaching, using curricula, textbooks, and pedagogy all developed in the West, but yeah, I think learning about intersectional feminism through her was definitely a turning point in terms of my gender, sexual and ethnic identity.

Chris: How has that connected to your teaching career up to now?

Yuzuko: Actually, I didn't know if I wanted to be a language teacher up until I joined the teaching practicum at the end of my master's program. But that experience changed my whole perspectives on teaching, and I still remember the very first day when I started teaching with my own class and students, and I immediately knew I loved teaching. It was that quick. You know, it's interesting some teachers had this 'calling,' like a sense of mission or they always knew they wanted to be a teacher. For me, it might sound shallow, but at least initially, I just loved that feeling when I was teaching, like I felt in control, and I was being someone that I always wanted to be, someone who is caring but strong, flexible yet in charge, things like that. So, I guess you could say that the performative aspect of my teacher identity is close to my ideal self, and I think that's kind of connected to my whole language learning experience, too. After that, it was like a natural process for me to become interested in incorporating critical issues, especially gender and sexuality, you know, things that I learned and cared about, into my teaching. But I am still in the stage of trying to figure out how to do it.

Chris: I'm curious what the term 'critical' means to us? What is 'critical'? And how does it differ from typical, uncritical forms of language teaching and learning? What makes teaching 'critical'?

Yuzuko: I think it's basically to challenge the students, challenge their belief system and what they take for granted. But I don't have much chance to do that in my required classes. I try to do that more in my advanced classes, elective classes with advanced students. But in any classes, especially from the perspective of feminist pedagogy, I don't think criticality is just about what to teach but also about how to teach (Vandrick, 1998). For example, how I, as a teacher, pay attention to the gender dynamics in the classroom and also internalized misogyny (hooks, 2000) within myself. I realized that I had subconsciously paid more attention to male students, and had certain gendered expectations on how they behave, so I've been trying to be critical about it and trying to change that.

Chris: So, just having the awareness of how you interact with various students?

Yuzuko: Yeah, and also I incorporate things like gender-neutral pronouns for grammar classes and female-centered stories and movies for reading classes and things like that.

Chris's path and definition of criticality

Chris: I think the defining force of my life has been anxiety. If there is one thing that's sort of shaped who I am and where I've gone, it's been anxiety. I was a sensitive kid, emotionally. And though it's difficult to explain, I think that my experience with anxiety has something to do with this sense of justice, injustice, fairness, unfairness, that has kind of driven me in terms of my political or academic interests. In particular, I was really fascinated by white/black race issues in America. And at a young age, I was obsessed with the era of the Civil Rights movement in the US, from the history to the novels and music of that era. And I think part of it is related to this hypersensitivity that I have, maybe being more aware than I would have been without that kind of anxiety. So, in some ways, the whole anxiety thing for me also relates to my interest in social justice issues, particularly, like I said, race in America at that time. I should be clear about what I mean by that. I didn't experience discrimination at all. But I think that having all this anxiety created a greater sensitivity to, and awareness about, a lot of things.

Yuzuko: Are there other things that influenced the development of your critically oriented view of the world?

Chris: I had many role models who had a big impact on me, starting with my parents. In terms of gender issues, I think that living mostly with a single mother and an older sister definitely had some impact on my understanding, maybe, of what women face in society. I have memories of my mom coming home from work and just being so exhausted that she would just go up to her room, lie in bed and read the paper, do some work. Additionally, she had experienced strong anxiety when she was a kid, too, and empathized with me, so I think for the first 13, 14 years of my life my mom was definitely my protector, my main caretaker, caregiver, security guard. So witnessing her struggle financially while dealing with a messed-up kid, I think, gave me respect for the challenges women, in general, and single mothers, specifically, face.

Yuzuko: How about your dad?

Chris: He also had a huge impact on me, albeit in a different way than my mom. He didn't know what to do about my anxiety. But a lot of my sense of right and wrong, fair and unfair, came from him. He was a prosecutor, but he didn't do it because he liked throwing people in jail. He really believed that he was helping people by prosecuting people who hurt others. So, I think I probably absorbed some of that from him as well, that there is just and unjust, right and wrong, and it shouldn't apply only to certain classes of people. He also told me stories of his time during the Vietnam War that tied into my interests in the Civil Rights movement. While he was there, he said the scariest part was actually the racial tensions between black and white American soldiers. It was 1968, 1969, so the time that included the death of Martin Luther King and the race riots, and it was a very intense time socially back in the States and that carried over to the war. Anyway, while he was there, his commanding officers asked him to play a sort of mediator role between some of the African American soldiers and white soldiers because they saw him as sort of a neutral, mediating presence. Also, he used to talk about our ancestors who had a house on the Underground Railroad that helped escaped slaves around the time of the Civil War. I don't know if that's something that you inherit in your DNA or where that comes from, but those stories of family 'doing the right thing' really impacted me.

Yuzuko: So, what does being a critical teacher mean for you?

Chris: I think the critical part means increasing awareness and at least providing opportunities for students to engage in activities that relate to not just important social issues, but social inequity and inequality, with the goal of getting them thinking in a way that will make the world a more equitable place.

Yuzuko: But in terms of issues involving social justice and inequity for those students that you have taught, what are they? They might not think they have any problems in their lives, or in this society.

Chris: Well, in the case of Japan, things like growing economic inequality.

Yuzuko: Yeah, but it may not directly affect them.

Chris: It doesn't necessarily have to affect them personally. Whether you're on top or on the bottom, you're still a part of this system. So, it does affect them. Other issues are sexual harassment and assault, equity in gender roles, development of critical media literacy and building awareness of dominant historical and media narratives, and questioning them. Diversity issues. Immigration. Japanese identity issues. I think there are a lot of issues that are out there. And, I think more than we might expect, students do have a knowledge base and awareness of these issues.

In spite of our very different histories and identities, we both somehow found ourselves embracing principles of critical ELT. It was interesting to note the different foci that first attracted us to social justice issues. For Yuzuko, it was the encounter with intersectional feminism which takes a critical stance on race, and issues of gender and sexuality, while Chris was 'obsessed' with a narrow aspect of race relations in the United States. Thus, it would seem, one's initial attraction to social justice issues may vary, but once it becomes apparent, one's awareness of other issues is capable of expanding significantly. As the above narratives also illustrate, however, we indeed identified certain similarities in our backgrounds that may, in part, help to explain some of our shared values as teachers.

The most salient similarity appears to be the impact that certain individuals had on our lives and value systems. These individuals stand out as key figures in our narratives as people who, knowingly or not, willingly or not, shaped the way we interpret the world.

Theme 2: Critical teaching – the importance of context

While Theme 1 illustrates both our seemingly opposite backgrounds yet similar goals toward adopting (or trying to adopt) a more critical approach to language teaching, Theme 2 focuses on the importance of context in critical ELT, and how each of us negotiates our positioning (or act of being positioned) as critical language teachers, and the local and global constraints that we have encountered through our respective career paths. We use 'context' in the expansive sense to include classrooms, teachers' offices, departments and the teaching institution as a whole. Although the following excerpts refer to our working context at the time of data collection, it is important to note that the purpose of the discussion is not to criticize a particular language program or target certain individuals, but rather to raise awareness of the injustice that is prevalent throughout the ELT field in Japan.

Yuzuko: In my current situation, I have very limited opportunities to create my own content. They don't monitor me on a daily basis or anything, so technically you can do whatever you like, but we do have required commercial textbooks and I do want to use them because students pay for the textbooks. So, in my head, I think a lot of time critical aspects and critical pedagogy can happen only in its own course, like you have to create everything from scratch. But my question is, is it possible to include certain aspects of criticality into the existing course, cuz that's what I would probably have to do in my current situation. But it's difficult sometimes, for example, in one chapter the topic is school rules, you know, modals for duties and obligations or something like that. And after we cover the grammar topic and we suddenly start talking about relevant social issues ... like bullying? Like you know, how can you combine them or transition well with a flow, because most of the textbook topics are not critically-oriented, so I wonder how is it possible, you know?

Chris: Yeah, there is the ideal, for us, what we imagine we would like to do if we had everything going for us, you know. And then, there is reality in that there are so many different constraints. So, I think a lot of people who are interested in maybe trying out a little critical stuff, the first obstacle they face is some sort of curricular constraint, and people also see their students' linguistic abilities as constraining.

Yuzuko: It can definitely be a challenge, yeah.

Chris: In my case, the context I worked in last semester was really ideal for experimenting with critical ELT. I've taught in a number of different contexts over the years, but most of that time was spent just trying to figure out how to teach. My attempts at critical ELT didn't really begin until the teaching I did during my PhD program. Still, this last semester had a number of qualities that made it an ideal situation. First, I was an emergency hire for two courses, and was told, quite clearly, that it would only be for one semester. So, as long as I showed up to work, I don't think the supervising professors really cared what I did in class. I could really experiment freely, with no real constraints, and the students were fantastic. There were really no issues with students' language level or motivation. In the first-year required course, they had already spent a semester together and had developed a very good rapport. When I asked them if there were things they didn't do the previous semester that they wanted to do this semester, one of the things they said was that they wanted to share their own thoughts and opinions more. So, it was ideal. We negotiated a syllabus. I negotiated for both classes, actually. So that was one bit of critical pedagogy that I tried (Breen & Littlejohn, 2000; Crookes, 2013). They had never done it before, but both classes actually did well in terms of negotiating either the type of assignments or the grading allocation. So, again, that's the ideal situation for me, where students take ownership over their own classes.

Yuzuko: Right.

Chris: For the first-year class, in terms of their discussion and presentation topics, I gave them wide leeway, just requiring that their topics be somehow academically-oriented, something that could fit within the context of a university course, or a controversial issue, or an important current event or topic in the news. I left it vague, and then had them submit proposals. And a lot of the proposals they submitted were already critically-oriented, dealing with issues like gender equality, LGBTQ rights, refugee issues and more. So, essentially, they brought in the perfect type of critical content that also fit in very well with the particular academic skills the course was designed to develop (Crawford-Lange, 1981). I helped with the presentation, organization and analysis of arguments, but, in comparison to your situation, they brought with them advanced linguistic skills, greater motivation and a broader view of the world and the social issues that exist. In all of those ways, my teaching context was almost the complete opposite of yours, and probably the best situation I can imagine for doing critical ELT. The downside, of course, was that I had no job security, bonuses, or benefits.

The contrast between Chris and Yuzuko is particularly striking when it comes to the differences between their workplaces and their respective institutional and programmatic constraints and affordances. Yuzuko's position is relatively more stable as a full-time instructor. However, this relative job security also comes with more limitations on her autonomy to make her own decisions about what she can and cannot do in her classroom. In contrast, because Chris's contract was only for one semester, he was free from any supervision and had significantly more freedom to explore his own teaching interests as a critical language teacher. Therefore, he explained that he was able to employ a variety of methods. He was also able to generate more student-oriented classrooms where his main role was to facilitate the discussions, challenge the students' own thinking, and suggest alternative possibilities. However, the price of this opportunity for his critical exploration was the absence of job security.

In the following excerpt, the topic shifts to the constraints on Yuzuko's work opportunities due to her ascribed status as a 'non-native' English speaker. Although she prefers labeling herself as emergent bilingual (García & Kleifgen, 2018), today's ELT field in Japan still regards her as a 'non-native' English speaker, which in turn affects the content of classes that she teaches. The discussion about her language status is then connected to the debate over English-only policies, which are currently dominant in the ELT field in Japan.

Yuzuko: There are certain things that I just am not allowed or not trusted to do, like I've requested to teach these advanced elective classes where teachers can basically bring their own contents into the classroom, with no required textbooks because I thought it would be a great opportunity for me to start incorporating, like, more critical aspects into the classroom, but every time they were like, 'That has never happened. You cannot do that'.

Chris: Really? Did they give you the rationale?

Yuzuko: Because I am not a 'native' English speaker.

Chris: They literally told you that?

Yuzuko: Well, they didn't say that to my face, but I heard that they said that none of the 'non-native' English speakers have ever taught those classes. I mean, I guess, that's part of their marketing strategy that students can actually learn 'real' English from 'real' English teachers, whatever that means, you know?

Chris: So, there is no recognition of the benefits of having bilingual teachers in the classroom (e.g. Goldenberg & Wagner, 2015)?

Yuzuko: There is not much concept of bilingualism, and we do implement the English-only policy on the official level, but there is some leniency in how to interpret that in the classroom, though.

Chris: I think that's very common in Japan and it just demonstrates not only how behind the times the 'native' English teachers are who are often at the supervisory level, but also demonstrates how behind the times professors, who are often Japanese, are that oversee these programs.

Yuzuko: It's a complete package.

Chris: In spite of the large amount of research that shows the benefit of bilingual teachers and translanguaging in the classroom (e.g. García & Wei, 2013), if the goal is to develop students who can actually communicate in the target language.

Although it was not explicitly stated, this is evidence that native-speakerism is still pervasive in her language program, where teachers who are labeled as 'non-native' English teachers are seen as not having the skills and abilities, at least not to the same degree as 'native' English teachers, necessary to teach classes where content is the focus of the class. Chris pointed out the connection between such discriminatory practice with English-only policies and how such ideologies are predominant in Japanese ELT (Kubota, 1998). He further speculates that the promotion of English-only education is anachronistic and does not take into account a wide variety of research showing the advantages of including bilingual teachers and translanguaging in language classrooms.

The last snapshot of our dialogue is centered not within the classroom or the curricular expectations of a department or institution, but rather within the context of the workplace itself and interactions with coworkers. Specifically, this dialogue focuses on how to navigate potentially confrontational encounters, especially in relation to the notion of sexism in the workplace, and who is best positioned to confront such situations. The discussion between us illustrates not only how pervasive such situations are, but also how imperative it is to take actions in order to achieve positive changes.

Yuzuko: You know, in any work places, there will always be challenging people to work with. But what bothers me the most is that most people may think it's a problem, but they don't really do anything. They remain quiet or they kind of like laugh it off. And they will never call them out or most of them will never take the initiative to show me their support. And that happens quite often as a woman living in Japan and as a minority at a workplace (Nagatomo, 2012), and it can be challenging.

Chris: Do you get it in the office, I mean, do you experience in-your-face sexism?

Yuzuko: Most of the time, it's not that explicit, only when we are socializing and mingling. For example, at one party, one of the teachers jokingly told me that it is my responsibility as a woman to get married and have kids soon, and everyone there was just... laughing nonchalantly, like it's not a big deal. And I remember I just wanted to point out how offensive and backward that comment was, but because it upset me so personally and emotionally, I wasn't really able to come up with any ways to raise awareness of it in a non-offensive, productive way. This is just my theory, but I'm not sure if women can change the attitude or beliefs of men who are already sexist. I guess it's not impossible, but it almost seems counterproductive to me. And the more I encounter this type of situations, the more I started to feel like, maybe those who are not on the immediate receiving end of problematic actions or behavior in an incident, maybe people who are closer on the social spectrum to the perpetrator should be able to speak up to them, in this case, a sexist man, to resolve the situation more effectively and efficiently and possibly bring some positive changes in the long run in the mind of the perpetrator and also the bystanders. I guess that's one of those things that those with social privilege can do by taking advantage of it, you know?

Chris: I had a similar experience at a former workplace, and now that I think about it, I was one of those who did nothing to stop it. I had a coworker who often said sexist things, particularly when he was drinking, but also in the workplace at times. We had many people in a single office, with very cramped working spaces. One day in the office, he made an off-hand, sexist comment. The person sitting next to him was a very nice woman, and an American guy sitting behind him had had enough. He openly confronted the sexist coworker, saying something like, 'Hey, what the hell are you talking about? You can't say that, there are women here and that's rude to say.' The other guy tried to explain it away as a joke, but with little effect. So, finally someone called him out on it, and I think you are right because, at least in the office, I never heard him say anything sexist again. You know, I've talked about that story often, but never thought about my own complicity in letting it happen until hearing your story. It's hypocritical of me to encourage my students to explore critical and feminist perspectives in the classroom, but then do nothing about it in the teachers' office a few doors down the hallway.

This dialogue was shown in order to display not only Yuzuko's encounter with microaggression (Sue, 2010) in a comment that she directly received at a social gathering as a joke based on her gender and age, but also to show her starting point to critically examine her social and professional positioning. She points out that such a subtle form of discrimination is not only problematic, but also covertly maintained by the lack of counteraction by other colleagues. On top of her concerns about the emotional impact on her, she also points out the issue of the legitimacy of her claim from the viewpoint of perpetrators. This concern was supported by Chris when he shared a similar story from a former workplace, where the situation was solved rather calmly when a fellow teacher, in this case a white, American male, directly confronted another man for making inappropriate comments in the workplace and pointed out that his behavior was unprofessional and needed to stop. Through the dialogic process of duoethnography, Chris also came to the uncomfortable realization that he was silently complicit and essentially hypocritical for promoting critical thought and action in the classroom, without practicing it himself in the teachers' office.

Theme 3: Wrestling with the issue of legitimacy as a critically oriented teacher

The issue of legitimacy as a critical teacher was a recurring theme for Chris in our dialogues. Many of his worries about critical language teaching concerned whether he has the right, and the right personal characteristics, to conduct critical ELT in a foreign country where English is not a prominently used language. To some extent, this is related to the frequently-voiced concern from non-critical teachers that lessons that explicitly address socio-political issues could result in the indoctrination of students toward the teacher's own biases. As the excerpts below illustrate, this is a concern that critical teachers wrestle with as well.

Chris: So, as I explore my own criticality and identities as a teacher, one thing that I struggle with is that I'm the perfect image of everything that's 'normative.' I'm white, male, American, a so-called 'native-English speaker,' heterosexual, middle-class, able-bodied...and here I am in a foreign country where English is not a prominent language trying to be a 'critical' teacher of a language many would call hegemonic, and I embody that hegemony in so many ways. So, even if I do believe in critical classrooms, am I the right person to be addressing these issues in a Japanese ELT class? I don't know. I don't know if I'm the best person to do it. In fact, I know I'm not the best person to do it, but will that stop me? Should that mean I stop trying to teach critically about race, about identity, about culture, about colonialism or postcolonialism? And I think the answer that I've come up with so far is, yes, I can, but I can only address these topics in a way that reflects my understanding and experience. As long as I'm approaching it in the way that I understand it, and not as *the* definitive approach, then that's what I want to do. But it's still an issue that I struggle with.

This theme arose for Chris once again while we were discussing what we had gained from this project.

Chris: So, I think the nice thing about this project is our positionings, so to speak, are so completely different.

Yuzuko: It's so opposite!

Chris: Yeah, truly. On a general level, we have very similar goals in the classroom. We have very different constraints on us, social and occupational. We have different claims to legitimacy, and I think as a critical teacher, you have core pieces of yourself that qualify you in a way that I could never be.

Yuzuko: Like I would be positioned as a woman and 'non-native' English speaker?

Chris: Right, so you have certain aspects of your positionality that, in my mind at least, give you more legitimacy and authenticity as a critical teacher. I feel like, on the surface level, even though these are deeply-held, deeply personal issues to me, I don't have the same level of legitimacy, or the same right to be a critically oriented teacher.

Yuzuko: That's interesting. You know it's kind of related to my experience with the sexist coworker that I mentioned above, but I felt the opposite way. I feel that because these issues, whether it's about sexism (Nagatomo, 2012), internalized misogyny (hooks, 2000), bi-erasure (Erickson-Schroth & Mitchell, 2009), or native-speakerism (Holliday, 2005), are such personal issues that affect me emotionally, I almost feel like I am not in the right position to do so, you know? First, it's because I am not sure if I can maintain this teacher-face, because as a teacher I would like to be fair and respectful to diverse ideas and opinions in the classroom and workplace, and also, again, if the purpose of critical language education is to raise awareness and hopefully produce some positive changes for a more just and equal society, can I change the mind of those who are consciously or unconsciously part of the problem or those who have no imperative to solve these issues in a practical sense? Because I identify as feminist and am very critical about these issues, I feel like this position might erase my legitimacy in the eyes of these people because I have my own agenda, in their mind, I am already biased against them. Why would they listen to me and possibly change their mind?

Though originating from different sources and expressed in different ways, the concerns about legitimacy expressed above by both Chris and Yuzuko demonstrate the type of awareness and constant self-reflexivity that is required of critical language teachers. Contrary to images of critical teachers as dogmatic partisans indoctrinating students with their own political biases and belief systems, we believe that most critical teachers are hypervigilant and reflexive when it comes to both the content and methods they employ in their classrooms. As Pennycook (1999) mentions, this self-reflexivity, or inward-facing criticality, is an essential component of critical language teaching practice.

Post-Project Reflection

In lieu of a traditional conclusion, we felt that a post-project reflection would provide a better accounting of our research process and findings, while also adhering more closely to the principles and practices of duoethnography. As such, this section aims to explore two broadly defined areas that stand out to us upon completing this project: one that concerns the research process, and a second that focuses on the practice of critical English language teaching and research.

Reflecting on the research process

In terms of the research process, the first thing that stood out for us was the degree to which the initial theme of the research changed during the research and writing process. Qualitative research of all kinds is often defined, in part, by its inherently emergent quality (Denzin & Lincoln, 1994) and this duoethnography was no exception. Yuzuko originally conceived of this project as an exploration of two English language teachers' lived experiences with issues of gender and sexuality. Since duoethnography often works well by pairing researchers with clear differences of some kind (Sawyer & Norris, 2013), Yuzuko asked Chris if he would like to participate, as they were friends, and were English teachers that differed in terms of gender and sexual orientation. In fact, the first two interviews were conducted with this purpose in mind. In examining the data, however, it became apparent that the larger, emergent theme was that of critical ELT, and how our identities led to different experiences, opportunities and obstacles. As a result, the focus of our dialogues began to shift and sharpen in focus. While gender and sexual identity remain important aspects in our dialogues, they became part of a larger exploration of critical English language teacher identity. We feel that this expansion of focus was not only beneficial for the research project, itself, but also for the development of our individual understandings of ourselves and our critical teaching practices.

Additionally, we found that conducting and recording multiple face-to-face interviews gave us the time and space to deeply consider our narratives, and the degree to which they truly reflected the meanings we intended to express. For example, after the first interview in which Chris described his background and how he perceived its relationship to his development into a critical language teacher, he asked to amend his original narrative, as he felt it didn't accurately express his intended meaning and personal understanding. If we had only met once or twice, it is likely that our dialogues would have focused only on the original (and clearly worthy) choice of topic of gender and sexuality, but we would not have had the ability to refine our initial descriptions, nor reached the depth of introspection, reflexivity and ultimate focus that we achieved through multiple sessions. Similarly, the act of sharing the same physical space throughout most of the writing process allowed for a truly collaborative exchange of ideas about the structure and presentation of the research in written form. Considering the fact that we were writing for an English language publication, with all the standards of 'native' English normativity that accompany it, the act of writing together allowed for extensive collaboration, negotiation and co-equal meaning making.

Reflecting on criticality in teaching and research

Nevertheless, as we engaged in the writing stage of this research, we both became acutely aware of the politics of English academic writing standards. Of course, it is always important to consider the consistency of writing styles and the accurate representation of voice when it comes to co-authoring a piece together. But as we discussed during the writing stage on multiple occasions, we came to the consensus that the consistency in writing and adherence to standardized English academic writing are two interconnected, yet separate entities. Therefore, it was imperative for us to consider how to determine where to draw boundaries of 'acceptability,' since Chris is labeled as a 'native' English speaker and writer, whereas Yuzuko is not. Kubota (2013) critically scrutinizes the western-centered writing standard and expectations in the applied linguistics field, and the way in which it might produce a power imbalance that disfavors 'non-native' English writers. Although this political issue of academic writing may not directly affect the outcome of research projects, it is essential to bear in mind the pressure that exists to produce writing that achieves certain standards of English academic writing, which further reflect the hegemony of a certain form of English (Hartse & Kubota, 2014). With that in mind, we refer to this final draft as the 'native-ized version,' in spite of our critically-oriented concerns of representation, authenticity and legitimacy as teachers, researchers and authors.

On a final note, one topic that arose often in our discussions (both recorded and not) during the project, but was not presented above, was our shared concern as critical teachers that many mainstream English teachers believe that language education is not an appropriate space for critical or feminist pedagogies, believing that language education should remain politically and culturally 'neutral.' However, as Canagarajah (1999) argues, the history of second/foreign language education has been, and remains, inherently political in nature, and every language classroom is full of ideological and political connotations, whether it relates to what is being taught in class or how a class is conducted (Benesch, 1993). Extensive review and discussion of our research led us to a few conclusions. First, teachers differ in their backgrounds, interests, contexts and preferred approaches to ELT, and no one should feel obligated to teach in a manner that feels wrong or uncomfortable to them, and therefore critical approaches to ELT are not for everyone, nor for every context. Second, we would like to reiterate that the ultimate goal of critical language education is not to indoctrinate or brainwash students with certain political views or agendas, but rather to help foreground issues of power and inequality, nurture their awareness of these issues, and acquire the skills to deconstruct and analyze social issues that are often normalized or systematically erased in our daily lives. Finally, it is our hope that this project will help to further promote the pursuit of social justice and equity in the field of language education and research, as well as inspire and empower other teachers to adopt their own forms of critical English language teaching in Japan.

References

Baudrillard, J. (1994) *Simulacra and Simulation*. Ann Arbor, MI: University of Michigan Press.

Beauvoir, S. (1953) *The Second Sex* (1st American edn). New York, NY: Knopf.

Benesch, S. (1993) ESL, ideology, and the politics of pragmatism. *TESOL Quarterly* 27 (4), 705–717.

Bourdieu, P. (1991) *Language and Symbolic Power*. Cambridge: Polity Press.

Breen, M.P. and Littlejohn, A. (eds) (2000) *Classroom Decision-Making*. Cambridge: Cambridge University Press.

Canagarajah, A.S. (1999) *Resisting Linguistic Imperialism in English Teaching*. Oxford: Oxford University Press.

Collins, P.H. and Bilge, S. (2016) *Intersectionality*. Cambridge: Polity Press.

Crawford-Lange, L.M. (1981) Redirecting second language curricula: Paulo Freire's contribution. *Foreign Language Annals* 14 (4), 257–268.

Creswell, J.W. (2007) *Qualitative Inquiry and Research Design: Choosing among Five Approaches* (2nd edn). Thousand Oaks, CA: Sage Publications.

Crookes, G.V. (2013) *Critical ELT in Action: Foundation, Promises, Praxis*. New York, NY: Routledge.

Denzin, N.K. and Lincoln, Y.S. (1994) *Handbook of Qualitative Research*. Thousand Oaks, CA: Sage Publications.

Derrida, J. (2016) *Of Grammatology* (G.C. Spivak, trans.) (14th Anniversary edn). Baltimore, MD: Johns Hopkins Press.

Erickson-Schroth, L. and Mitchell, J. (2009) Queering queer theory, or why bisexuality matters. *Journal of Bisexuality* 9 (3–4), 297–315.

Fairclough, N. (1989) *Language and Power*. London: Longman.

Fanon, F. (1963) *The Wretched of the Earth* (1st Evergreen edn). New York, NY: Grove Press.

Farrell, T.S.C. (2015) *Promoting Teacher Reflection in Second Language Education: A Framework for TESOL Professionals*. New York, NY: Routledge.

Foucault, M. (1977) *Discipline and Punish: The Birth of the Prison*. Harmondsworth: Penguin.

Freire, P. (1970) *Pedagogy of the Oppressed*. New York, NY: Herder and Herder.

García, O. and Kleifgen, J.A. (2018) *Educating Emergent Bilinguals: Policies, Programs, and Practices for English learners* (2nd edn). New York, NY: Teachers College Press.

García, O. and Wei, L. (2013) *Translanguaging: Language, Bilingualism and Education.* Basingstoke: Palgrave Macmillan.

Giroux, H.A. (1983) *Theory and Resistance in Education: A Pedagogy for the Opposition.* South Hadley, MA: Bergin & Garvey.

Goldenberg, C. and Wagner, K. (2015) Bilingual education: Reviving an American tradition. *American Educator* 39 (3), 28–32.

Habermas, J. (1987) *The Philosophical Discourse of Modernity: Twelve Lectures* (F. Lawrence, trans.). Cambridge, MA: MIT Press.

Hammond, K. (2006) More than a game: A critical discourse analysis of a racial inequality exercise in Japan. *TESOL Quarterly* 40 (3), 545–571.

Hashimoto, K. (2013) The Japanisation of English language education. In J. Tollefson (ed.) *Language Policies in Education: Critical Issues* (pp. 175–190). New York, NY: Routledge.

Hartse, J.H. and Kubota, R. (2014) Pluralizing English? Variation in high-stakes academic texts and challenges of copyediting. *Journal of Second Language Writing* 24, 71–82.

Häusler, A.H., Leal, P, Parba, J., West, G.B. and Crookes, G.V. (2018) 'How did you become political?': Narratives of junior researcher-practitioners in applied linguistics. *Critical Inquiry in Language Studies* 15 (4), 282–301.

Hill, J.H. (2008) *The Everyday Language of White Racism.* West Sussex: Wiley-Blackwell.

Holliday, A.R. (2005) *The Struggle to Teach English as an International Language.* Oxford: Oxford University Press.

Holliday, A.R. (2015) Native-speakerism: Taking the concept forward and achieving cultural belief. In A. Swan, P. Aboshiha and A.R. Holliday (eds.) *(En)countering Native-Speakerism* (pp. 11–25). New York, NY: Palgrave Macmillan.

hooks, b. (1994) *Teaching to Transgress: Education as the Practice of Freedom.* New York, NY: Routledge.

hooks, b. (2000) *Feminism is for Everybody: Passionate Politics.* London: Pluto Press.

Horkheimer, M. (1972) *Critical Theory: Selected Essays.* New York, NY: Herder and Herder.

Kubota, R. (1998) Ideologies of English in Japan. *World Englishes* 17 (3), 295–306.

Kubota, R. (2011) Questioning linguistic instrumentalism: English, neoliberalism, and language tests in Japan. *Linguistics and Education* 22 (3), 248–260.

Kubota, R. (2013) Dislimiting second language writing. *Journal of Second Language Writing* 22 (4), 430–431.

McMahill, C. (1997) Communities of resistance: A case study of two feminist English classes in Japan. *TESOL Quarterly* 31 (3), 612–22.

Nagatomo, D.H. (2012) *Exploring Japanese University English Teachers' Professional Identity.* Bristol: Multilingual Matters.

Nelson, C. (2009) *Sexual Identities in English Language Education: Classroom Conversations.* New York, NY: Routledge.

Pennycook, A. (1999) Critical approaches to TESOL. *TESOL Quarterly* 33 (3), 329–348.

Pennycook, A. (2001) *Critical Applied Linguistics: A Critical Introduction.* London: Routledge.

Phillipson, R. (1992) *Linguistic Imperialism.* Oxford: Oxford University Press.

Said, E. (1978) *Orientalism* (1st edn). New York, NY: Pantheon Books.

Sawyer, R.D. and Norris, J. (2013) *Duoethnography: Understanding Qualitative Research.* Oxford: Oxford University Press.

Sue, D.W. (2010) *Microaggressions in Everyday Life: Race, Gender, and Sexual Orientation.* Hoboken, NJ: John Wiley.

Tsuda, Y. (1998) Critical studies on the dominance of English and the implications for international communication. *Japan Review* 10, 219–236.

Vandrick, S. (1998) Promoting gender equity in the postsecondary ESL class. In T. Smoke (ed.) *Adult ESL: Politics, Pedagogy, and Participation in Classroom and Community Programs* (pp. 73–88). Mahwah, NJ: Lawrence Erlbaum Associate.

Vandrick, S. (2009) *Interrogating Privilege: Reflections of a Second Language Educator.* Ann Arbor, MI: University of Michigan Press.

4 Personalisation and Professionalism: Managing the Relationship Between Teacher and Learner as People

Richard Pinner and Ema Ushioda

Introduction

In this paper, we look at how relationships between teachers and students are managed at both personal and professional levels, paying particular attention to the point of intersection between these two realms. Drawing on Ushioda's (2009) *persons-in-context relational view* of motivation, self and identity, we analyse our own relationship between one another as supervisor/supervisee. This framework, originally intended to describe L2 motivation, but here applied more generally to identities in context, sees meaningful interactions as emergent from 'relations between real persons, with particular social identities, [within] the unfolding cultural context of activity' (2009: 215). In other words, we take a holistic look at the identities that we bring with us to interactions, avoiding the tendency to reduce people to the sum of their mere contextual identity (e.g. learner, teacher, supervisor, supervisee). In doing so, we examine interactions at several levels, incorporating multiple aspects of identity and interpersonal dynamics. Of course, in presenting this duoethnographic retrospective analysis of various situations, we are only able to expose the complexities and uniqueness of each encounter, and as such we do not seek to provide any kind of generalisations or rules of thumb for managing this rather 'thin blue line' between personalisation and professionalism with regards to student-teacher relations, by which we mean an often invisible barrier with shifting borders between what is acceptable and what is not in a professional context. Rather, we advocate very much a 'case-by-case' approach, yet with strong underlying ethical principles and guidelines, which we feel are what lie at the heart of healthy, mutually rewarding, productive and personally authentic relationships in institutional educational settings.

In order to start off this chapter, we thought it would be important to explain who we are and how we came to know each other. The most important information about our relationship is that Ema supervised Richard's PhD at Warwick University between 2013 and 2017. We first met in August 2010 at the XIVth International CALL Conference in Antwerp, where Ema was giving a plenary talk on motivation and CALL. At that stage, Richard had just completed his master's degree at King's College, London, having researched teachers' attitudes and motivations relating to the use of CALL for his MA dissertation. Following our conversations during the conference, we kept in periodic email contact as Richard moved to Japan to take up a teaching position at Sophia University in Tokyo and then subsequently applied to do a PhD at the University of Warwick. Richard began his PhD on 1 February 2013, registering as a part-time student since he was working full-time in Tokyo. This meant that much of the PhD supervision process was conducted at distance via email and Skype, though we had face-to-face meetings at least once a year when Richard visited the UK or when Ema visited Japan.

The research question in focus in this paper revolves around how personal and professional identities are negotiated between supervisor and supervisee, and what factors influence the decisions to foreground or prioritise either of these two identities. Teaching is essentially a very personal endeavour (Dinham & Scott, 2000; Dörnyei & Ushioda, 2011; Richardson & Watt, 2006), and as such we argue that both personal and professional identities come into play when negotiating such relationships. Our interest in the spectrum of personalisation and professionalism emerged quite naturally as a result of our existing interest in themes of identity, motivation and authenticity and also as a result of our own interactions with one another as our relationship evolved during the course of Richard's PhD and the subsequent contact we had afterwards. In this chapter we will tell the story of how we managed the two overlapping registers of professional and personal discourse in our own relationship with each other. We then go on to discuss how teachers and students might utilise duoethnographic methods in their own research, and what existing methodological toolkits there are for teachers wishing to explore this relationship further.

What follows is a more personal account of how we see each other, in light of the focus of this chapter and the personal/professional relationships that we manage as fellow teachers and as former supervisor/supervisee.

Richard's account of Ema

Although I first properly met Ema in Antwerp, I knew her work from my MA and had also seen her give a plenary talk at IATEFL in 2010, which was the first time I ever attended a proper teachers' conference. Ema's plenary was really fantastic, and I instantly liked her for her ability to not only write in an engaging way but also present in a way which kept the audience's attention and put the theoretical parts into perspective through the use of stories and personal examples. I now realise that what Ema does is to frame things within a narrative so as to be clearer for people. Furthermore, the public sharing of personal information by teachers, what Henry and Thorsen (2018) call 'self-disclosures', has been shown to be an important aspect of teacher–student relationship forming, having particular relevance for motivation. During my PhD I found that through Ema I made many contacts in the field of L2 motivation and was able to pursue my own research agenda with a great deal of guidance. Several times, mainly at conferences, I was able to socialise with Ema and get to know her personally. She also briefly met my wife and son when we came to campus, and also had dinner with me and my parents the night before the graduation ceremony. By the time I finished my PhD, I felt that although I could no longer call Ema my supervisor, I could undoubtedly call her a friend and a close colleague. This was very important to me; when a student particularly likes a teacher, then it is essential that the teacher reciprocates this admiration in the form of acknowledgment or mutual validation. As Goffman states 'there is hardly a performance, in whatever area of life, which does not rely on the personal touch to exaggerate the uniqueness of the transactions between performer and audience' (1959: 50). In other words, as students we feel that we must appear special to the teacher in some way, that they must remember us and that they must have meant all the encouragement they gave us from their hearts. When students get particularly motivated by a class and by a teacher, they of course begin to personally invest in that course, and as such the stakes are raised in terms of potentially face-threatening behaviours as a greater personal investment means a greater personal risk in the face of failure or lack of recognition. In other words, once a student begins investing in a class which is due in particular to the relationship with the teacher, the student will naturally require some form of validation in order to continue with their investment and maintain their motivation. Without this validation, the student is likely to perceive their efforts in the class as having gone unnoticed, and withdraw as a natural reflex. Upon writing this reflection, I wonder if I perhaps sought out Ema not just based on her academic credentials but more personally because I felt confident that she would be able to provide the kind of nurturing and supportive supervision that I needed. I wonder how much these two aspects are actually united in the personal/professional interrelationship.

Ema's account of Richard

I remember that when I first met Richard at the CALL conference in Antwerp in 2010, he struck me as a personable and courteous young man who seemed both a little excited and a little shy to talk to me. I don't recall our initial face-to-face conversations as being extensive or 'chatty', and I don't think I really got to know Richard until we started communicating by email in the months and years that followed, as Richard moved to Japan and then began his part-time PhD with me. In fact, our working relationship has largely been built through the medium of emails plus occasional Skype meetings, with opportunities for face-to-face interactions limited to around once a year or so.

In this sense, I have got to know Richard primarily through the way he writes and what he writes – in his emails, his academic writing for his PhD and publications, his entertaining written summaries of our tutorial discussions, as well as other forms of writing such as his blog (http://uniliterate.com/) and creative writing pieces (including the odd poem that cropped up in interim drafts of his PhD thesis in place of academic prose). Richard is a gifted, engaging and creative writer, and an impressively prolific one. After all, how many part-time PhD students with full-time teaching positions can also embark on a separate research monograph and succeed in getting it published (Pinner, 2016a) while doing their PhD, and yet still manage to complete their doctorate a year ahead of the normal minimum registration period?

Regarding our principal mode of interaction by email, I have always found Richard's emails engaging, quite conversational in tone, and very much infused with his personality so that they are never simply matter-of-fact and business-like. His emails are often quite lengthy, in a rambling yet entertaining and humorous kind of way, and sometimes have quite amusing subject headers (such as 'Where is all that stuff I promised?' or 'Turning to the dark side?' or 'Wobbly but without need of a walking stick'). In fact, I think wit and humour have been a significant feature of our email conversations as research supervisor and supervisee and as colleagues and friends since then (including the email conversations through which we have been developing this duoethnography). Humour (often self-deprecating) is a characteristic of Richard's communication style that I particularly warm to, perhaps because of my upbringing in Ireland where wit and humour are part of the cultural fabric of life.

I think this element of humour in his communication style and in our interactions has been an important part of the 'bonding' in our personal/professional relations. It has contributed to a shared sense of perspective where we can see the funny side of issues that may be quite serious for Richard (e.g. certain challenges that he faced during his PhD), which can help take the edge off some of the stress or pressure. The use of humour has also tempered and facilitated potentially difficult or face-threatening discussions in our interactions as supervisor–supervisee. For example, I can recall the email exchange when Richard first raised the critical question of that 'thin blue line' in teacher–student relations. In his email to me, he was clearly uncomfortable about challenging my view that, as teachers and as researchers, we should try to understand language learners holistically as 'people' or 'persons-in-contexts', rather than as just L2 learners. By framing his critical question to me in a very entertaining manner (e.g. 'Don't worry, I'm not going to go against it and say that we need to see our learners as nothing more than learning blobs of flesh who should be treated like caged chickens or anything', October 2014 email), he made sure that his question would be received in good humour by me, and that I would respond candidly and engage him in genuine discussion, as I did. A couple of emails later, he wrote: 'I love how you took my rambling email and turned it into an erudite question 'the appropriateness or indeed the ethics of encroaching too much on students' personal world'. Later in this paper we will revisit this episode in greater detail.

Method and Data Types

As this is a book about duoethnography, we have the privilege of being able to write our account without the necessity of justifying the method or explaining it to unfamiliar audiences, as this is already done elsewhere in the volume (see Lawrence & Lowe, this volume). We call this a privilege because, as Bell (2002) has argued, much of the struggle of qualitative research is that justifying the approach often takes a serious amount of effort and a considerable percentage of the word count, leaving precious little room for data and discussion, which also require considerable word allowances in qualitative research. However, some explanation of the individual methods we used are certainly needed, because there is no 'fixed blueprint' and the method is 'always emergent and uncertain' in duoethnographic inquiry (Norris & Sawyer, 2012: 25). Much like Richard's PhD, the majority of this paper and the discussions leading up to it were conducted via email and skype, at a distance of over 6500 miles. While this has an impact on the types of interactions we had, it also left a very useful trail of content (data) which allowed for an accurate retrospective of our interactions that provided a useful record of the development of our relationship (see Nabavi & Lund, 2012; Sawyer & Norris, 2012 for other studies conducted through mixed digital mediums). In addition to this, each of us also traced back through our other forms of correspondence, which included a much more diverse range of texts and sources. Some of these, as mentioned by Ema in her account of Richard, were such things as tutorial summaries, comments on early drafts and even audio recordings of some of our past tutorials. In this way, much of the main data for this study bears a resemblance to netnography (Kozinets, 2015); a fusion of ethnography and digital-based inquiry, generally used to examine issues of interaction facilitated through information communication technologies.

Finally, when the theme of the study had been agreed and some of the main points for discussion had been decided, we conducted a Skype call on 8 March 2018 in which we discussed the main points. This was then transcribed by Richard and used to form the backbone of the study. As this was being written, we emailed back and forth the draft and made changes and comments as well for clarification. In this way, the actual process of writing the paper served as a secondary stage of data analysis. Within narrative inquiry, this process is usually referred to as 'restorying' and it involves successive reiterative writings of a narrative in order to gain a deeper critical perspective and make sense of past experiences (Foote, 2015). So, this study is very much process-oriented and as such it follows the conventions of duoethnography (Norris *et al.*, 2012). In this way, the construction of this paper can be mapped to the four steps of *currere*, as outlined by Pinar (1994), which are; regressive, progressive, analytical and synthetical. In other words, we looked back at our relationship through introspection, we moved forward through dialogic discussion, we worked together in analysis and identifying the key themes, and finally we produced the finished synthesised report of those findings. Of course, the concept of synthesis at this stage is somewhat misleading, as what we are describing are relationships which are dynamically constructed through the unfurling context. This is appropriate, as the concept of *currere* lends itself well to both of our prior research interests (see for example Pinner, 2016b, 2018; Ushioda, 1993, 2009, 2011) – and in this way our ethical approaches seem to have naturally meshed to form the method underlying this dialogical approach to qualitative inquiry. Ethical principles are likewise identified as the key finding in this paper, when looking at the central research question about how the 'thin blue line' between professional and personal identities are managed.

Reflections on Persons-in-Context

During our discussions and looking at the data and content of our relationships, it was possible to see how the two strands of 'personal' and 'professional' entwined and were both mutually supported by our activities as teacher and supervisor. For example, in one particularly relevant email (entitled 'Turning to the dark side?'), which Ema mentioned in her account of Richard, the themes at the centre of this inquiry (professionalism and personalisation) first began to form as questions relating to how we manage our personal and professional identities with one another. The email is worth including in full here, although it has been slightly modified for clarity.

Richard's Email to Ema questioning her own work

From: Pinner, Richard
Sent: 28 October 2014 03:21
To: Ushioda, Ema
Subject: Turning to the dark side?

Dear Ema,

> How are you? I've not been in touch much but I have regularly been thinking about you and not wanting to leave things on ice for too long. Of course the PhD is now at an all-consuming mad place where I feel that

I am nearly going to be at the end of the data collection stage soon (week 5 of the last 14-week semester already…. How can this be?) and I thought it might be good to tell you what I've been up to and how my ideas are developing.

As usual I have some new hypotheses rattling around, and of course one of them can only be explained with a visual diagram of a tree… how clichéd huh? But I'd like to talk about all these things nonetheless. Also, the reason for my scary sounding subject line about turning to the dark side is that I've been thinking a lot about the *persons-in context relational view* which is basically the main thing that spoke to me in all the reading I've ever done and one of the main reasons why I approached you to be my supervisor (there are other reasons too but that was a big one as you know) and anyway I've started to think that there might be a thin blue line somewhere in there and I'd like to hash this out with you. Don't worry, I'm not going to go against it and say that we need to see our learners as nothing more than learning blobs of flesh who should be treated like caged chickens or anything, but I am currently REALLY trying to connect with my class and to learn about them as people, like REALLY to see them and learn about the people who make up the class. I drew an iceberg and the bit jutting out of the water is what I see and know about in class…. But of course there is a limit to how personal you can be and this is something that I've started to think about as being an important reality in the authenticity question…. It would be actually inauthentic to try to be too close or to befriend the learners when really they are just learners, especially those students who do not want to make a personal connection with the teacher. People may not want to talk about their personal lives with a teacher! And of course there is a professional boundary as well. So I've been thinking about this. It doesn't go against your calls for person in context at all, I think it complements it but I'd like to talk about all this in a tutorial as I wrote in my journal that my world had turned upside down when I first thought of that!

So, I know that this email will make you smile and sigh because it's long and breathless, but I hope that it has piqued your interest and I'd be grateful of a chance for a tutorial to see if you can help reign me in a bit.

Love as always,

Richard

We intended to look at this email and to extract which parts could be coded as being primarily 'personal' and which 'professional' (relating to the PhD), but looking at the email it is clearly difficult to demarcate one type of discourse from the other. For example, the opening starts with a generic 'how are you' and explains that Richard has not been in touch for a while, which could easily belong to an email between friends. However, later, Richard questions Ema's concept of the *persons-in-context relational view* and (as discussed previously in Ema's account of Richard) does so in a humorous and non-threatening way, clearly invoking both personal and professional identities at the same time. Often, although the content of the email relates to professional topics, the style is still very personal and informal. In addition, the length (575 words in the original) is possibly a marker of politeness, since hedging and indirectness are seen as polite forms in English (Brown & Levinson, 1987).

In Ema's reply, we can see now looking back that the email is quite a bit shorter (219 words, less than half as long), and generally more on-point. It takes the 'rambling' words of Richard's email and re-expresses them in more academic terms.

Ema's first reply to Richard's email

From: Ushioda, Ema
Sent: 28 October 2014 18:17
To: Pinner, Richard
Subject: RE: Turning to the dark side?

Hi Richard

> The image of students as learning blobs of flesh who should be treated as caged chickens is quite compelling ... ;-)
>
> Well, it's good to hear from you again and know that you continue to be very active in your thinking and your teacher-researcher life. The point you raise – i.e. about the appropriateness or indeed the ethics of encroaching too much on students' personal world – is certainly an important one. I think it's one reason why I find the concept of 'transportable identity' attractive (as developed in Keith Richards' 2006 paper analysing classroom talk, following Zimmerman, 1998), since it relates to aspects of identity and their personal world that students (and teachers) may choose to invoke in the classroom. In other words, there will be many (private) aspects of our identity and personal world that we (as students or teachers) will not want to bring into play in the classroom.
>
> Cheers
>
> Ema

Despite the more academic tone, in the first line Ema indicates her reciprocation of Richard's humour with an emoji and perhaps some gentle teasing of the 'student as battery-hen' image he used in his email. Despite this, there are clearly differences in the tone of each email. Richard signs his with 'love as always' whereas Ema retains a more professional distance by simply signing off with 'Cheers' (although note how this is in itself an informal and friendly use of language). Next, we will focus briefly on the theme of love and its fit within the bonds of a professional relationship. Challenging the idea that emotions can impair professionalism as a 'myth',

Barcelos and Coelho (2016) make an excellent case for the place of love in the classroom, arguing that love is essential for a passion for teaching, a motivation and source of energy for being attentive to others, for creating a 'positivity resonance', and even for facilitating spiritual and mental growth with our students. From this definition, we can both recognise that we draw on aspects of love in order to propel us through the more challenging and emotionally taxing interactions that we may have in the course of our professional lives, because we are humans with professional roles, we do not merely tread a 'thin blue line' but rather we must draw boundaries and know when to re-draw them in a constant process of social interaction which is guided by ethical principles and philosophical beliefs.

Thinking About Thinking About our Relationship

In Richard's reply to Ema, some of these issues are clearly stated rather explicitly, and actually he pitches the idea of working with Ema on a paper that looks at these issues. Here is an extract from the email.

Richard's Reply (extract)

> I love how you took my rambling email and turned it into an erudite question 'the appropriateness or indeed the ethics of encroaching too much on students' personal world'. If you are remotely interested in working with me on a paper perhaps that could be the theme... I would love to be able to put my name next to yours in the bibliography one day... but I know that might be uncomfortable for you as my tutor perhaps. And the irony of signing my last email with 'love as always' wasn't lost on me either, in fact I think I intentionally try to make our relationship more a personal one... I think I do that because I tend to look far ahead, and I am actually a little worried about what will happen to me when I cease to be a PhD student and can no longer legitimately ask your advice in the 'big massive favour' way which is embedded already in the current roles we both have. I suppose I am trying to frame myself as a friend because that way there is less of a sense of finality about it.

Here, Richard clearly expresses his desire to continue the relationship with Ema even after the PhD supervisor/supervisee relationship is over. In Ema's response, she directly addresses these questions, again using her customary good humour, albeit rather less 'gushing' than Richard's.

Ema's reply (extract)

> Re maintaining our relationship and co-authoring something in the future ... I don't think I would say no ... ;-) And in fact co-authoring with current/former PhD students is something that we are actively encouraged to do ...

In framing the response as 'something we are actively encouraged to do', Ema is clearly situating this proposed new 'friendship' or 'lasting relationship' from an institutional setting and maintaining the situated identities that are bestowed on us from the context of our professional relationship (Zimmerman, 1998). Despite this, in the Skype conversation we had (notably, after the supervisor/supervisee relationship has played out), this issue was approached now from a slightly different angle, and with a notably different tone.

First Skype Extract

Richard: I find when I'm working at X University (where I am just a part-time lecturer) for example I can be I guess less guarded about what I say because I don't feel like I represent the institution as much as at my full-time job. I don't know, do you have any experiences like that? I think, going back to what you were saying earlier that I think it's not the case that you maintain a kind of close friendship or relationship with *all* former students.

Ema: I think it depends very much on the kind of working relationship you had with each person but also in terms of what they are doing and how active they are in remaining in touch with you, so I think in all cases the students, the PhD students that I have fairly, sort of, what I would call regular interactions with tend to be those who themselves want to continue that interaction. So it's not something that I as a sort of former PhD supervisor would actively seek out and try and follow up and see how people are doing, because in some senses I kind of feel I… I don't want to continue, you know, for my former PhD students to think that I'm still kind of their supervisor so things like exchanging Christmas cards for example I only kind of write back to or respond to students who send me Christmas cards but I don't make a point of sending them Christmas cards or initiating that process.

Richard: Yes possibly also because of the power asymmetry of the teacher–student relationship. If you seem to be the one doing the kind of coming on and wanting to create that then obviously because you're, you're in the power situation there, it's harder for them to refuse whereas if they send you a Christmas card that's their choice right from the start.

Here, it is clear that we are both discussing our situated identities from a rather meta perspective, and in doing so are both on more equal ground now as practicing teachers who are reflecting on our work as educators.

Changing by Looking at Change

As we composed this paper together, we also found our relationship went through yet another change, which raised new issues such as the ethical and moral question of how much of ourselves to reveal in our writing. Dashper quite rightly notes that, while the act of writing can be a form of self-discovery, 'the decision about how much, what and how to reveal in relation to personal issues, weaknesses and experiences in pursuit of academic goals is one that requires careful consideration and constitutes a very personal decision' (2015: 522). Here Dashper is referring to autoethnography, but this 'personal decision' is even more foregrounded when composing a duoethnography, as there are not one but two people now involved, both of whom may have different interpretations and different levels of privacy. In creating this study and revisiting the development of our relationship, many personal stories have been uncovered, but not all of them have a place in this published chapter and thus again the negotiation of personal and professional is enacted even as we put words onto the page.

As Ema stated at the start of this paper in her account of Richard, one of the striking things about our relationship was that, although it was primarily a textual and distance relationship, it contained many different genres of writing (poetry, stories, formal and informal). Richard sent Ema not only samples of his academic work, but also stories and poems too. Ema, likewise, would reciprocate by buying Richard the occasional cake or Guinness, and in face-to-face interactions we often shared many personal anecdotes and shared many meaningful exchanges. Clearly, just like during discourse, in the texts and emails we sent each other, we would often enact various transportable identities during the interactions, which have been shown to be important because 'the interactional consequences of [invoking transportable identities] can be significant' and can become a 'potent aspect of interaction' (Richards, 2006: 63, 68). However, transportable identities only really describe at a transactional level the types of interactions that were taking place. In order to more fully understand how the personal and professional limits of a working relationship are constructed, we must look in more detail at the types of interpersonal interactions taking place and approach them from a teacher's perspective in examining what place these have in terms of the wider development of an individual. In other words, we must look at social and emotional intelligence as a construct that affects teachers' ability to foster meaningful interpersonal relationships with their students, and in particular ask how this is important for learning.

Social and Emotional Intelligence

The notion of EQ (emotional intelligence), as opposed to IQ (intelligence quotient), has been gaining prominence in educational settings recently. Emotional intelligence is defined basically as our capacity to manage our emotions, to recognise our own feelings and especially to understand the feelings and emotions of others (Goleman, 1998: 317). Emotional intelligence can manifest itself in the form of certain abilities, such as 'self-control, zeal and persistence, and the ability to motivate oneself' (Goleman, 1995: xii). As important as this seems, of perhaps even far greater relevance to teachers is the related issue of social intelligence, which is connected to our ability to manage relationships with others, to have fruitful and enriching interactions with others, and of course our capacity for empathy and understanding others' emotions and points of view (Goleman, 2006). In a fascinating study by Gkonou and Mercer (2017), it was found that teachers had generally high levels of social and emotional intelligence, and this correlated strongly with gender (females scoring more highly than males) and experience, with the authors stating that the more experience a teacher accrued, the higher their scores on the questionnaire which measured these abilities. So, from this it could be inferred that teaching develops our social intelligence, and that social intelligence is necessary for teachers in order to do their work. Certainly, in our work together and in the discussions we had in composing this paper, these interpersonal skills were very much highlighted. For instance, in our Skype discussion, Ema mentioned her 'emergency bottle of whiskey' which she keeps in her office, and when colleagues (notably male ones) come to her due to some problem they are having, she has on occasion felt it necessary to open. Of course, this is a rather amusing example but it actually points us towards a much more serious and important issue – the role of academic support.

Reflections on our Roles for Providing Support

Ema's reflections on support

> As a postgraduate supervisor, I think it's fair to say that the support and guidance I offer may often extend beyond academic support and guidance. Of course, we know that one of our responsibilities is to provide pastoral care for our students, but I think it's only when we start working with individual students that we come to appreciate how complex and challenging their lives and personal circumstances can be, and how these factors may impact on their academic work. The PhD process for a full-time student is three to four years, and for a part-time student can be as long as seven years (at our university). This is a sizeable chunk out of a person's life, and all kinds of things can happen during this time. Students may experience financial constraints, difficult family responsibilities, bereavement, marital strain, health concerns, very serious medical problems, and of course mental health issues. As a supervisor, I sometimes find myself having to consider how to help students who experience such life challenges, and in some cases this help may extend beyond the student to include their family as well. After all, many of our students come from

overseas and some may bring family with them, or have left their family behind, and may struggle to support themselves and their dependants on a limited studentship. As a research supervisor, it is sometimes difficult to know how much (non-academic) support it is appropriate to give to one's students, where our professional boundaries and commitments should lie, and when our compassion and moral obligations as fellow human beings should stretch beyond such boundaries.

Richard's reflection on support

I have often benefitted from Ema's generosity, from free drinks and dinners to personal contacts and introductions, and yet shortly after embarking on this paper in various discussions with friends I realised quickly that having such a close relationship with a PhD supervisor is by no means the norm. In fact, it seems that it is at least as common if not more so to have very little contact with a supervisor. One colleague reported that his PhD supervisor knew almost nothing about his topic and had very little impact on the shape of his study, offering guidance only on structural aspects of the writing. Another of my colleagues stated that he had actively disliked his PhD supervisor and they had very little contact. Yet another colleague, who like me had studied mainly at a distance while living in Japan, had barely known his supervisor and generally found their input to be more of a distraction than a guide. Despite this, perhaps due to the working culture of the Centre for Applied Linguistics at Warwick, closely working with supervisors and having amenable relationships between staff and students seemed to be an important part of the dynamic. In my experience of talking with other PhD students, almost all of them reported great levels of satisfaction at their relationships with their supervisors, although it was also generally known that Ema was a bit special in that respect.

But... (there's always a but)

However, Ema also acknowledges that she is by no means close with all of her students, nor does she maintain contact with everybody she has supervised. Managing this was something we discussed at length, and one of the clearest strategies for constructing appropriate relationships that do not violate the personal/professional divide is by not initiating contact with students, but rather only reciprocating when a student reaches out. Ema used the example of sending Christmas cards, but clearly this expands to all aspects of developing a relationship with someone. Due to the marked power asymmetry of the teacher/student relationship, not initiating closeness was seen as an important ethical matter because doing so could be construed as an abuse of that power, and thus 'the ball is very much in the student's court' as Ema put it.

Our mutual awareness of this, and our concern for the ethics of such relationships, is likely to be a consequence of the fact that both of us have quite highly developed sensitivities to interpersonal relationships. This is also very likely to be the reason why colleagues recently elected Ema to take the role of Head of Department, because her highly developed social and emotional intelligence make her an obvious choice for such an important role that requires dealing with people and managing relationships for an entire group of colleagues. Likewise, Richard displays similarly high levels of sensitivity to personal relationships, and indeed this became the focus of his PhD when he began to investigate the synergistic relationship between teachers' and students' motivation (Pinner, 2017, 2019).

Although this emerged as a very salient aspect of this study, it was not particularly surprising since 'human beings have a pervasive drive to form and maintain [positive and lasting] interpersonal relationships' (Baumeister & Leary, 1995: 497). Our mutual interest in these issues is likely to have been what led Richard to seek out Ema initially as his supervisor, which was mentioned previously. Such relationships of course form the backbone of positive group dynamics, which are an absolutely essential aspect of good quality classroom life (Dörnyei & Murphey, 2003; Murphey *et al.*, 2012). In learning about social and emotional intelligence, teachers can strive to create supportive and safe environments for learners, which is thought to be especially significant to EFL 'given the social and interpersonal nature of language teaching' (Gkonou & Mercer, 2017: 6).

Individuals in context: Case-by-case

Another of the findings that emerged through the writing of this paper was the importance of personalising relationships and expectations on a case-by-case basis. This was not surprising, because the nature of both of our academic work focuses on people in context, and recognising them not merely as students but as real persons, with their own needs and histories, their own beliefs and drives, and their own emotions (Pinner, 2016a, 2018; Ushioda, 2009, 2011, 2016). It is also important to recognise 'individuals as fundamentally social and relational beings' (Mercer, 2015: 74), because in doing so we can acknowledge the importance of our subject: *language*. At the heart of language teaching must lie a fundamental drive to communicate with others, to talk to different people outside of our immediate community and to connect with people who may well have very different ways of seeing the world.

Reflecting on what we learned from this inquiry, we realised that we both seem to prioritise interpersonal relationships at local and contextual levels. Here, we are referring to Ema's definition:

> by local contexts of learning, we mean more than just the physical, social or virtual setting, however defined. Local contexts of learning embrace also the micro-level of dynamic interactions, relations, practices and shared histories and experiences in particular classrooms as shaped and orchestrated by particular teachers. (Ushioda, 2013: 236)

For this reason, one of the key understandings we arrived at during this study was that the boundaries of a healthy personal/professional relationship between teachers and students need to be managed at an individual level, and this is very much case-by-case. We can offer no generalisable strategies or rules for managing this 'thin blue line', but of course our decisions regarding how we manage these interpersonal relations must be informed by our own guiding ethical code, by our own philosophies and beliefs as educators, and of course by our own personalities and unfurling contexts.

Duoethnographies for ELT Research

This paper has focused mainly on our own relationship as PhD supervisor and supervisee, and although we have discussed our work with English language students, we felt that we should specifically reflect on the usefulness of duoethnographies for ELT research. It is perhaps worth noting that Richard's PhD was an autoethnography focusing on his own classroom practice. As supervisor, Ema clearly had a very important and guiding influence on the development and writing up of this piece of research, but that would not traditionally fit the description of a duoethnography. However, in producing this paper it has been an interesting experience to reflect on just how much we have informed one another's thinking on various matters.

The method of duoethnography is very new to both of us, and yet it makes intuitive sense in some ways as it simply provides a medium for the process which we undertook naturally as supervisor/supervisee. The method which we have utilised for this paper pays particular focus to the narrative of our developing relationship to one another. Specifically, we found that reflecting back on the interactions between us as supervisor and supervisee, we were able to trace areas of interest as they had arisen, and to recognise the importance of the way our understandings increase through a dialogic process. This is not always apparent, especially if one is writing a single-authored paper, as we might not always recognise how others have played a key role in shaping our thinking on a certain point.

The relationship between supervisor and supervisee is certainly an interesting one, in that it is characterised by its uniqueness in many ways. As Ema mentioned in her reflections, different people might need different types of support and this brings out a different dynamic in the relationship. For Richard, what he wanted in a supervisor was a nurturing and yet challenging relationship, which is perhaps why he sought out Ema, having been drawn both to her writing on this subject and her manner in person. In conducting this duoethnography, we have both learned a great deal about how we construct our identities and manage the 'thin blue line' between personal and professional identities.

Certain approaches utilised by teachers and being advocated within the research methods literature certainly do seem to provide a good toolkit for those wishing to conduct duoethnographic research for ELT. One such method is Exploratory Practice (EP), which is 'a form of practitioner research in which learners as well as teachers are encouraged to investigate their own learning/teaching practices, while concurrently practising the target language' (Hanks, 2017: 3). EP mainly starts with a 'puzzling' process, in which participants begin identifying areas of their own practice that they would like to learn more about, specifically framing them as 'why' questions so as to avoid framing anything as a 'problem'. From here, participants develop a line of inquiry which leads them through a process of reflection and focusing, until they arrive at a more informed understanding of why they act in certain ways or hold certain beliefs. Evidently, there is here a very metacognitive element to EP which fits in well with Ema's 'small lens' approach to researching language learning motivation (Ushioda, 2016). Clearly, this would seem to be a useful framework for making use of a dialogic method of inquiry. Students could either form pairs or threes to undergo this process as a group rather than working individually, with the obvious advantage here being more opportunities for discussion, hence target language production and exposure.

Similarly, evidence-based reflective practice is intended to be 'a more collaborative, dialogic approach to reflection' (Walsh & Mann, 2015: 353). Learning is seen as primarily a social activity, and learning is a 'dialogic process in which language, in particular, plays a key role' (Mann & Walsh, 2017: 189). Thus, if we are doing research, we are likely to already be engaged in some form of dialogic narrative of understanding, and as such we can quite easily begin to find collaborators and co-authors to work with in order to question and expand upon our own experiences of the world, and to probe our realities together in a way that can expand on the veracity of our individual stories by combining them with others.

Conclusion

In writing this paper, we have once again come to a better understanding of our beliefs about the nature of personal and professional relationships, and at the same time facilitated a change in our relationship which moves us forward into new experiences. We have gone from supervisee/supervisor to co-authors. We have also changed our job titles, experienced personal events in our own lives, and been there for others who may have needed our support and counselling. A key finding is that, for us, the personal/professional 'thin blue line' was not something static, but something that has been constantly re-drawn with the crayon of our own ethics and beliefs. Generalising somewhat, we could be tempted to advise that this is a person-to-person and case-by-case set of inner principles, and is likely to be the case for any teachers and students whose work finds them nearing the nexus of personal and professional relationships. For both of us, this has been a very personal inquiry and as such we hope that the reader will also find something personal to take away from it. In the end, we can certainly say that working with people as people, and not merely as learners or teachers, seems to be the only way for those of us with a strong personal connection to our work to function as professionals.

References

Barcelos, A.M.F. and Coelho, H.S.H. (2016) Language learning and teaching: What's love got to do with it. In P.D. MacIntyre, T.S. Gregersen and S. Mercer (eds) *Positive Psychology in SLA* (pp. 130–144). Bristol: Multilingual Matters.

Baumeister, R.F. and Leary, M.R. (1995) The need to belong: desire for interpersonal attachments as a fundamental human motivation. *Psychological Bulletin* 117 (3), 497–529.

Bell, J.S. (2002) Narrative inquiry: More than just telling stories. *TESOL Quarterly* 36 (2), 207–213.

Brown, P. and Levinson, S.C. (1987) *Politeness: Some Universals in Language Usage.* Cambridge: Cambridge University Press.

Dashper, K. (2015) Revise, resubmit and reveal? An autoethnographer's story of facing the challenges of revealing the self through publication. *Current Sociology* 63 (4), 511–527.

Dinham, S. and Scott, C. (2000) Moving into the third, outer domain of teacher satisfaction. *Journal of Educational Administration* 38 (4), 379–396.

Dörnyei, Z. and Murphey, T. (2003) *Group Dynamics in the Language Classroom.* Cambridge: Cambridge University Press.

Dörnyei, Z. and Ushioda, E. (2011) *Teaching and Researching: Motivation* (2nd edn). Harlow: Longman Pearson.

Foote, L.S. (2015) Re-Storying life as a means of critical reflection: The power of narrative learning. *Christian Higher Education* 14 (3), 116–126.

Gkonou, C. and Mercer, S. (2017) Understanding emotional and social intelligence among English language teachers. *ELT Research Papers* (Vol. 17.03). London.

Goffman, E. (1959) *The Presentation of Self in Everyday Life.* New York: Anchor.

Goleman, D. (1995) *Emotional Intelligence: Why it can Matter More Than IQ* (2006 edn). New York: Bantam.

Goleman, D. (1998) *Working with Emotional Intelligence.* New York: Bantam.

Goleman, D. (2006) *Social Intelligence: The New Science of Human Relationships* (2006 edn). London: Arrow.

Hanks, J. (2017) *Exploratory Practice in Language Teaching: Puzzling About Principles and Practices.* London: Palgrave Macmillan.

Henry, A. and Thorsen, C. (2018) Teacher–student relationships and L2 motivation. *The Modern Language Journal* 102 (1), 218–241.

Kozinets, R.V. (2015) *Netnography: Redefined* (2nd edn). London: Sage.

Mann, S. and Walsh, S. (2017) *Reflective Practice in English Language Teaching: Research-based Principles and Practices.* London: Routledge.

Mercer, S. (2015) Social network analysis and complex dynamic systems. In Z. Dörnyei, P. MacIntyre and A. Henry (eds) *Motivational Dynamics in Language Learning* (pp. 73–82). Bristol: Multilingual Matters.

Murphey, T., Falout, J., Fukada, Y. and Fukuda, T. (2012) Group dynamics: Collaborative agency in present communities of imagination. In S. Mercer, S. Ryan and M. Williams (eds) *Psychology for Language Learning: Insights from Research, Theory and Practice* (pp. 220–238). London: Palgrave Macmillan.

Nabavi, M. and Lund, D.E. (2012) Tensions and contradictions of living in a multicultural nation in an era of bounded identities. In J. Norris, R.D. Sawyer and D. Lund (eds) *Duoethnography: Dialogic Methods for Social, Health, and Educational Research* (Vol. 7, pp. 177–197). London: Routledge.

Norris, J. and Sawyer, R.D. (2012) Toward a dialogic methodology. In J. Norris, R.D. Sawyer and D. Lund (eds) *Duoethnography: Dialogic Methods for Social, Health, and Educational Research* (Vol. 7, pp. 9–39). London: Routledge.

Norris, J., Sawyer, R.D. and Lund, D. (eds) (2012) *Duoethnography: Dialogic Methods for Social, Health, and Educational Research* (Vol. 7). London: Routledge.

Pinar, W.F. (1994) *The Method of Currere Autobiography, Politics, and Sexuality: Essays in Curriculum Theory 1972–1992* (pp. 19–27). New York: Peter Lang.

Pinner, R.S. (2016a) *Reconceptualising Authenticity for English as a Global Language.* Bristol: Multilingual Matters.

Pinner, R.S. (2016b) Trouble in paradise: Self-assessment and the Tao. *Language Teaching Research* 20 (2), 181–195.

Pinner, R.S. (2017) Social authentication and the synergies between teacher and student motivation: An autoethnographic inquiry into the interaction between authenticity and motivation in English language teaching at a Japanese university. (PhD Doctoral Thesis), University of Warwick, Coventry, UK.

Pinner, R.S. (2018) Re-learning from experience: Using autoethnography for teacher development. *Educational Action Research* 26 (1), 91–105.

Pinner, R.S. (2019) *Social Authentication and Teacher–Student Motivational Synergy: A Narrative of Language Teaching.* London: Routledge.

Richards, K. (2006) 'Being the teacher': Identity and classroom conversation. *Applied Linguistics* 27 (1), 51–77.

Richardson, P.W. and Watt, H.M. (2006) Who chooses teaching and why? Profiling characteristics and motivations across three Australian universities. *Asia-Pacific Journal of Teacher Education* 34 (1), 27–56.

Sawyer, R.D. and Norris, J. (2012) Why Duoethnography: Thoughts on the dialogues. In J. Norris, R.D. Sawyer and D. Lund (eds) *Duoethnography: Dialogic Methods for Social, Health, and Educational Research* (Vol. 7, pp. 280–306). London: Routledge.

Ushioda, E. (1993) Redefining motivation from the L2 learner's point of view. *Teanga (Journal of the Irish Association of Applied Linguistics)* 13, 1–12.

Ushioda, E. (2009) A person-in-context relational view of emergent motivation, self and identity. In Z. Dörnyei and E. Ushioda (eds) *Motivation, Language Identity and the L2 Self* (pp. 215–228). Bristol: Multilingual Matters.

Ushioda, E. (2011) Motivating learners to speak as themselves. In G. Murray, X. Gao and T.E. Lamb (eds) *Identity, Motivation and Autonomy in Language Learning* (pp. 11–25). Bristol: Multilingual Matters.

Ushioda, E. (2013) Motivation and ELT: Looking ahead to the future. In E. Ushioda (ed.) *International Perspectives on Motivation: Language Learning and Professional Challenges* (pp. 233–239). New York: Palgrave Macmillan.

Ushioda, E. (2016) Language learning motivation through a small lens: A research agenda. *Language Teaching* 49 (4), 564–577.

Walsh, S. and Mann, S. (2015) Doing reflective practice: A data-led way forward. *ELT Journal* 69 (4), 351–362.

Zimmerman, D.H. (1998) Identity, context and interaction. In C. Antaki and S. Widdicombe (eds) *Identities in Talk* (pp. 87–106). London: Sage.

Part 2

Duoethnography for Reflection and Teacher Education

Part 2: Duoethnography for Reflection and Teacher Education

In the second section of the book we move away from research to focus on teacher development in the form of reflection and different forms of teacher education.

In Chapter 5 Ben Smart and Charlie Cook use their respective positions as an experienced and novice teacher to investigate the various issues that teachers face at different stages in their careers. In this innovative duoethnography they reflect on their own reflections in order to gain new insights and understandings into their own and each other's experiences and philosophies.

Next, in Chapter 6 Nick Kasparek and Matthew W. Turner reflect on their experiences of teaching special educational needs (SEN) learners to offer a much needed and unique insight into an area of research that has hitherto been under-researched in ELT. By taking us through their journeys from tentative awareness, to active participation and beyond, they provide a thought-provoking account that teachers in similar situations can relate to and draw on.

In the final chapter in this section Matthew Schaefer and Peter Brereton use the process of duoethnography to reflect on their roles and identities as program managers and teacher trainers. In doing so they pose a number of questions surrounding the very nature of professional development and call into question some of the everyday practices of teachers, trainers and training programs.

As with the first section, the diversity of approaches each pair of authors have taken highlights the reflexive diversity of the duoethnographic method. In addition to this, it is hoped that the honesty and openness of the conversations allow for the reader to become the 'third participant' in the conversations that provide a framework and inspiration for other teachers to carry out their own reflections.

5 Professional Development Through Duoethnography: Reflecting on Dialogues Between an Experienced and Novice Teacher

Ben Smart and Charles Cook

Introduction

One of the aims of this paper is to address the gap that exists between novice teachers' need for support and the lack of that support in many educational institutions (Farrell, 2012). In addition, teachers who are further into their teaching careers often acknowledge a degree of 'stagnation' (Huling & Resta, 2001) that can hinder their further development. Duoethnography is yet to be consistently applied as a professional development tool in higher education institutions, therefore this study attempts to make a case for its application in this area. It is believed that through the collaborative discourse of a duoethnography, an experienced teacher and a novice teacher with some shared working context will be able to address, and potentially resolve, some of the issues that they are facing at the current stages of their teaching lives.

The working context of the participants, Ben and Charlie, will be set out initially, before the academic motivations for engaging in this duoethnography are discussed, with reference to the relevant literature. Finally, the authors' personal reasons for wanting to do this project together will be explained.

The Study

Context of the study

Ben studied BA English Language and Linguistics at a university in the UK before moving to Japan in 2006 to work for a large *eikaiwa* (private language school) chain. He returned to the UK in 2011 to study for an MA in Applied Linguistics. He came back to Japan in 2012 and briefly worked for a different large eikaiwa chain. Ben started working at a mid-sized women's university in Tokyo, Japan in April 2013. He is employed, with two others, as an instructor on a compulsory course, which all second-year students take four times a week. The course has no fixed textbook or prescribed syllabus, and the three instructors on the course are asked to design course structure, lesson content and assessments, as well as sharing the teaching of all the students over the year, and thus have a very close working relationship. In April 2017 Charlie joined the team. Prior to being employed at the university, Charlie worked as an international student assistant at a UK university and taught occasional conversation classes. Subsequently, he volunteered in India where he also taught infrequent casual-style English classes. He gained his CertTESOL in the summer of 2017, moved to Japan and started working at the same university as Ben the following spring. Data collection began for this duoethnography after we had been working together for five months. There are no mentoring or other professional development systems in place in the department for non-tenured staff, and as a result we were both interested in exploring ways to stimulate our own professional development.

Motivations for the study

Before reviewing some studies that examine the problems that novice practitioners face and how they can be helped, and in so doing explaining some of the reasons for engaging in this duoethnography, it will be necessary to provide a working definition of the important terms, *novice*, *experienced* (and *expert*) and assessing their suitability for describing the participants in this study.

'Novice' teachers are generally considered to be those who have just started in the profession or who are still in training, although as Farrell (2012: 437) points out, 'there is no full agreement as to the exact definition of when teachers cease to be novices in terms of time teaching'. Farrell (2012) suggests that teachers with up to three years' teaching experience could still be considered novices, while Gatbonton (2008) opts for two years as a reasonable cut-off, and Tsui (2003) for one. Whichever researcher we follow, we can feel fairly confident in calling Charlie, with less than six-months teaching experience at the start of the project, a novice. It stands to reason that an experienced teacher is anyone who is no longer a novice, and again, by any of these standards, Ben, with more than 12 years' teaching experience, is clearly not a novice. We have, in this study, opted for the term 'experienced', rather than 'expert', to describe Ben. In her study of expertise in language teaching, Tsui (2003) acknowledges that it can be problematic identifying 'expert' teachers and she points out that experience is not necessarily synonymous with expertise. She reports on other studies that have identified expert teachers through recommendations or researcher-screening. Thus, without such external endorsements, 'experienced' was chosen to describe Ben, although this is not necessarily to deny his expertise.

A lot has been written about the challenges for novice teachers when they embark upon their teaching career. In his article introducing the *TESOL Quarterly* special issue on Novice Professionals in TESOL, Farrell (2012: 436) explains that '[t]oo often, novice teachers are left to survive on their own in less than ideal conditions, and as a result some drop out of the profession early in their careers'. He goes on to list lesson planning and delivery, identity development and classroom management as some of the challenges these novice teachers face from the moment they walk into their new jobs, 'often without much guidance from the new school or institution'. Novice English to Speakers of Other Languages (ESOL) educators may face additional problems relating to intercultural stress, cultural misunderstandings stemming from unfamiliarity with the diversity in the classroom or the school environment, as well as stress, frustration and isolation (Brannan & Bleistein, 2012).

It has been argued that 'the success of new teachers is critically linked to their first teaching experiences and the opportunities they are given to talk through issues they face in the classroom' (Pitton, 2006: 2). Whether formal or informal; external or internal, assistance and support from authorities or colleagues is understood to help novice teachers negotiate the early years and aid their socialisation into the profession (Farrell, 2009). In many institutions, this support may take the form of mentoring. Many researchers examining the role of mentoring in the socialisation process have shown benefits for both novice teachers (e.g. Brannan & Bleistein, 2012; Mann & Tang, 2012; Winter & McGhie-Richmond, 2005) and experienced teachers (e.g. Huling & Resta, 2001; Winter & McGhie-Richmond, 2005). Mann and Tang (2012: 484) conducted a case study into the socialisation and experience of four novice teachers in their first year of teaching in Hong Kong. They discovered that only one of the four mentor-mentee relationships in their study displayed 'evidence of a partnership based on professional and interpersonal collaboration', with the others being more like 'hierarchical apprenticeships' in which encouraging conformism seemed to be the primary role of the mentor. Mann and Tang (2012) suggest that, for the mentors, the procedural, rather than reflective, nature of the mentoring relationship may have been caused by the experienced teachers viewing mentorship as a duty, rather than as a choice. Nonetheless, the novice teachers reported that interaction with their mentors was useful for their professional development. Brannan and Bleistein (2012: 536), in a study exploring novice teachers' beliefs about teacher efficacy, also found that novice teachers valued support from mentors and colleagues (as well as family). They conclude that 'if novice ESOL instructors identify people who will be both pragmatically and affectively supportive, they may feel more positive about their teaching experiences and abilities'. Meanwhile, Huling and Resta (2001) report on a number of studies which have shown the positive effects that mentoring relationships can have on the experienced mentors, including: growth in self-esteem, increased confidence in professional relationships, an ability to define their beliefs about teaching more clearly, getting new teaching ideas and being able to engage in more objective reflective practice. A further study in which novice teachers and experts collaborated is Winter and McGhie-Richmond (2005). As in other studies, both the novices and experts held positive views about the collaborative discourse in which they discussed case studies on educating children with special needs.

A key theme across these studies and others like them is that creating opportunities for novice and experienced teachers to communicate directly about their work can be enormously beneficial to one or, often, both practitioners. It is with this in mind that we believe duoethnography could be a valuable professional development tool for novice and experienced teachers alike. Unlike with mentoring programmes, in which the experienced teacher is often required to be a mentor, rather than volunteering to be one, and so may not engage fully in the experience (Mann & Tang, 2012), participants in duoethnographies are equal in their enterprise. In duoethnographies, the participants are 'working in tandem to dialogically critique and question the meanings they give to […] epistemological concepts' (Sawyer & Norris, 2013: 2), thus providing equal opportunities for growth.

In addition to the general reasons relating to professional support and socialisation, especially for the novice teacher, outlined above, we also each have some individual motivations for wanting to engage in a duoethnography and expectations of the benefits we could gain from doing so, which will be discussed below.

Personal expectations

Ben: My personal reasons for wanting to engage in a duoethnography with Charlie are twofold. First, a very practical reason: I want to help him improve as a teacher so that our shared students can get the best learning experience. This isn't to say that I envisage this duoethnography as being an extended training session in which I impart my wisdom and he listens (cf. Mann & Tang, 2012), but rather that I hope by talking equally, openly and at length with an experienced colleague in a (private) forum dedicated to talking about teaching, he will be motivated to explore and reflect on his own practice and beliefs in such a way that will encourage him to experiment with new approaches and ideas in the classroom. The second reason is a personal one: I want to challenge my own beliefs about teaching and be motivated by a fresher, younger colleague's outlook. I have been teaching roughly the same course at the same university for five years and I would admit that I have, to some extent, been 'going through the motions' in some of my own teaching practice. Huling and Resta (2001: 3) warn of 'stagnation in the adult years' and suggest that reflective practice (in mentoring) can 'provide an opportunity for renewal and regeneration necessary for all adults'. I hope that this study will give me a chance to re-evaluate some of my long-held, perhaps subconscious, teacher beliefs through being challenged by someone whose beliefs are still forming (Gatbonton, 2008; Woods, 1996), to see things in a different way.

Charlie: My expectations are that I have something concrete to gain from the duoethnography, primarily in the areas of general teaching methodology and knowledge broadly applicable in EFL, but also context specific knowledge (about teaching female Japanese undergraduates). I also hope that it will improve my confidence: as Moran and Hoy (2007: 954) suggest 'the support of colleagues and of the community made significant contributions to explaining variance in novice teachers' self-efficacy beliefs.' It is my prediction that I may be more flexible than Ben in being able to change my opinions or being open to new ideas. I am concerned about potential flashpoints regarding issues at work coming up in the duoethnography and am not convinced that it will necessarily further the productivity of our working relationship; indeed, I fear it could possibly degrade it. Whether it will be positive or negative, I am certain that engaging in the duoethnography will change our personal and professional relationship in some way. I have some anxiety about entering into a dialogue about methods, teaching practice and so on, with someone with far more experience than me, and expect at times it will be difficult to be completely truthful because of a desire to appear always professional and competent.

Data Collection and Analysis

In this section the distinct two stage process of our duoethnography data collection and analysis will be laid out in detail so that other practitioners can follow our lead in conducting their own similar duoethnography, or use it as context against which to define their own duoethnographic study.

Stage 1

The first stage comprised primary data collection from two sources: a written, online message thread and a face-to-face discussion around reflective lesson diaries that was recorded on a Dictaphone and from which relevant passages were transcribed. Of the two sources, the online conversation generated the bulk of the data. Similar methods were employed by Lowe and Lawrence (2018) and Lowe and Kiczkowiak (2016) and we felt computer-moderated conversation an adequately flexible and dynamic space in which to enact our transformation of understanding. As noted by Winter and McGhie-Richmond (2005: 120), 'computer conferencing places different demands on the contributors while providing a record of participant interactions. This is normally absent from face-to-face [...] dialogue, and allows for greater interaction, and reflection on decisions.' Concurrently, using online messaging as our primary medium of conversation catalysed a more rigorous investigation of both partners. We found it to be a space in which new, complex and often incomplete understandings could be posited and examined, and in which such development of understanding could be charted. Following Sawyer and Norris's (2013: 43) assertion that 'collaborators [should] seek to provide each other with sufficient detail in their discussions', messages on our online thread were long and detailed, with many supporting examples. The average length of each message was 651 words; the response time usually spanning between a couple of days and a week. In the end, the total word count was slightly in excess of 25,000 words.

Although face-to-face data collection is more commonplace than written in duoethnographic practice (e.g. Breault *et al.*, 2012; Krammar & Mangiardi, 2012; Norris & Greenlaw, 2012), we felt online written communication sufficient until a concern arose that our long, often formal messages over-represented some parts of our personalities (our academic backgrounds, for example) and under-represented others. In duoethnography, '[t]he research story unfolds in bits and pieces; both content and the structure develop throughout the process' (Norris & Sawyer, 2017: 6) and the addition of a face-to-face dialogue was such a development to ours. Duoethnographies frequently make use of significant objects and documents, or 'artefacts', to create further critical tension between participants (Sawyer & Norris, 2013: 64), and as such we decided to focus our additional, face-to-face dialogue on reflective lesson diaries, which were written, following some guiding questions, after each of the three lessons we taught in one day. This was a document that could act both as a duoethnographic artefact while also being widely accepted as a vehicle for reflection in its own right (Lee, 2007; Richards & Lockhart, 1994). We discussed the reflective diaries in an hour-long recorded conversation a few days after the lessons in question to give ourselves a chance to review each other's diaries to find some interesting similarities or differences before talking about them.

Stage 2

Once the teaching semester had finished and we were both satisfied that we'd covered enough interesting and pertinent topics to a satisfactory degree in our primary dialogue, we began stage two; that is to say, we began the dialogues which would form the main part of this chapter. We had decided that the best way to analyse and synthesise over 25,000 words and hour-long audio recording of primary data would be to have a further dialogue about our initial conversations. We felt that in reflecting on our original ideas in this way, we might be able to take a more objective view of the primary data, and we hoped that new themes would emerge as we discussed our experience of doing the duoethnography and noticed any changes that had occurred in our thinking in the time that had passed since the original data was collected.

To give the stage two dialogues some focus we followed Newby's (2010) first stage of coding and each, individually, reviewed all the data and made notes of potential categories into which we could organise the data. At this stage, so as not to be overly/adversely influenced by previous research, we allowed 'the coding system to emerge from [the] data' (Newby, 2010: 464). Between us we noted over 15 (fairly narrow) potential categories. From this we chose three broader categories on the basis of the number of occurrences of the topic in our primary dialogue, as well as our subjective feeling about the importance and relevance of the topic. The broad categories which emerged in this first stage of collaborative coding were:

- professional development through experience;
- current teaching practice;
- relationships and roles.

Once these categories had been decided we returned to our primary data and read through it carefully in order to find quotes related to the three themes (Newby [2010] calls this 'tagging') and copy them into documents which were shared over Google Docs. These quotes were then used as the 'jumping off' points for our secondary dialogues. Our aim was to support our discussion in the secondary dialogues with illustrative quotes from the primary dialogues in order to add some transparency to the process, as well as because we wished to streamline the presentation of our own personal revelations in order to more fully represent some of the dynamics, shifts and U-turns that brought those revelations about. Secondary dialogues, as with primary dialogues, were computer-mediated for the reasons outlined in stage 1, above. Finally, secondary dialogues were edited for length and fluency.

Discussion

This section will be divided into three sub-sections as discussed above. First, we explore how our lived experiences inform our values and teacher beliefs. We then examine the impact of our dialogues on our current teaching practice. Finally in this section, we discuss the effect that doing this duoethnography has had on our personal and professional relationship.

Dialogues

Professional development through experience

In the original dialogue several areas of experience that are said to most influence teacher beliefs were explored, including past learning experiences, non-educational working experiences, (teacher) training, and early language teaching experiences (Borg, 2006; Farrell, 2009; Freeman & Freeman, 1994). Two areas stood out as most influential and interesting: learning experiences at school and early teaching experiences.

Ben: I'd like to begin this part by reflecting on my early teaching experiences, which I suggested have had the biggest influence on where I see myself as a teacher now. In our dialogue I wondered 'how different my teaching style would be had I not started in eikaiwa. If I'd come straight in to this university context in which I now work, would I be a very different teacher?' In our recorded conversation I note that in many of the responses I wrote when reflecting on my classes that day, 'I talk more about student interaction [than lesson content] so perhaps my focus lies here more'. I think this shows the emphasis that I place on building rapport through interacting with students, and I believe that this is something I learned to do in eikaiwa, where teacher enthusiasm is often emphasised over knowledge of content and teaching skills (Nuske, 2014).

Charlie: Do you think this focus on interaction is something you were explicitly aware of prior to this duoethnography, or was it something of a surprise to you?

Ben: Quite early in our dialogue I responded to a comment of yours thus: 'Reading your comment about the fact that you find understanding the students to be a difficulty made me realise that that's my biggest strength.' The use of 'made me realise' suggests that it was something of a revelation, but looking back on a Personal Statement that I wrote when I was applying for a job to teach Japanese people in London in 2011, I notice that I focus quite a lot on this aspect of my teaching and how I developed 'a strong understanding of Japanese culture [...] and learning styles' during my time in eikaiwa, and that many of my students becoming my private students 'is testament to the rapport that I developed with my students'. I also note that 'During the CELTA course I was especially praised for ... my rapport with learners', so I can't say that it was surprising, but I guess strengths and weaknesses are an area of my practice that I don't often explicitly think about unless asked to do so. I suppose that if I were a good reflective practitioner I would personally consider these things more often.

Charlie: So do you think that through the duoethnography, rather than discovering new traits in your practice, you recognised strengths you had 'normalised' into your day-to-day teaching?

Ben: Yes, as well as encouraging more general reflective practice, a big benefit of our dialogues has not been about getting 'new' ideas, or discovering 'surprising' things about myself, but rather being made to explicate and then re-evaluate the things I do in the classroom and the beliefs I have about teaching. It's been interesting to connect those things to my own experiences in a way that I'd not consciously done before. For example, while I believed my early ELT teaching experiences have had the biggest influence on my teaching, in our dialogue I point to several other experiences which I see as being important in shaping my teacher beliefs. For example, I explained how my own 'apprenticeship of observation' (Lortie, 1975) at school had influenced me: 'my most memorable teachers at school were the ones who were prepared to allow a little silliness in class (within reason) and who could join in laughing with us. They were enthusiastic about their subject and they also created a good rapport. [...] I can definitely see how that has had a major influence on the way I teach. I'm all about the fun! I believe primarily that if the student is enjoying being in the class they'll get more out of it.' I was interested in what you had to say about your own apprenticeship of observation in our original dialogue. How do you feel about it now, reflecting on what you said then?

Charlie: I'm surprised I didn't have the insight then to connect my bad experiences in high school because of poor class discipline to my then pre-occupation with maintaining control despite stating it as the reason I dropped languages: '[..] my [Modern Foreign Language] teachers were [...] hopeless at controlling the class and I hated those lessons so much [...] I dropped it as soon as I could.' It's through the duoethnography I came to recognise how it had impacted on me: 'I've never connected that concern to my own experiences of chaotic classrooms in high school, but on reflection I did loathe those classes, and it makes sense that I'd put high priority of maintaining control in the classroom.' Still, reflecting again, this preoccupation was compounded by other factors, for example advice from a colleague on my first day about asserting my authority because of my age and my general preconceptions about teaching in a university. I should point out that it's not only negative learning experiences that may have influenced me and I acknowledged that at university 'the crucial combination my favourite teachers displayed was of passion and competence.' I like to think that I can aim to display the same qualities in my teaching.

Ben: So in a similar way to many of the native-speaker novice (pre-service) participants in Warford and Reeves' (2003) study on novice TESOL teachers' preconceptions about teaching, you had not related your EFL teaching experiences to previous learning experiences. I should admit that it's only through my course on Professional Development for Language Teachers that I took as part of my MA that I became aware of the 'apprenticeship of observation'. I'm glad that I was able to introduce it into our original dialogue to help you become aware of some interesting influences that you hadn't thought about before. I think this shows a benefit for a novice of doing a duoethnography with a more experienced colleague. If your learning experiences had been an unconscious influence, what was your conscious feeling about what had had the biggest influence on where you see yourself as a teacher now?

Charlie: I think I believed that my current practice is primarily informed by recent experiences and a handful of critical incidents (Farrell, 2008) from the last academic year. For example my mishap '"deciding" to try some more hands-on classroom management with the one class I felt was most out of my control, ... [which] ironically had the opposite effect, and after that the [class] respected me less.' Doing this duoethnography has confirmed this, and by digging around in my past experiences I've been able to see key areas of potential growth. For example, to draw from my own CV, which I wrote when applying for this job, I wrote something similar to you about 'extensive experience working with and building working relationships with Japanese undergraduates in the UK'. The context amuses me because when I wrote that, I believed it wholeheartedly. However, in our original dialogue I wrote, 'One of the hardest things I'm finding is understanding the students, and knowing what subject or activity will motivate them', hence demonstrating how my perceptions of my skills changed rapidly when I moved to Japan. It's demoralising to realise something like that now, but also feels like a liberation. To improve one needs to acknowledge there are areas to improve in. I feel like this has been a good forum in which to do that.

Ben: So do you think that it has been beneficial for you to be doing this duoethnography alongside your first year of teaching?

Charlie: Absolutely, unlike you I feel that discovering surprising things about my own developmental experiences and how they have influenced me, or have the potential to influence me, has been an important and immediate benefit. I've been able to chart some changes to my own teaching practice that came as a direct result of discussions in our original dialogue. *(These will be discussed more in the next part.)*

This section explored how Ben and Charlie's experiences, including Ben's early teaching experiences at eikaiwa schools in Japan, and Charlie's negative experiences in high school language classes, have shaped some of their teacher beliefs. The dialogue touched on some of the areas of concern for novice teachers that were noted by Farrell (2012), such as classroom management. Ben was able to use some of the advanced knowledge he gained from his MA course to help Charlie explore the reasons behind his reactions to some early classroom critical incidents, and Charlie, through the dialogue, was able to notice changes in his own practice and emphasis in the classroom as he developed his teacher identity.

Current teaching practice

The discussion of current teaching practice spanned a broad range of topics, such as classroom discipline, culture, methodology, interaction and teacher talk, among other themes.

Charlie: I think that some of most rewarding parts of our dialogue were when we disagreed, for example about the role of a teacher. Between your assertion that you 'don't believe that our actions influence the future actions of students in a long-term way' and mine that 'without doubt we are role models to the students because of our visibility [and positions of responsibility]' there was a lot of room for change. One result of the conversation was I started to worry less about the micro-aspects of my role. Does the opposite hold true for you?

Ben: I agree that the times when we disagreed were the most rewarding. As the experienced participant, this holds especially true for me. Many of the issues about the role of the teacher were things that I'd not thought about before, and it's interesting that my immediate reaction to some of them was so direct, strong ('really', 'absolutely'), and negative, for example: 'I really think you shouldn't worry so much about giving them this amazing real-life rounded experience. Your job is absolutely not to teach them life lessons!' Interestingly, it is only now, reappraising these original reactions, that I'm feeling a more sympathetic stance towards your point of view and questioning my own. Do you think the 'softenings' of your positions in these disagreements were more immediate during the dialogue?

Charlie: I think the speed at which my opinion changed varied from case to case; in some situations, it was easy to appreciate your position quickly, as occasionally evidenced in the dialogue with statements from me like: 'writing this has made me think I'm too serious in class!' Other times I was more stubborn. Overall, I think my flexibility was dependent on my level of personal investment; for example, I explained that my ideas about role models 'seeded when volunteering in India', which was quite a significant period of personal growth for me. As a result, I suppose I was more reluctant to re-evaluate those ideals. Following that line of thought, it suggests that my relative inexperience in teaching allows me to be more flexible. Do you think your teaching practice has become more cemented over the years?

Ben: I think it's precisely because of the experienced teacher's more fossilised beliefs that doing a duoethnography can be helpful. With many of those issues, my beliefs only made themselves known to me as I was writing my responses to you, so I think it's good that I was first given the opportunity to explicate those (hidden) beliefs through our primary dialogue, and then reflect on them later.

Charlie: There were also some areas that I found particularly stimulating in our primary conversation that we agreed on, for example about culture. One example I gave was about students not asking questions about their assessment feedback. It was reassuring to hear you resonate with me when I was charting my reaction from indignancy: 'Well, then why didn't you check with me!?', to a more productive mindset: 'this is a cultural difference and it is my job [...] to make sure that difference doesn't have a negative effect on the student's learning experience'. Do you think that you gained any further insight about culture in the classroom via our duoethnography or did my lack of cultural experience in Japan mean that part of the discussion was less fruitful for you?

Ben: I think your lack of cultural experience made the discussion more fruitful! I was reminded of all the internal struggles I had about student reticence when I started my teaching career in Japan. I did resonate with your comments around the feedback problem saying: 'Since that is obviously a harmful [...] habit, I think it's our duty, at least in our classes, [to break it and] encourage a change in that behaviour. In this case, rather than being angry with the students for not having checked, or annoyed with ourselves for some perceived failure, we can just try to think of ways that we could improve the situation for next year'. However, despite the tone of the comment, the reality is that I'd long since largely given up on trying to encourage students to follow-up on their feedback in many classes. I think that being reminded of this issue has made me reconsider my attitude.

Charlie: I'm glad to hear that our discussion has reinvigorated you to try new approaches in the coming year, and I hope that maybe seeing more of your process of trial and error will make me feel more comfortable engaging in my own. I also think that our discussion was aided by your introduction of the idea of 'critical incidents' (Farrell, 2008). I was interested to hear some detailed, explicit examples of how you might deal with particular situations relating to classroom discipline, for example, '[Student's Name] put your phone away or I'll throw it out the window!'

Ben: That's a good point. I think one key thing that our dialogues have done is allowed/encouraged us to talk about areas of our teaching practice that we might otherwise not have talked about together in the same kind of detail, if at all. Especially with the focus on some critical incidents and more general classroom examples, we have both been able to see more about how the other works. It must be good to get to know more about your co-teacher's style, especially when you work as closely together as we do.

Charlie: I agree. I think I've also gained more awareness of some of the pitfalls that can be found in our teaching context through talking about specific examples, although it might be interesting to revisit both conversations in a year, to see how many of those pitfalls I ended up in anyway. As a final point, I think it's worth noting that topics that produced more debate, like culture and the role of the teacher, were ones I had already formed opinions about in some depth, leading me to hypothesise that my inexperience in other areas such as methodology led to less dynamic and interesting dialogue. If duoethnographers 'seek critical tension, insights and new perspectives' (Sawyer & Norris, 2013: 4), I posit a lack of understanding on one side could undercut the process. What do you think?

Ben: I'm not sure about that. I think you did have opinions on other things like methodology, but they were unexplored, implicit opinions, which you'd never really had any need to talk about in any detail before. You said yourself, 'When I was on my TESOL course I never thought about 'the hidden curriculum' (Lowe & Lawrence, 2018) at all, and just swallowed what I was told wholesale without really questioning it. I strongly believed that the methods they taught were the most superior and the leading edge of language teaching, viewing other methods as old-fashioned and outdated.' So I think that while our discussions on some of the topics might not have been 'dynamic' and long, they are definitely important areas to explore, in order to get to those implicit beliefs and challenge them, for both the novice and the experienced practitioner alike.

This section has shown how a novice teacher's concerns about the day-to-day practicalities of teaching can be eased by engaging with an experienced colleague (Brannan & Bleistein, 2012; Mann & Tang, 2012). It has also explored how an experienced teacher's perceptions of their own current teaching practice can be challenged by a less experienced colleague: like the experienced teachers mentioned by Huling and Resta (2001), through the dialogues Ben was able to (re)define some of his beliefs about teaching through objective reflection that he might not otherwise have done.

Roles and relationships

The nature of teacher beliefs about classroom roles was a recurring theme in the original dialogues. The working relationship of the participants was also constructed and reconstructed through the conversations and will be discussed in this section.

Ben: I believe there have been several positive changes in our working relationship since we started this project, but I think (and correct me if I'm wrong!) that one of the most important things is that you have started to feel less inhibited about asking me for advice or making suggestions.

Charlie: I wholeheartedly agree that's the case. Again, it's difficult to identify explicitly what development occurred as a result of this duoethnography and which happened because of other events. Regarding myself, I think broadly speaking two areas of change could be identified. The first is increased confidence and self-assurance through primary experience, resulting in less inhibition about asking questions for advice (from anyone in the EFL profession, not just you). In our primary conversation I wrote about the 'social vulnerability of being a novice', which also applies to me. Secondly, and pertinently, I think our duoethnography catalysed our relationship to become more open. Especially reading about your previous experiences in EFL, both good and bad, helped me relate to your opinions and positions. I was wondering, though, whether, perhaps because I have less teaching experience to contextualise my current views, you still find it difficult to relate to my positions/ideas when they arise?

Ben: In the middle of our primary dialogue I comment that 'my first teaching experience was somewhat different from this, so it is sometimes hard for me to know where you're coming from with the decisions you take. This dialogue is helping me to understand and appreciate those decisions in a useful and positive way.' I think this comment shows that doing this project has actually made it considerably easier for me to understand your positions and ideas, and has in some way neutralised the potential 'problems' of the novice/experienced dichotomy.

Charlie: I feel that much like our real-life workplace situation, our duoethnography spanned social and professional modes of interaction. One of the things I found particularly useful was how, when speaking about your past experiences, you contextualised our workplace's history. I feel like knowing this 'meta' information helped me to feel more comfortable at work, which was something surprising that I wasn't expecting to get out of the project. Am I right in saying this was unintentional on your part?

Ben: Since an important part of a duoethnography is about relating past experiences with the present, it's natural that I would explain something of my past working contexts (including at our university) in our dialogue. I'm glad that it had the bonus by-product of contextualising some of your feelings about the job, although that wasn't necessarily my primary aim in introducing the topic. I'm somewhat surprised that this kind of talk about our university hadn't come up before in regular conversations (i.e. outside of the duoethnography), or maybe it had but the context of talking about it here made you better able to directly connect that history with your own current working situation?

Charlie: You're completely right that the contextual information had come up in previous conversations at least a couple of times, I'm sure. Perhaps subconsciously I put more trust in things I read than things that are said, especially when those said things are often mixed in with various other conversational flak: jokes, gossip, small talk, etc. Our dialogue was also private (at that stage), so I knew that you were not filtering information for the benefit of anyone else present.

Ben: One thing that I noticed when reading back over our primary dialogue was that I was, I think consciously, trying to make it as casual as possible. I did this by making jokes ('Trust you to bring nihilism into this! Keep it out of your teaching or you'll get nowhere!'), swearing a fair amount (e.g. In my first full turn: 'First, my immediate reaction on reading your comments was along the lines of "Oh, shit! Do I do that?" and I felt pretty uncomfortable realising that I probably do'), and by being fairly direct and honest in my comments about colleagues or our work environment ('It became clear that she was basically awful'). I think I did this to try and put you at your ease, and to try and dispel this unwanted feeling that you have that I am in some way your boss ('I definitely think of you as my "boss" within our team'). I did worry that you wouldn't be as open as you could be because of how you felt about our different statuses. You mentioned at the end of our primary dialogue that, looking back, you didn't always feel like you said the truth, and, I think I'm fair in saying, your generally more formal responses throughout suggest that I wasn't totally successful in putting you at your ease?

Charlie: Not totally, although I do appreciate your effort! I didn't actually notice any of that conscious colloquialism in your responses (until now that you've brought it up). As you say my responses were often more formal than yours – slight unease could be extrapolated through that. And now that I write it, 'slight unease' is a pretty accurate descriptor of how I often felt writing my responses. The process of doing a duoethnography makes both parties vulnerable and there has to be trust to create new understanding from the tension between two views.

Ben: I wonder, then, to what degree doing this study has brought about that trust and whether your feelings of 'slight unease' have lessened over the course of the study or stayed about the same? I also wonder to what degree your views of our professional relationship have changed since, quite early in our primary dialogue, we had an exchange in which I strongly disagreed with the label of 'boss', which was one of several labels that were attached to me (by one or other of us) in the conversation:

> **Charlie:** 'Perhaps one thing that complicates our professional and social work atmospheres is the lack of an enforced hierarchy between us.' [...] 'In that sense, you've got the job of juggling "Boss" "Mentor" and "Peer" hats, whilst I've got the job of staying open minded to greeting whichever Ben might be interacting with me.'
>
> **Ben:** 'I'm definitely not your boss – I consider us professionally equal. I don't mind being considered a mentor (although I feel the pressure of the tag), definitely a peer and hopefully occasional friend.'

Charlie: I think that this study certainly brought about a higher level of trust and openness between us, however, I think (from my side at least) that it is still contained within a hierarchy I project onto our professional relationship. I strongly disagree that we are professional equals, primarily because I think to say so is a disservice to yourself!

Ben: Technically, of course, we are professional equals in that we have the same job title and the same salary at the same university. The only thing that separates us is our experience. So although I somewhat understand the feeling of awe that you have when you gaze upon me at my work (there's me with that joking again), I think it's something of an opportunity missed if you've held back in any way in this project, even subconsciously, because you fear any repercussions due to a non-existent hierarchy.

Charlie: You make a valid point about the potential rewards of the duoethnography being affected by one or both parties not giving their full opinions. I don't think that problem has particularly impacted our study however, and I don't think I ever held back in any area that could yield an interesting contrast or comparison. But that's not to say that I didn't often feel slight trepidation when writing.

Let me end this section by reiterating that I feel our professional and personal relationship has changed during the course of this duoethnography. I feel more comfortable asking questions and indeed challenging your ideas, which I feel is more productive for both of us. To come back to an earlier quote, you said '[t]his dialogue is helping me to understand and appreciate [your] decisions [about teaching] in a useful and positive way.' Is there anything else, caveats or otherwise, you'd like to add to that?

Ben: Nothing to add, except that I agree with both my past self, and with you! We definitely know more about each other ('s thinking), and that can only be helpful when having a close working-relationship. And I agree that the breaking down of enough barriers to make you feel more comfortable challenging my ideas is great for both of us.

This final section looked at how the working relationship of the participants has changed as a result of engaging in the duoethnographic process.

It was noted that in Mann and Tang (2012), some of the relationships between mentors and mentees were hierarchical rather than collaborative, which perhaps made the relationships less beneficial to the experienced practitioner. The efforts made by Ben to ensure a collaborative and equal dialogue were shown to have had some success, but issues of (perceived) hierarchy may still have had an influence on the openness and course of the conversations. Nonetheless, both Ben and Charlie agreed that positive changes have occurred in their working relationship as a result of this study. These will be discussed further in the final part of this chapter, below.

Conclusion

This final section will begin with our own personal reflections on how we feel the experience has benefitted each of us in both the short-term and, potentially, the long-term. This will be followed by some key points of advice for practitioners like us who wish to engage in their own duoethnography. Finally, ways to follow-up on the project will be suggested.

Personal reflections

Ben: I'd always thought of myself as a good reflective practitioner and believed that I was always looking for ways to improve my practice, whether it be, for example, through reading academic literature, or discussing the previous week's lesson in a weekly meeting with my colleagues. Doing this project has made me realise that my 'reflections' were sometimes shallow, and tended to focus more on content of lessons rather than on how and why I do what I do in the classroom. The areas of concern for Charlie, as a novice teacher, were often things that I'd long since stopped consciously thinking about (for example, classroom 'discipline', or the role of 'culture' in our classes), and being made to explicitly state my beliefs about certain issues, or what I would do or have done in certain classroom situations, for example, was a useful exercise for making me re-analyse my feelings about those, perhaps recently neglected, areas of my teaching. As I said before, these 'revelations' were not immediate, and have largely come through reflecting on the primary dialogues that we had, so I've yet to know if they will have a significant influence on my practice, but I hope that I will start the next academic year with a more personally reflective mindset.

Charlie: Having set out into the project with more concrete expectations about the potential rewards, I think the outcome of the study has been less surprising for me than for Ben. It would be impossible to argue that the project has had a negative or negligible effect – it has certainly already improved my teaching capacities and most pertinently encouraged me to engage in reflective practice consistently as I move forward with my teaching career. As well as the immediate benefits of practical, immediately applicable advice from a more experienced teacher, it has also opened my eyes to broader phenomena in the TESOL profession such as native-speakerism, debate around use of L1 in the classroom, approaches to methodology, and training and development. I honestly feel that I've benefited from every stage of the process, including both dialogues and the process of writing up the duoethnography for academic publication. I'm also glad that Ben was able to benefit from the project, and it wasn't just a one-way street of advice and encouragement from him to me.

Advice for practitioners

Duoethnographies are very personal accounts and as such the scope for making generalisations about the findings may be limited. The purpose of this study was not to discover some new categorical differences between the beliefs or practice of novice and experienced teachers, but rather to discover the ways in which doing a duoethnography could support the professional development of a novice teacher and an experienced teacher. As can be seen from our personal conclusions above, we both, in somewhat different but equally valuable ways, feel that doing the study has been of enormous benefit to our own development of teaching beliefs and teaching practice, as well as our working relationship. Consequently, we would highly recommend that other novice and experienced teachers who work closely together, have similar roles, or work in similar institutions, embark upon similar projects. With this in mind, below is some basic advice for practitioners wishing to engage in a duoethnography like ours to follow:

- **Set a time period over which to record the primary dialogue(s).** We conducted our primary dialogues over the course of one semester (15 weeks). We could have probably continued it for three years!
- **Find a variety of ways to communicate.** Although the majority of our primary dialogue was conducted via a computer messaging application, as explained in the methods section, doing so can make responses 'unnatural' in length and style, as well as slow. Recording additional audio of a real-time conversation meant that we presented each other with less filtered opinions. However, tagging recorded conversations was more time-consuming, so a variety of data collection methods is recommended.
- **Be aware of issues of 'status'.** It may be more difficult to conduct an open and honest dialogue if one participant is in a professionally subordinate role (Mann & Tang, 2012). In our study Charlie admitted finding it difficult to be completely open because of a professional status difference that he perceived to exist, despite Ben's insistence in the dialogues that there was no such difference.

- **Explore opportunities for secondary dialogues.** For Ben, the experienced practitioner, in particular, the most useful 'realisations' from a professional development point of view came when reflecting on the primary dialogues and writing about those reflections in the secondary dialogue, so this is considered to be a crucial part of the duoethnography process here.
- **Publish your duoethnography.** Every teaching situation, and every teacher, is different, and we all have something to learn from our fellow professionals' experiences.
- **Publishing need not be the end of your project.** A duoethnography need not finish after the project has been written-up. The possibilities for recurring follow-ups are numerous, as we will illustrate below.

Future directions

Sawyer and Norris (2013: 107) assert that 'duoethnography is not just about reporting one's life but also about taking action on the temporary conclusions or ambiguous insights gleaned.' Although our conversations generated new ideas and understandings of our work context and practice, rarely did these translate into immediate, concrete changes in that practice, and these 'temporary conclusions' and 'ambiguous insights' will require further focus to follow up on, so both participants agreed it would be valuable to revisit the dialogues again in the future to assess whether actions have been taken and new conclusions reached.

We suggest that a six-monthly follow-up meeting may be sufficient to maintain positive developmental momentum for both of us, not only for external motivation, but also to maintain the dynamic tension that made us discover these hidden meanings and new interpretations in the first place. Having set the precedent for using duoethnography as a tool for professional development within our relationship, we expect that it will be easier to begin a useful and productive dialogue once again in the future. There should be no barrier to the continuing productivity of such a relationship, as due to age, experience and other factors, there is likely to continue to be a significant enough divergence between the two participants' lived experience to produce worthwhile contrast and construction of new meaning through comparison of experiences and ideological positions.

References

Borg, S. (2006) *Teacher Cognition and Language Education: Research and Practice.* London: Continuum.

Brannan, D. and Bleistein, T. (2012) Novice ESOL teachers' perceptions of social support networks. *TESOL Quarterly* 46 (3), 519–541.

Breault, R., Hackler, R. and Bradley, R. (2012) Seeking rigor in the search for identity: A trioethnography. In J. Norris, R.D. Sawyer and D.E. Lund (eds) *Duoethnography: Dialogic Methods for Social, Health, and Educational Research* (pp. 115–137). Walnut Creek, CA: Left Coast Press, Inc.

Farrell, T.S.C. (2008) Critical incidents in ELT initial teacher training. *ELT Journal* 62 (1), 3–10.

Farrell, T.S.C. (2009) The novice teacher. In A. Burns and J. Richards (eds) *The Cambridge Guide to Language Teacher Education* (pp. 182–189). New York, NY: Cambridge University Press.

Farrell, T.S.C. (2012) Novice-service language teacher development: Bridging the gap between preservice and in-service education and development. *TESOL Quarterly* 46 (3), 435–449.

Freeman, D.E. and Freeman, Y.S. (1994) *Between World: Access to Second Language Acquisition*. Portsmouth, NH: Heinemann.

Gatbonton, E. (2008) Looking beyond teachers' classroom behaviour: Novice and experienced ESL teachers' pedagogical knowledge. *Language Teaching Research* 12 (2), 161–182.

Huling, L. and Resta, V. (2001) *Teacher Mentoring as Professional Development*. Washington, DC: ERIC Clearinghouse on Teaching and Teacher Education.

Krammar, D. and Mangiardi, R. (2012) The hidden curriculum of schooling: A duoethnographic exploration of what schools teach us about schooling. In J. Norris, R.D. Sawyer and D.E. Lund (eds) *Duoethnography: Dialogic Methods for Social, Health, and Educational Research* (pp. 41–70). Walnut Creek, CA: Left Coast Press, Inc.

Lee, L. (2007) Scaffolding collaborative exchanges between expert and novice language teachers in threaded discussions. *Foreign Language Annals* 42 (2), 212–228.

Lortie, D. (1975) *Schoolteacher*. Chicago: University of Chicago Press.

Lowe, R.J. and Kiczkowiak, M. (2016) Native-speakerism and the complexity of personal experience: A duoethnographic study. *Cogent Education* 3 (1), 1264171.

Lowe, R.J. and Lawrence, L. (2018) Native-speakerism and 'hidden curricula' in ELT training: A Duoethnography. *Journal of Language and Discrimination* 2 (2), 162–187.

Mann, S. and Tang, E.H.H. (2012) The role of mentoring in supporting novice English language teachers in Hong Kong. *TESOL Quarterly* 46 (3), 472–495.

Moran, M. and Hoy, A.W. (2007) The differential antecedents of self-efficacy beliefs of novice and experienced teachers. *Teaching and Teacher Education* 23, 944–956.

Newby, P. (2010) *Research Methods for Education*. Harlow: Longman.

Norris, J. and Greenlaw, J. (2012) Responding to our muses: A duoethnography on becoming writers. In J. Norris, R.D. Sawyer and D.E. Lund (eds) *Duoethnography: Dialogic Methods for Social, Health, and Educational Research* (pp. 89–114). Walnut Creek, CA: Left Coast Press, Inc.

Norris, J. and Sawyer, R.D. (2017) *Theorizing Curriculum Studies, Teacher Education & Research through Duoethnographic Pedagogy*. New York: Palgrave Macmillan.

Nuske, K. (2014) 'It is very hard for teacher to make changes to policies that have become so solidified': Teacher resistance at corporate eikaiwa franchises in Japan. *The Asian EFL Journal* 16 (2), 283–312.

Pitton, D.E. (2006) *Mentoring Novice Teachers: Fostering a Dialogue Process*. California: Corwin Press.

Richards, J.C. and Lockhart, C. (1994) *Reflective Teaching in Second Language Classrooms*. Cambridge: Cambridge University Press.

Sawyer, R. and Norris, J. (2013) *Duoethnography: Understanding Qualitative Research*. Oxford: Oxford University Press.

Tsui, A.B. (2003) *Understanding Expertise in Teaching*. New York, NY: Cambridge University Press.

Warford, M.K. and Reeves, J. (2003) Falling into it: Novice TESOL teacher thinking. *Teacher and Teaching: Theory and Practice* 9 (1), 47–65.

Winter, E.C. and McGhie-Richmond, D. (2005) Using computer conferencing and case studies to enable collaboration between expert and novice teachers. *Journal of Computer Assisted Learning* 21 (2), 118–129.

Woods, D. (1996) *Teacher Cognition in Language Teaching*. Cambridge: Cambridge University Press.

6 Puzzling about Special Educational Needs in EFL Teacher Development: A Duoethnographic Inquiry

Nick Kasparek and Matthew W. Turner

Introduction

This chapter explores the thoughts and experiences of two teachers of English as a foreign language (EFL) in relation to supporting learners who have special educational needs (SEN). While some English language teaching (ELT) professionals might be able to draw upon significant specialized support and knowledge, many more are likely to find working with SEN learners initially puzzling, thereby sparking for them a continuing professional development (CPD) process. While the teaching of SEN learners has been written about widely in mainstream educational studies, EFL teachers are less likely to find such resources in their specialized literature. As the teaching of SEN learners requires significant specialization and individualization, there is a need for more qualitative accounts like those presented in this chapter. Our duoethnography will thus attempt to trace the development of our thoughts, feelings and orientations within the profession regarding teaching SEN learners. The reflective process of juxtaposing our histories and ideas has given us a better understanding of the complexity of SEN, broader inclusive educational practices, our own teacher identities and the professional challenge of working with SEN learners in English language teaching settings; at the same time, it has revealed new puzzles. We hope that our documented process informs others on similar developmental journeys.

The Study

Background and context

As relatively privileged (white, cisgender, male, cognitively 'normal,' currently able-bodied, middle-class) EFL teachers with almost no formal training in SEN, we recognize that we still have a great deal to learn about SEN education. As such, rather than attempt to present an authoritative or universal account, our reflections here attempt to provide a revealing window into our ongoing process of learning to become SEN educators. In this chapter, we focus primarily on a period of accelerated professional development regarding SEN education beginning when we worked together teaching the same compulsory oral English communication course at a private university in Tokyo, Japan (2013–2017), especially when we collaborated to teach one learner (whom we call 'Fumi') who had a significant learning difference. Fumi was officially designated as a SEN learner, as she apparently did not produce any spoken language, perhaps due to extreme anxiety. This meant that 'normal' participation in our mainstream English communication course seemed impossible, and our university program asked the two of us and another teacher to adapt and teach the course especially for her, aided by our program managers and the university SEN support staff. We thus received a great deal of support and assistance in radically adapting our oral English course for her as a one-on-one course that instead used writing as the medium of communication, and this adaptation proved remarkably successful. This experience led us to reflect together on our other experiences with SEN learners, even after we started different jobs at different universities. We subsequently made a presentation on the topic at an academic conference (Turner *et al.*, 2017), and the topic of teaching SEN university students frequently came up in our social conversations as well. We found some potentially interesting differences in our thinking about this subject, so we decided to delve deeper into our beliefs, choosing this project as a way not only to articulate and make sense of our thoughts on the subject and on ourselves as emergent SEN educators, but also to share our story with others, especially other similarly-positioned ELT professionals teaching at the university level.

Data collection and analysis

Primarily between March and June 2018, our initial inquiry unfurled, like other duoethnographic research, 'in bits and pieces; both the content and the structure develop[ed] throughout the process' (Norris & Sawyer, 2017: 6). We began this process with alternating interviews to prompt our investigations of our lives as curricula, in hopes that this dialogic examination would help us reconceptualize ourselves and our practice (see Sawyer & Norris, 2016). We then analyzed emerging themes on a shared online document. We continued to develop and supplement our discussion with new questions, comments and responses, thereby offering each other 'a new and destabilizing lens' (Sawyer & Norris, 2016: 3). We also messaged each other through *Facebook* and reviewed and reflected on our teaching materials and notes from our collaborative teaching experience with Fumi. In tandem with our ongoing data collection, we highlighted areas of growing importance and relevance, which subsequently informed how we eventually chose, through the 'collaborative approach of duoethnography [that] defers closure' (Norris & Sawyer, 2017: 7), to structure and present this chapter.

Chapter structure

The data from all our interactions led us to create five overarching sections through which to present our ideas. The first section, rather than presenting a formal literature review, establishes our current understandings of SEN through our individual engagement with the literature; rather than constructing a unified voice, the literature review is 'blended into the written study' (Sawyer & Norris, 2013: 20), as we 'intentionally highlight [our] different voices to promote a multiplicity of perspectives' (Sawyer & Norris, 2016: 8). The first sections highlight our understandings of SEN and formative memories of related issues stretching from our childhoods to our early teaching years. The central section then focuses on our reflections on our shared experience of collaborating to co-teach Fumi. The fourth section explores our concerns around SEN definitions and related activities. Finally, the fifth section imagines what the future of SEN education could be, both for the field of ELT and for ourselves professionally.

We have chosen to present our duoethnography as a conversation, in a similar way to a previous duoethnography in the field of ELT by Lowe and Kiczkowiak (2016), taking turns to respond to themes and each other.

Dialogues

Understandings of SEN

In this first section, in lieu of a traditional literature review, we blend the literature that has informed each of us into our discussion of our emergent understandings of SEN (see Sawyer & Norris, 2013).

Nick: I had very little familiarity with the term SEN until you introduced it to me, probably because it is a more popular term in the UK than in the USA.

Matthew: I wasn't particularly familiar with SEN either, but my general understanding is similar to Delaney's (2016: 12): students have special educational needs if 'they have significantly greater difficulty in learning than the majority of students of the same age and special educational provision has to be made for them.'

Nick: The way you describe it reminds me of the broader concept of 'inclusive education,' an idea I was a little more familiar with, and as I've since read, often focuses on disability and special educational needs (Messiou, 2017). Inclusion also entails, however, accommodating other traditionally excluded identities such as ethnic minorities, LGBTQ+ students and students dealing with poverty. My understanding of SEN is that it too is a broad, umbrella category, but it seems more focused on particular types of needs.

Matthew: I certainly agree that inclusive education likely encompasses SEN, and from my understanding, the terms are often conflated. After all, any provisions that would need to be made are done so in the spirit of, and to maintain, inclusivity and equity. However, any provisions made are highly dependent upon learners' conditions; for example, I have personally had experience with instructing a hearing-impaired learner (Turner, 2017), and I am aware of others working in the field of second language learning that have written about their practice more formally (Mayer, 2009; Swisher, 1989). As well as this, the teaching of sight-impaired and color vision disabled learners has been documented (Enjelvin, 2009; Moriya, 2016). These examples could fall under the category of sensory and/or physical impairments, with other categories including cognition and learning needs; communication and interaction difficulties; and social, emotional and mental health difficulties (Connor, 2017). Some examples of note here are the teaching of languages to learners on the autism spectrum (Wire, 2005), and to those who suffer from dyslexia (Gallagher, 2017). It is also my understanding that the use of the word 'difficulty' could be problematic too, and indeed, descriptions and categories of SEN may differ across teaching settings, such as a nation or a specific institution. Some scholars, such as Kormos and Smith (2012), and Kormos (2016) prefer a term like specific learning differences (SpLD), which seems to emphasize individuality and differences in ways of experiencing and interacting with the world. It also seems important to note that from personal experience, some learners may exhibit SEN-like characteristics, yet not be formally classified as needing classroom modifications or accommodations. There may also be learners that identify, or have been identified as SEN who require little in the way of changes to classroom practice. It seems that the plethora of SEN characteristics are not always clear cut, but far-reaching, and the definitions of SEN itself may be quite fuzzy.

Nick: Right, and while some relatively hidden differences would certainly be categorized as part of SEN, the fuzziness risks a blending of SEN with identities that would seem to have little to do with learning; your mention of *learning* differences thus seems like the key element to emphasize for more clarity and focus. I'd primarily associated SEN with intellectual differences, especially in the form of what I now know is referred to as 'cognitive diversity' (O'Donovan, 2010), but as you say, students with sensory and physical impairments certainly warrant accommodation aided by specialists if they attend mainstream schools.

Matthew: Given the dynamic nature of working with SEN learners, it is my understanding that teachers and learners are required to make use of support networks, primarily in non-SEN settings. In my experience, these networks commonly take place between different stakeholders, namely the teachers, students, managers and with other members such as parents and dedicated support workers. Support networks may vary depending on the educational setting; for example, there are those influenced by legislative governmental initiatives (Ortiz & Yates, 2001), those specially created for specific institutions (Young *et al.*, 2019), and those proposed for personalized support as a CPD process (Lowe, 2016).

Nick: Support networks and specialists do seem vital, and this has long been my understanding of SEN professionally: it is its own specialist field with professionals dedicated to developing ways to meet different learners' needs. Although I was vaguely aware that mainstreaming, or placing SEN students in regular classes, has been an important trend in education systems throughout the world (McConkey *et al.*, 2016), I had thought of non-specialist teachers' roles as just being open and welcoming to specialist support staff. Experience and development through professional networks have recently led me to see a more proactive role for mainstream university EFL teachers, but also to take a more skeptical view of what Tomlinson (2012) has called the 'SEN industry' and what others see as a 'medical model' of identifying disabilities (Hamayan *et al.*, 2007). Just as those outside our field often seem guilty of viewing language education as a straightforward technical skill and not a true discipline in its own right, I seem to have taken a simplistic view of SEN as a technical challenge for other specialists. I still have the sense that we should be mostly deferring to other experts and their research, but rather than viewing this as a technical task to accomplish, this now means reading and learning about the approaches and controversies in the field, some of which you've already highlighted.

Matthew: Yes, I think that as non-specialist teachers, support from experts should be sought at different points in the process, but I wonder about difficulties with this. I imagine that some teachers don't have the privilege of having access to academic materials in which these works are often housed, and I wonder how open an would be to bringing in someone with sufficient knowledge who could offer dedicated time and training to helping non-specialist teachers? And I wonder to what extent teachers really get the chance to work with SEN learners. From our understanding, teachers would be required to make their own connections in reading between mainstream educational work in SEN and ELT settings. However, all this being said, I feel that teachers could adequately support their SEN learners without much outside expertise, as long as some informal collaborative and/or personal plan for development is followed. From experience, I think that traditional practitioner research models of inquiry commonly used in the field of ELT such as action research (see Burns, 2010) together with reflective practice (see Mann & Walsh, 2017) could very much apply, and potentially yield greater understanding and development into classroom practice. Of course, any insights gained and subsequent changes being made as a result of classroom enquiry should be justified and principled.

Nick: That's true, but it still seems important for all of us teachers to at least gain familiarity with key concepts from SEN and decode their acronyms. For instance, I've benefited from reading through my graduate studies about IEPs (individualized education programs), RTI (response to intervention) and MLE (mediated learning experience) to name a few. These are particularly focused on how teaching requires individualized planning, assessment and responsiveness for all. I have also started to recognize the pernicious 'deficit view' regarding differences (Messiou, 2017), and see SEN education as something like 'universal design,' that is, as a good for everyone (Burgstahler, 2008). SEN education then starts to look like simply working to provide the best educational environment and experience possible for all the students who happen to be in our classroom. I've come across the same quotation in several articles: 'MLE is not only for the handicapped, it is for all of us since it's MLE which makes us human!' (Bruner cited in Poehner, 2008: 60). Outdated terminology aside, this encapsulates the ethos that shapes my understanding of SEN professionally: as a teacher, my responsibility is to help mediate the learning experiences of all the students in my classroom according to their needs.

Our understanding of SEN thus dovetails with ideals of inclusive education and teaching that is responsive to learners. However, SEN is its own specialized field, since it deals directly with learning differences and accommodating students who would struggle if their teachers ignored these learning differences. This understanding of SEN still deserves some critical scrutiny, but it provides an orientation and ethos toward accommodation rather than exclusion or seeing students as failing or disruptive 'problems.'

Formative SEN experiences and teaching experiences

While reading some specialized literature and working directly with SEN learners have been very influential on our personal development and understandings of SEN, our life curricula began long before we even consciously thought about teaching SEN learners. Our sociocultural contexts began shaping our ideas and attitudes before we learned the terms, and our experiences continue to affect our approaches today. Moreover, the ways in which we learned to become teachers has influenced how we have thought about SEN.

Nick: I've actually learned a great deal about SEN from you and from our work together, so this has been an important part of my life curriculum regarding SEN. That's not to say that I hadn't thought about the underlying ideas before. I was vaguely aware of special learning difficulties and how teachers sought to include different learners in their classrooms. It just didn't seem directly relevant to me. Perhaps this goes back to my earliest exposure to SEN: hearing mean jokes about 'the short bus' and the ubiquitous insult of things and people being 'retarded' in elementary and middle school. Learners with special needs rode a separate bus and were taught in different classrooms, so I saw SEN learners as different and probably deficient, to the extent that I thought about them at all.

Matthew: Perhaps recalling some childhood school experiences, like you, there was often some exposure to peers with learning differences at school, and these outward characteristics were often points of ridicule and hardship for those affected. Recalling one particular example, I remember a school classmate who suffered from Tourette syndrome. His condition led him to often utter involuntary words and expressions during classes that often included taboo or curse words. While I and other class members found this humorous at times, this was of course unfortunate and not funny at all. There was actually a feeling of concern, and I recall coming home one day and explaining to my mother about my classmate's symptoms; she guessed correctly that he was a Tourette syndrome sufferer. I actually brought this term up with my classmate, and he acknowledged its accuracy. Before the year ended, my classmate gave a speech to the class about his condition; looking back, this may have really changed the way the class reacted to his condition, and perhaps triggered my developing interests in SEN issues.

Nick: My development was slower. It wasn't until my undergraduate educational studies courses that I learned about Gardner's (1995) ideas of multiple intelligences, and learning differences took on more of a positive connotation. I reflected more critically on how my particular intelligence had been arbitrarily valued by standardized assessments. Still, these issues seemed pretty distant, and I don't think I fully internalized the ethos behind the ideas. Embarrassingly, at times, my learning of terms, especially of labels such as 'developmental issues' outpaced my development. These are certainly better than derogatory terms, but I see now how they risk becoming co-opted as euphemisms.

Matthew: You seem to have gained some awareness of related terminology and how to articulate ideas of learning differences from your undergraduate years. I feel that I can identify my earliest interests with SEN back to when I made the decision to become a teacher. Having chosen a career in EFL and undertaken a teaching training course, although SEN actually didn't feature at all, this is still a worthwhile time to reflect on. My Trinity Certificate in Teaching English to Speakers of Other Languages (CertTESOL) course, although this may not be everyone's experience, didn't include a focus on the potential challenge of instructing SEN learners. This course took a broad approach in seeking to equip trainee teachers with the procedural knowledge and 'nuts and bolts' of how to deliver lessons. As novices, we were perhaps more focused on ourselves and how we would cope as teachers, than *really* being attentive to what was happening with the groups of individuals we were learning to teach. Trinity College London (2016: 5) states that one objective is for candidates to develop an 'awareness of the learning needs of individuals or groups of learners, and of the motivation of learners in a variety of cultures and contexts.' In my experience, this objective was linguistically focused, where for instance, we were expected to describe and diagnose learners' English language difficulties based on L1 influences. As a result, embarking on my first teaching positions, I recall having one or two younger learners in my class who I would now like to think I would attempt to offer differentiated support to. But at the time, I had a limited understanding of how to work with learners in a more sensitive and individualized manner. Looking back, I probably viewed them as disruptive, and had yet to develop any pastoral skills.

Approximately five years after completing my initial CertTESOL course, I decided to take the Trinity College London's Licentiate Diploma in TESOL (DipTESOL). As expected, this course explored pedagogy more thoroughly, with greater attention paid to learners' individual variables to and group dynamics. I recall writing some coursework on 'emergent language,' an idea central to Meddings and Thornbury's Dogme ELT (2009). I observed how teachers expressed awareness of learners' emergent language issues by paying attention to how teachers reacted to these developments. Looking back, I think this was perhaps a point when I started to critically question 'one-size-fits-all' approaches to communicative language teaching.

Along with this, trainees were encouraged to keep notes on students' styles of learning. For example, we were asked to observe how students behaved during different aspects of the class, noting whether they seemed receptive to listening activities or visual stimuli, for example. These traits were termed learning styles, which are considered to be 'a set of learner characteristics that influences their response to different teaching approaches' (Howard-Jones, 2009: 29). They also relate to thoughts around multiple intelligences, with Gardner (1995: 16), as you mentioned previously, arguing that 'the human species has evolved to be able to analyze at least seven kinds of information in the world,' with '[e]ach intelligence exhibit[ing] its own developmental trajectory.' These brain-based ways of looking at learning would see me making lazy and sweeping generalizations about my learners' supposed preferred ways of learning. Although recently being critiqued as neuromyths (Lethaby & Harries, 2016; Lethaby & Mayne, 2018), and scrutinized across the field of educational psychology as an exercise in paying attention to the affective output of learners (Krätzig & Arbuthnott, 2006), this was an important point in my journey towards my developing SEN awareness. This could be the first time that I consciously and meaningfully made remedial and individual adaptations to my classroom practice.

Nick: I think it's interesting how your studies seemed focused on teaching procedures at the expense of a broader ethos, since my studies were essentially the opposite. Academic educational studies for me were much more about developing a general philosophical, sociocultural and psychological approach to understanding education. I took an elective TESOL course that involved some teaching practice, but most of the course centered on a historical approach to understanding different methodologies. I didn't have much procedural knowledge when I started my first full-time teaching position; instead, I synthesized my reflections on education and teaching, the language-teaching methodologies that I had studied in theory but not in practice, and classroom-management strategies from an educational psychology class. I never had a 'one-size-fits-all' model, so I often just had to respond to what seemed to be working for different groups of students and make things up as I went. When I taught one-on-one in language schools, this was even more the case, since I would develop a kind of IEP for each new student. I feel like I learned to teach more through intuition and experience than professional training. I was a mid-career teacher when I started my MEd studies, and even in this more praxis-oriented program, the emphasis was on inclusive education and being better advocates for traditionally-excluded students, especially English language learners in the US. In my understanding, still, SEN learners had their own advocates, and I just wasn't particularly involved with that field.

Matthew: There are certainly some resonances here, particularly your feeling that SEN learners may have their own advocates, and that these may be in parallel with, and detached from traditional educational settings. It seems useful to consider what happens when a SEN learner enters a non-specialized environment, the kind of which they may not be used to. When I taught my first SEN learner, this is what happened. Without going into too much detail here, as the teaching/learning process has been documented elsewhere (Turner, 2017), my first experience of working with a SEN learner was a hearing-impaired student who had elected to take an oral English discussion class, rather than be exempted. Before any teaching had started, I remember meetings focussed on the question of if she could, and even should, participate in the class. I recall some nebulous ideas being suggested, one being that she may wish to participate in an online messaging discussion instead of face-to-face exchange. Luckily, this was a nonstarter, and our department set in motion an IEP for the learner. Over the duration of the course, to my surprise, I found myself getting more personally involved than I had anticipated, and was amazed at how much was actually possible – and was achieved. Although both personally and departmentally, there was a sense of underpreparedness, I felt that with the right amount of flexibility and creative planning, the course objectives and outcomes could largely be met, without too much disruption. I think my experience here is reflective of our previous university department's broader attempts to proactively increase accommodation efforts with SEN learners.

Nick: Your point about the learners themselves making the choice to be included in regular classes seems really important, since we should certainly strive for equal access. When our department started to pay more attention to identified SEN learners in our classrooms, I started to make some connections with my previous course readings, but I still didn't really apply them to my case. Although some of my students had mobility limitations, these were very easily accommodated. However, I started learning about your experience with teaching a hearing-impaired learner, and other teachers' experiences with SEN learners who needed more creative and significant accommodations, and I started to wonder what I would do to be an effective teacher for such learners. It was thus fortunate that our shared experience of teaching an officially identified SEN learner provided one good model for radically adapting a course, and this experience and this duoethnography have encouraged me to read and think more critically about SEN.

We were both influenced by negative experiences and portrayals of disability in our formative years, though there were glimmers of emerging awareness of how limited our perspective was. Likewise, we were only rarely challenged to think about the implications of SEN on our own lives and teaching. While one of us was helpfully exposed to learning differences in formal courses, even then, it did not always seem particularly relevant to English teachers. Reflecting on our past experiences, there may have been students who would have benefitted from our taking a more SEN-informed approach. Still, at the time, to the extent that we thought about it, teaching SEN learners seemed a distant prospect, since we lacked the expertise.

Our experience of co-teaching one SEN learner

As mentioned previously, we felt underprepared when we were asked to co-teach and help adapt an English communication course around one SEN learner, Fumi, who apparently did not speak, but we were reassured by the existence of a helpful support network. We and our colleague Matt were each assigned a five-lesson section of the course to teach, one after the other, and we took a highly collaborative approach to adapting a unified course for Fumi (see Turner *et al.*, 2017). This positive experience led us to reflect on how we could also better accommodate our future SEN learners.

Nick: When I got the email from our managers, I felt vaguely honored to be trusted as one of the teachers of this special course, but at that time, I didn't realize how radically we would need to adapt the course for Fumi. I think if I had known that then, I would have been pretty intimidated, since I felt like I didn't know much at all about SEN education.

Matthew: I remember feeling reassured when I learnt I would be teaching Fumi with you, and with Matt who had taught her the previous year. I wasn't too aware about what took place during the previous attempts to teach her, but came to learn a lot about what could and couldn't be done. I feel that her previous teachers realized, the hard and unfortunate way, that mainstreaming did not seem to work for Fumi, and that she could not fully take part in classes with other students. We knew that we were lucky that we could build on this experience, helping ensure that Fumi could at least achieve some of the primary learning outcomes of the course. Looking back on my experience teaching with you and Matt, I think I wanted to show to everyone that even more could be achieved. I remember wanting to improve on what had taken place before, wanting to make some innovative impact through our efforts. Collaboration was certainly important for this process; it was through collaboration that we not only found out what each other was doing in the classroom with Fumi, but to some extent, collaboration allowed us to work with the learner and her support workers more constructively. I recall making a lot of notes during meetings, documenting mentions of Fumi's life, her condition and her interests. Looking back, I felt this is where we had the most success. For example, related to our previous work together on developing humor-focused language learning activities (Kasparek & Turner, 2016; Turner & Kasparek, 2017), I remember you and I searching online for more information about her favorite anime, and then talking about how we could not only incorporate this into lesson materials, but also imagine how it could be used as a vehicle to motivate and stimulate Fumi's communication.

Nick: Once I started talking with you, I also came to approach this teaching challenge with more hope. It was a relief to learn that I'd be working with you and Matt. I also felt like we had a good chance to improve on previous efforts and to address challenges in creative ways. The anime example stands out for me too, as an instance of attempting a playful approach to reduce her apparent anxiety and give her a less stressful way to engage with the course content, but I remember that we waited until your portion of the lessons, the second five lessons, to try that out.

Since I had Fumi for the first five lessons of the 15-lesson intensive course, I was pretty worried about whether Fumi and I could really co-create a comfortable atmosphere. Not wanting to ruin the rest of the course, I erred on the side of caution, reducing the pressure as much as possible, while still maintaining the expectation that she would nonetheless practice interacting in English. In some ways, it was like a return for me to teaching one-on-one courses to very 'shy' students in my previous job. One key challenging difference from those experiences was that we had a unified curriculum to teach Fumi and clear institutional expectations to meet. This highlighted that to the extent that the course was universally designed, its universe did not include a learner like Fumi. Fortunately, the other key differences were that I was not alone in creating Fumi's IEP and that we were informed about her learning differences before we began teaching her.

This gave us time to learn from SEN specialists, program managers, her previous teachers, each other and from the literature. From the literature, it became clear that we should use a fairly standard research cycle, and to help formalize this cycle, I found a collaborative inquiry approach of iteratively (re-) defining the fundamental puzzle, planning, enacting strategies, observing and adjusting (Schnellert & Butler, 2016). A significant focus of our collaborative inquiry involved planning and enacting strategies of substituting speaking activities with written activities, then monitoring progress and making adjustments. I was struck by how my expectations for what constituted success changed, growing more ambitious as the course progressed. For instance, I was encouraged by how Fumi responded somewhat playfully to some of my more facetious questions and comments in our practice dialogues, and it was a relief to be able to report to you that you could go ahead with the anime character dialogues as we had hoped.

Matthew: Once Fumi's IEP was formed, and you had taught her the initial classes, I also felt that some experimentation could take place. The experiments I tried were aimed at building up rapport and developing meaningful interaction. I remember bringing some chocolate to class and asking if she'd like some. Although she didn't take it, I left it on the table, and I believe she took it herself when I had left the classroom. I also gradually tried to make more eye contact with her over the process, as well as sometimes gently asking her to say target language phrases. Perhaps my attempts here show that although I was subverting the agreed IEP a little, I felt that our support network had ensured a much more comfortable environment for both Fumi and ourselves as teachers, and provided a space for potential development.

Nick: I think this kind of safe experimentation, scaffolded by each other and the support network, also allowed for our own development regarding SEN education. Although I recognize that other SEN learners would need very different accommodations, I felt like I finally understood at least one successful process for SEN accommodation. At the same time, the experience and our subsequent writing and talking about it also highlighted more specific gaps in my reading and led me to seek out more literature on not only SEN education in EFL, but also on critical disabilities studies and inclusive education. Many of the sources that I have cited in this chapter are articles and books that I have only found thanks to our experience with Fumi and our conversations inspired by it. I've also become more attuned to SEN-related issues in media such as podcasts and in conversations with others. Some of this reading and listening, along with my subsequent experience, has also simultaneously raised and complicated some new nuanced concerns about SEN. For instance, Fumi's official designation as a SEN learner could, on the one hand, be criticized as conforming to the medical model, but on the other, her designation led to support for all of us and ultimately improved her MLE.

Matthew: In line with your newfound discoveries of media and literature around SEN-related issues, I too am thinking about different ways of immersing myself in the world of SEN. In my current faculty, I have become aware of a group of students who are learning sign language in order to support hearing-impaired peers, and I have started to informally learn along with them. So, partly through our shared experience with helping Fumi, I am undertaking new activities that I may not have previously considered, and learning that there are many dimensions of engagement that could be worth exploring.

In this section, we reflected on our collaborative teaching experience with one SEN learner. It emerged that we remember it positively both in terms of supporting the learner and of being supported and learning a great deal ourselves. One highlight of the experience was the creativity and experimentation that our collaboration and our support network fostered. Our experiences suggest that with the right support network and IEP in place, even teachers with limited knowledge, training and experience regarding SEN instruction can use their flexibility and creativity to meet ambitious educational goals.

Our lingering concerns with SEN

We both identified 'fuzziness' in the concept of SEN, and we expressed some discomfort about 'SEN' as a label. In this section, we present our discussion of what we still find potentially problematic about SEN in our professional development.

Nick: Although SEN seems very worthy of focus, I do still have a few broader socio-political worries. One worry relates to 'accommodation,' and the admission inherent in the term that our institutions are not really universally designed, since we only need to accommodate those who are otherwise excluded in the institution's basic design. I worry that mainstreaming pressure might lead to more labeling and medicalization in our 'normal' schools and become a way of disinvesting in excellent SEN-focused schools that impart a sense of pride in that part of their identity, such as deaf schools with a vibrant culture. I feel like we all need to make more of an effort to listen to what advocacy groups and SEN learners actually want, while also keeping in mind that SEN is a spectrum and that creating a more diverse society seems an admirable end in itself. This tension relates to my biggest practical worry for myself regarding teaching SEN learners: that I have a persistent case of 'neurotypical syndrome,' a satirical condition I've come across in my reading, which is described as 'a neurobiological disorder characterized by preoccupation with social concerns, delusions of superiority, and obsession with conformity' (*ISNT: Institute for the Study of the Neurologically Typical* cited in O'Donovan, 2010: 182). For instance, I still struggle with suspicions that I am somehow lowering my expectations and standards for SEN learners, especially when their mental health issues are hard to distinguish from an apparent lack of effort and engagement. I think for my further development as an EFL teacher of SEN students, I will need to engage with critical disability studies more and grapple with my own possible 'syndrome.'

Matthew: I understand your worries here. You highlight that although there are some problems with the SEN label, it could be observed as acting as an introduction to other areas of progressive educational principles. I feel that my orientations to SEN have been practical, and focused on the pedagogical challenges that learners who possess a physical or mental difference generate. Yet, I worry to what extent choosing to overtly focus on SEN as a feature of my CPD might be more of a personal endeavor, rather than a more genuine attempt to innovate or bring about larger changes to education. For example, I've chosen to write up my experiences in an autoethnographical style in the past, so this was heavily focused on looking at, and analyzing myself throughout the teaching procedure. I've also talked of limitations in the literature, and the marginal focus there is in the field of ELT. Although any kind of work in this area has and can have mostly constructive outcomes, I'm still questioning what my genuine intentions are. Of course, this isn't exclusive to SEN per se, and I'm sure that there have been practitioners that have conducted research activities into their classrooms principally for extrinsic purposes such as meeting publication requirements.

Nick: I don't think it detracts from your projects at all that it is personal – my research obsessions stem from my own curiosity and whatever issues I'm working through, especially about how my ideals don't quite match up with my practice, and how my ideals conflict with each other. An example of the latter is my imagined worst-case scenario of SEN education cannibalizing inclusive education, even though I regard both as worthy ideals. First, I see how SEN might come to encompass nearly all forms of difference in Japan and thus become stretched too thin to support them all. For example, I envision university SEN offices being asked to assist not only students with physical disabilities and learning differences but also transgender students and those with serious mental illnesses, when it seems clear that students with any of these differences would need very different forms of specialized support. University offices and teachers would need to triage their support in response, so then the SEN learners with the most influential advocates or 'sympathetic' conditions would gain outsized attention. I think to avoid this scenario of preferential inclusion, we would again need to keep the ethos of universal design and its focus on universal inclusion, while also allocating more resources for various specialists. There would undoubtedly be resistance, though, to allocating these resources in tight economic conditions, especially if we take a deficit view of SEN.

Matthew: I wonder if there could be a stigmatic aspect present too. Especially in for-profit English language schools, I could imagine that raising the issue that a child might have cognitive learning differences for example, could be seen as a potential disruption to business, as well as something that might bother parents. It shouldn't be like this of course, and any maneuvers such as this by the teacher I would think would be welcomed by related parties. I do wonder however if there may be some pressure to not express issues if they arise. Of course, there are formalized frameworks and codes of practice when it comes to mainstream education, but I think it might be a completely different process in industry-based teaching settings, or in countries where the working conditions may not be immediately familiar to the teacher, such as a British teacher like myself working in Japan. On the other hand, our experiences at our previous institution showed that by triggering a process of officially identifying a learner as having special educational needs, suitable provisions and accommodations can be made. These feelings also correspond with the narratives presented in Shepherd *et al.* (2017). Although this process should perhaps be dealt with delicately, effective outcomes are certainly possible.

This section explored some of our concerns regarding the label of SEN and its potential tension with other pressures and ideals involved in contemporary education. As relatively novice SEN teachers, we have begun to explore how SEN instruction and thinking about SEN issues can be a CPD activity, but we have also started to question the motivations and ideologies underlying our educational institutions as well as our own thoughts and practice.

Directions for the future

We have emphasized throughout this chapter that we are still new to teaching SEN learners, and still open to significant development and change. At the same time, our experiences and reflections have clarified some gaps in our education and development as EFL teachers, and we believe that these gaps could also be instructive for others. In this section, we explore some directions we might take in our own journeys toward becoming better teachers for our students, and some directions that we feel the field of ELT could take to better prepare future teachers for SEN education.

Nick: Personally, throughout this duoethnography, I've become more inspired to respond the best I can to my students, to continue reading about and discussing SEN issues, and to advocate for inclusive education and universal design for learning (UDL), especially among fellow (and future) EFL teachers who might have even less background in SEN education.

Matthew: Talking about ELT teacher training courses, I wonder to what extent issues related to SEN and inclusivity could be incorporated. Although I think it will remain marginal, given the low amount of SEN learners in mainstream EFL classes, I'm hopeful that there could be some increased emphasis. I imagine it would need to be framed around practical accommodations that the trainee teachers would need to make. However, I wonder if a new teacher could cope with the extra commitments of supporting SEN learners in the classroom? If someone had shown me an example of this 12 years ago when I was in the very early stages of my career, I wouldn't have fully understood it. I feel like teachers need to have good amounts of procedural and reflective knowledge of their practice before they can begin to reconfigure, adapt, and modify it. Yet, if an ethos or overt focus on inclusivity and difference was introduced at a pre-service stage, teachers may instinctively begin to think about this from the outset. I may look for ways to involve myself with suggesting increased SEN focus on pre-service training courses such as CertTESOL, or research more deeply and critically the question of why this currently isn't the case.

Nick: I suppose it depends on the teacher's personality, but from my own experience, I feel that a privileging of ethos over procedures can work. I was certainly overwhelmed, and this might have stemmed from my lack of professional training. Nonetheless, I think if given some space to teach flexibly and responsively, teachers can find their own ways. I had moments of self-doubt, but I also never felt like I was lacking any of the components I needed to simply get through a class. I would imagine that the ethos would be harder to discover on one's own.

Matthew: Having a SEN learner in a classroom, whether physically-impaired or cognitively challenged, has taught me not to take things for granted. As explored previously with my experiences with supporting a deaf learner and our experiences with teaching Fumi, comfortable elements of practice may need to be challenged and reexamined. For example, I learnt that I couldn't simply rely on my voice for instructions with a hearing-impaired learner in the room, but needed to deliver verbal instructions in combination with written support. So, I think my feelings have led me to feel that working with a SEN learner presents professional puzzles, leading teachers to reevaluate practice once again, prompting teachers to find innovative ways to deliver lessons, while looking to ensure inclusivity and quality.

Nick: I think that openness to puzzles is key. Our experience led me to view teaching and research in SEN as intricately connected. If I do encounter SEN learners in the future whose successful accommodation and inclusion seems elusive, I'd like to try 'collaborative' or 'inclusive research' with them (Nind, 2014;

Messiou, 2017). Put simply, this would mean involving the students in the action research projects.

Matthew: What you're saying here resonates with what I understand the work of Exploratory Practice (EP) (Allwright, 2003) to be. EP is form of practitioner research, which centrally looks to blend and synergize research and pedagogy. However, unlike other approaches to research, collegiality and co-enquiry relationships with learners are foregrounded. Enquiry is carried out through classroom practice, with learners invited to take on participatory roles in the process, and practitioners being transparent and honest about what they're investigating. Another tenet is the idea of puzzling about something of critical interest, with EP inviting practitioners to 'puzzle about their own experiences of language and teaching, and having identified puzzling issues, explore their practice together in order to develop their own understanding(s) for mutual development, by using normal pedagogic practices as investigative tools' (Hanks, 2017: 82). I feel that in future, I'd like to see more accounts of English language teachers 'puzzling' with their SEN learners, as I believe that in essence, the teaching of SEN learners is very much one professional puzzle. This duoethnography has perhaps revealed that, with very little outside help, provisional changes made in the classroom can yield positive learning outcomes and potentially support educational inclusivity. Another aspect of EP is the idea of making professional enquiry public, and less of a property of academia. In this respect, SEN learners should be viewed as primary informants of their own condition, and subsequently, seen as having the ability to lead their teachers to understanding their learning needs. So, like you mentioned, I think working alongside, and in collaboration with our SEN learners as co-enquirers would be an interesting and sustainable way to go about exploring the 'puzzles' related to the support of SEN learners in ELT. I'm being very idealistic here, and I'm sure that there may be a number of difficulties and limitations with this approach, however at its core, I think a lot can be learnt and gained from working closely alongside our SEN learners.

Conclusion

This chapter has examined through probing dialogues how we have developed and hope to continue developing as EFL teachers with SEN learners. While this discussion centered on our shared experience of co-teaching one SEN learner in a radically adapted course, and then presenting and writing about this important experience, we also attempted to trace the development of our ideas related to SEN education through our own life experiences and our engagement with the academic literature.

Our discussion encouraged us to think more deeply about some of the subtle influences on our ideas stretching from our childhoods to current trends in educational institutions and society, and it caused us to return to the academic literature and to notice more SEN-related issues in our daily lives and our media environments. Conducting this duoethnography helped us reframe our underpreparedness, our inchoate understandings, our concerns, our successes and our conflicting ideals as puzzles that inspired our curiosity and exploration.

Although differences emerged in our stories and ideas, with different emphases and concerns coming to the fore, so did more important and fundamental similarities, namely, that ELT professionals need an awareness of SEN issues, an ethos of inclusiveness and individualization, and ideally, a network of support. As more SEN learners are included in mainstream classrooms and as more students are officially designated as SEN learners, there will be more need and demand for ELT professionals, even those who feel ill-positioned to do so, to accommodate these learners in creative ways. We hope that this chapter adds to the dialogue that more and more ELT professionals will need to have in order to collaborate for their own professional development to become SEN educators.

This project began with the initial data collection stage in March 2018 and continued to evolve through to the end of the writing process in October 2018. While this duoethnographic inquiry accurately captures our thoughts, feelings and orientations in that particular period, our ideas about this complex topic have continued to develop since.

References

Allwright, D. (2003) Exploratory Practice: Rethinking practitioner research in language teaching. *Language Teaching Research* 7 (2), 113–141.

Burgstahler, S.E. (2008) Universal design of instruction: From principles to practice. In S.E. Burgstahler (ed.) *Universal Design in Higher Education: From Principles to Practice* (pp. 31–64). Cambridge, MA: Harvard Education Press.

Burns, A. (2010) *Doing Action Research in English Language Teaching: A Guide for Practitioners*. New York: Routledge.

Connor, J. (2017) *Addressing Special Educational Needs and Disability in the Curriculum: Modern Foreign Languages*. New York: Routledge.

Delaney, M. (2016) *Special Educational Needs*. Oxford: Oxford University Press.

Enjelvin, D.G. (2009) Teaching French to a non-sighted undergraduate: Adjusting practices to deliver inclusive education. *Journal of Further and Higher Education* 33 (3), 265–279.

Gallagher, N. (2017) EDC and disability: Reflections on creating an inclusive classroom. *New Directions in Teaching and Learning English Discussion* 5, 9–14.

Gardner, H. (1995) 'Multiple intelligences' as a catalyst. *The English Journal* 84 (8), 16–18.

Hanks, J. (2017) *Exploratory Practice in Language Teaching: Puzzling about Principles and Practices*. London: Springer Nature.

Hamayan, E.V., Marler, B., Sanchez-Lopez, C. and Damico, J.S. (2007) Reasons for the misidentification of special needs among ELLs. In E.V. Hamayan, B. Marler,

C. Sanchez-Lopez and J.S. Damico (eds) *Special Education Considerations for English Language Learners: Delivering a Continuum of Services* (pp. 2–7). Philadelphia, PA: Caslon.

Howard-Jones, P. (2009) Neuroscience, technology and learning (pp. 14–19). *Becta* (accessed 27 September 2018). See http://www.bris.ac.uk/education/people/academicStaff/edpahj/publications/becta.pdf

Kasparek, N. and Turner, M.W. (2016) Harnessing humorous outbidding for the rapid generation of content. In J. Rucynski (ed.) *New Ways in Teaching with Humor* (pp. 21–25). Alexandria, VA: TESOL Press.

Kormos, J. (2016) *The Second Language Learning Processes of Students with Specific Learning Difficulties*. Abingdon-on-Thames: Routledge.

Kormos, J. and Smith, A.M. (2012) *Teaching Languages to Students with Specific Learning Differences*. Bristol: Multilingual Matters.

Krätzig G.P. and Arbuthnott K.D. (2006) Perceptual learning style and learning proficiency: a test of the hypothesis. *Journal of Educational Psychology* 98 (1), 238–46.

Lethaby, C. and Harries, P. (2016) Learning styles and teacher training: Are we perpetuating neuromyths? *ELT Journal* 70 (1), 16–27.

Lethaby, C. and Mayne, R. (2018) A critical examination of perceptual learning styles in English language teaching. *International Review of Applied Linguistics in Language.* https://doi.org/10.1515/iral-2017-0067

Lowe, R.J. (2016) Special educational needs in English language teaching: Towards a framework for continuing professional development. *ELTED* 19, 23–31.

Lowe, R.J. and Kiczkowiak, M. (2016) Native-speakerism and the complexity of personal experience: A duoethnographic study. *Cogent Education* 3, 1264171.

Mann, S. and Walsh, S. (2017) *Reflective Practice in English Language Teaching: Research-Based Principles and Practices*. New York: Routledge.

Mayer, C. (2009) Issues in second language literacy education with learners who are deaf. *International Journal of Bilingual Education and Bilingualism* 12 (3), 1–11.

McConkey, R., Kelly, C., Craig, S. and Shevlin, M. (2016) A decade of change in mainstream education for children with intellectual disabilities in the Republic of Ireland. *European Journal of Special Needs Education* 31 (1), 96–110.

Meddings, L. and Thornbury, S. (2009) *Teaching Unplugged: Dogme in English Language Teaching*. Peaslake: Delta Publishing.

Messiou, K. (2017) Research in the field of inclusive education: Time for a rethink? *International Journal of Inclusive Education* 21 (2), 146–159.

Moriya, R. (2016) Raising awareness of language learners with color vision disabilities. In P. Clements, A. Kruse and H. Brown (eds) *Focus on the Learner* (pp. 161–168). Tokyo: JALT.

Nind, M. (2014) Inclusive research and inclusive education: Why connecting them makes sense for teachers' and learners' democratic development of education. *Cambridge Journal of Education* 44 (4), 525–540.

Norris, J. and Sawyer, R.D. (2017) Introduction: The efficacy of duoethnography in teaching and learning: A return to roots. In J. Norris and R.D. Sawyer (eds) *Theorizing Curriculum Studies, Teacher Education, & Research through Duoethnographic Pedagogy* (pp. 1–14). New York: Palgrave Macmillan.

O'Donovan, M.M. (2010) Cognitive diversity in the global academy: Why the voices of persons with cognitive disabilities are vital to intellectual diversity. *Journal of Academic Ethics* 8 (3), 171–185.

Ortiz, A. and Yates, J. (2001) A framework for serving English language learners with disabilities. *Journal of Special Education Leadership* 14 (2), 72–80.

Poehner, M.E. (2008) *Dynamic Assessment: A Vygotskian Approach to Understanding and Promoting L2 Development*. New York: Springer.

Sawyer, R.D. and Norris, J. (2013) *Duoethnography*. Oxford: Oxford University Press.

Sawyer, R.D. and Norris, J. (2016) Dialogic interdisciplinary self-study through the practice of duoethnography. In R.D. Sawyer and J. Norris (eds) *Interdisciplinary Reflective Practice through Duoethnography* (pp. 1–13). New York: Palgrave Macmillan.

Schnellert, L. and Butler, D.L. (2016) Teachers as self- and co-regulating learners. *Psychology Today, PsychEd Blog* (accessed on 29 September 2018). See https://www.psychologytoday.com/blog/psyched/201612/teachers-self-and-co-regulating-learners

Shepherd, K.G., Kervick, C.T. and Morris, D.M. (2017) *The Art of Collaboration: Lessons from Families of Children with Disabilities*. Rotterdam: Sense Publishers.

Swisher, M.V. (1989) The language learning situation of deaf students. *TESOL Quarterly* 23 (2), 239–258.

Tomlinson, S. (2012) The irresistible rise of the SEN industry. *Oxford Review of Education*, 38 (3), 267–286.

Trinity College London (2016) *Certificate in Teaching English to Speakers of Other Languages (CertTESOL) Syllabus – January 2016* (accessed 27 September 2018). See https://www.trinitycollege.com/site/?id=201

Turner, M.W. (2017) A teacher's journey of integrating a deaf learner into their class. *New Directions in Teaching and Learning English Discussion* 5, 253–262.

Turner, M.W. and Kasparek, N. (2017) Playing with perspectives: An academic preparation activity for creative thinking. *The Language Teacher* 41 (1), 23–24.

Turner, M.W., Kasparek, N. and McLaughlin, M. (2017) *Teacher collaboration to support SEN learners*. Paper presented at *JALT 2017*. Tsukuba, Japan.

Wire, V. (2005) Autistic spectrum disorders and learning foreign languages. *Support for Learning* 20 (3), 123–128.

Young, D., Schaefer, M. Y. and Lesley, J. (2019) Accommodating students with disabilities studying English as a foreign language. *Journal of Postsecondary Education and Disability* 32 (3), 311–319.

7 Developing Understandings of Reflective Practice and Teacher Training

Matthew Schaefer and Peter Brereton

Introduction

Reflective practice is something which is rightly felt to be important for language teachers as a means of ongoing assessment and re-evaluation of classroom practice (Farrell, 2008, 2016; Mann, 2005). Reflection can lead to more teacher autonomy and better awareness of strengths and weaknesses (Richards & Farrell, 2005), while also improving decision making in the classroom (Mann, 2005). In addition, it may allow teachers to have a better sense of their own effectiveness, which can have a positive impact on students' learning outcomes (Ross & Bruce, 2007). All of these benefits are typically included as aims of teacher education, so it is no surprise that many continuing professional development systems include reflective practice as a key component. As a result, most teacher educators are aware of the importance of reflection, for both encouraging and guiding its practice in others and for undertaking it themselves as a means to develop as trainers.

The two authors of this chapter, Peter Brereton and Matthew Schaefer (hereafter Peter and Matt), worked together as two of the four program managers of a large-scale academic English discussion course at a private university in central Tokyo, Japan. The course was a requirement for all first-year students at the university – roughly 4500 in number per year. It employed a strongly unified curriculum (Schaefer *et al.*, 2016), which meant that all 42 of the course instructors used the same methodology and materials to teach the same discussion skills, as expressed through set phrases, following the same lesson structure and using the same assessment methods. The course aims were to develop students' discussion skills and speaking fluency in the context of deepening their understanding of a range of contemporary topics.

The course instructors came from a variety of backgrounds in terms of qualifications and experience, although all had taught in universities or obtained advanced degrees in language teaching, or, most commonly, both. They represented a diversity of nationalities, and so called 'native' or 'non-native' speakerhood was not considered during the recruitment process (Schaefer, 2018b). Instructors were responsible for teaching only the discussion course and would typically have 12 to 14 lessons per week for a maximum of five years.

As program managers, we were responsible for evaluating and developing the course through internal research projects that led to ongoing curriculum design. We also maintained its unified nature by training and overseeing the professional development of the teachers. This included a five-day orientation program for new instructors, regular faculty development sessions, and lesson observations. These observations were summative in that they sought to ensure that all instructors were following the prescribed syllabus in order to best support students in achieving the course aims. However, they were also developmental in terms of helping instructors reflect on their own teaching practice in a way that could be beneficial for other teaching contexts. In addition, we were responsible for supervising instructors' professional development projects, which were, for the most part, reflective in nature. Examples included the keeping of a teaching journal and the design of a principled classroom activity. The program manager role occupied a somewhat unusual position within the discussion course center. Although there were a director and deputy director who had final say in decisions regarding large changes to the course, there existed no strict oversight of what the program managers did on a daily basis and no formalized professional development system for them to follow.

We both came to the program manager role after working as English language teachers and teacher trainers in a variety of contexts, including at public high schools and private language schools in, collectively, the UK, Ireland, France, Italy, Australia and Japan. Coincidentally, we also worked at the same International House school, albeit several years apart, in San Sebastián in the Basque region of Spain. We also both completed CELTA and Delta training courses before doing our MAs in language education. Matt was in the role of program manager three years longer than Peter, although there was no hierarchy among the four managers. In addition, Matt had been an instructor for one year prior to becoming a program manager, whereas Peter joined the discussion course center directly as program manager.

When asked to contribute a duoethnography to this book, we agreed primarily for developmental purposes. We had previously discussed the need for program managers in the center to undertake some kind of professional development, focusing on aspects of teacher training (e.g. post-observation conferences), program evaluation, and/or teaching. Although this happened regularly at an informal level, i.e. through talk among the four program managers, it was not standardized or systematized to the same level it was for instructors. Therefore, the opportunity to try a formalized piece of reflective practice was appealing. In addition, we had both been made aware of duoethnographies through recent publications and conference presentations (Brereton & Kita, 2019; Lawrence & Nagashima, 2019; Lowe & Kiczkowiak, 2016; Rose & Montakantiwong, 2018) and were curious about the process. It appealed to us partly due to its interactive nature, since, as colleagues working closely together, we were accustomed to discussing all aspects of the course we collaborated on. However, aware of the many similarities in our work backgrounds, we were also keen to seek ways in which we differed in our approaches to the same role. While program managers presented a united front to the instructors they supervised and the professors they answered to, behind closed doors disagreements had to be talked through before the best solution was reached. We felt that being more aware of our different perspectives, with regards to both principles and practice, would positively affect our discussions by allowing for more empathy and a broadening of our viewpoints. Therefore, we were interested in uncovering explicit differences in how we undertook aspects of the job we were both doing and exploring how those differences might influence the choices we made. Teacher training seemed an obvious aspect to focus on as it comprised many of the tasks of program managers. As such, we set out to explore the following questions:

(1) How similar and how different are our understandings of reflective practice, and how did our evolution as reflective practitioners influence our understandings?
(2) What is our role as teacher trainers in encouraging reflection in others?
(3) What role did training and reflection play in the development of our identities as teacher trainers?

This duoethnography was conducted when we were still working together in our roles as program managers. We had three 90-minute conversations over the course of about two weeks and the overall aim was to share our experiences of teacher training and reflective practice. We approached each discussion with a general theme in mind and some possible starter questions. The theme of the first discussion was how we had evolved in our own reflective practice, while the second focused on our experiences encouraging reflection in others, and the third looked at our developing identities as teachers and teacher trainers. In the days following each conversation, we produced broad transcriptions of them; in other words, orthographic representations that sought to capture only the content of what was said, but not features of speech such as pauses or mispronunciations. We then selected which sections of the discussions we felt were most relevant for this chapter and regrouped them under discrete headings, meaning that the original chronology of our interactions was not maintained. Finally, we edited these sections to more accurately express our thoughts and opinions, and, in place of a formal literature review, added references where appropriate.

Dialogue 1: Our Evolution as Reflective Practitioners

In this dialogue, we explore our understandings of reflective practice, with a particular focus on our 'evolution' as reflective practitioners. In doing so, we look at both the processes involved in reflection and the benefits that may result from it. As teacher trainers whose job involved leading and encouraging the reflective practice of others, this was a natural starting point for our discussion.

Peter: So, maybe a good place to begin is: why do we place so much value on being reflective teachers?

Matt: I think when I first heard about the concept of teacher reflection, my first impression was that all teachers are probably already reflective.

Peter: Yeah, whether they are aware of it or not.

Matt: Right. So, is what we call 'reflective practice' just the formalizing of a process that teachers already do?

Peter: I think it is. As soon as I come out of class I can't help but think about what went well and I tend to know instinctively if I've had a 'good' class or a 'bad' class. This feeds into subsequent lessons, where I obviously try to take steps to improve whatever didn't go so well. As a novice teacher though, looking back, I think this started off as quite subjective, perhaps based on a feeling I had when I left the classroom, thinking, 'Oh, that lesson went really well.' or 'That lesson was a real nightmare, but I have to teach it again tomorrow.' So, then you make some changes.

Matt: So, the first thing is an impression of 'good' or 'bad'. That's the first step: You come out of a lesson feeling good about yourself as a teacher or feeling bad about yourself.

Peter: Or at least feeling good or bad about the lesson. Especially if you're teaching it again, you've got a genuine reason to reflect then.

Matt: This is making me think of the evolution of the reflective teacher, in terms of the different stages we go through.

Peter: Well, for me it definitely started off as a fairly subconscious process.

Matt: That's interesting. I think I had a similar beginning, and perhaps the next step was to make that process more conscious. I remember initially that, while things were going badly in the lesson, I'd be aware of it, even if I was just thinking 'Okay, this is not good but I've got to somehow get through it.' And then I'd get to the end and think 'Okay, that was a terrible lesson.' or 'Actually, overall it wasn't that bad.' After a while, I became better able to identify which parts of the lesson were good or bad, or where exactly it started to go wrong, or deciding if it had been doomed from the start.

Peter: The interesting question that comes out of that is: Are we more reflective about bad lessons than we are about good lessons? If you came out of a lesson thinking the lesson had gone really well and the students had responded well to everything, would the same level of reflection be evident if you came out of class dejected because the lesson hadn't gone so well? In my early days of teaching, I know I'd spend more time reflecting on things that went badly than those that went well, although that might have been due to the number of bad lessons back then! Nowadays I'm happy with the vast majority of my lessons although I still feel it's the case now that I'll reflect more on the negatives; I don't know if there's necessarily as much reflection involved when you're happy with a lesson.

Matt: Yes, I think that was further up the evolutionary scale of being a reflective teacher for me too, where I started to consider why a lesson was good. I think another key step for me was when I went from reflecting on not only why it was bad, but starting to consider what changes could be made so it wasn't as bad the next time. I think this is at least part of what Schön (1983) referred to as 'reflection-on-action', where you're looking back on a lesson that's already happened.

Peter: I see. I think reflection also really helped me a lot with autonomy. Thinking back to those first post-CELTA teaching moments, it was odd not to have the safety net of tutors observing from the back of the room. I really valued that post-lesson discussion/reflection session at the end of each lesson on CELTA; it helped foster some really good habits in terms of reflection in my early teaching days. Even without the support of the course, it just seemed normal to spend some time considering how my lessons went and wondering what I could have done differently. That definitely helped make me more independent and, as I noticed themes over time, it made me more aware of my strengths and weaknesses. But does that development happen automatically, without that kind of support?

Matt: I wonder. Most teachers would eventually reach that point. As a more experienced teacher, what I think happens now is 'reflection-in-action' (Schön, 1983), where during the lesson, you start to realize things aren't going well so you make little adjustments at the time.

Peter: Absolutely. That was certainly something I wasn't capable of doing when I first started teaching; I think I often stuck to my lesson plan even if I felt that things might have been going off course. I just didn't have the skills, experience, or even the confidence to make major corrections. Once I developed my reflection-in-action though, which was in my second year of teaching, I started to enjoy my teaching a lot more, knowing I had the ability to control and manage the learning that was happening in the classroom. I see a very clear connection between reflection-in-action and in-class decision making and, in that sense, reflection had a very powerful impact on how effective I was as a teacher, as well as on how rewarding I found the job.

Matt: I think I also got to a point where I was reflecting on what was happening in the lesson, and I was able to anticipate issues that might come up and make changes before they happened.

Peter: Which, for me at least, was not something that I could develop quickly. As a novice teacher, I was so focused on the actual teaching that, even if I knew something wasn't going well, I don't think I was able to effectively adapt lessons at the same time. But I think that's so vital to successful teaching – being able to manage students' learning effectively while at the same time reflecting on how well the lesson is going and making adjustments based on emergent factors to improve the overall lesson.

Matt: I think an important part of that is also knowing where you want the students to end up by the end of the lesson in terms of learning outcomes. Or at least knowing where they could possibly end up. This is something that ideally happens at the planning stage, when your reflection is informing how you set lesson goals – the concept of 'reflection-for action' (Killion & Todnem, 1991). But I sometimes wonder if all these terms are part of the formalization of reflection and therefore kind of off-putting for some people.

Peter: I think the idea of getting started with 'formal' reflection can be quite confusing. Especially if you're reading the literature on it, but you're not in the habit of finishing a lesson and dedicating time to reflect on how it went.

Matt: That's a good point. Our own development as reflective practitioners was a gradual 'evolution'. While we started out with the 'safety net' of our tutors in our initial training, our development as autonomous reflective teachers was a gradual and natural movement from a subconscious process to a conscious one. A lot of our early reflection was inspired by fear, worry, or insecurity, but this eventually gave way to a more principled consideration about how to improve our practice. As managers though, we have set up a more formalized system for our teachers to reflect on their teaching. So, I suppose our discussion raises the question: how can a natural process such as this be effectively encouraged in others, and what are effective ways to do that?

Dialogue 2: Encouraging Reflection in Others

In this dialogue we take up the question posed at the end of the previous section, regarding ways of encouraging others to engage in reflective practice. Our experiences as teacher trainers act as a lens through which we can consider the effects of different strategies on the development practices of our teaching staff.

Matt: Reflection is a central part of what we do, but our last discussion caused me to question whether we're actually training teachers how to be reflective, or whether we are just assuming, 'By doing this task, you are therefore being reflective.'

Peter: I guess the question here is: are we aiming to *train* them to reflect, or to help them to *develop* their reflective practice? Is it coming from us, or is it coming from them?

Matt: Or do they already have the skill and we're just formalizing it? And my other question is, by formalizing it for them, does that help them, even if they never do any sort of formal reflective practice afterwards? Has it ultimately helped them become more reflective teachers?

Peter: A lot of literature seems to suggest that training is required to build teachers' reflective skills (Burns *et al.*, 2016; Farrell, 2016; Walsh, 2013), so I think, as trainers, we can help teachers learn about the principles and the different forms and shapes that reflection can take. Ultimately, though, as facilitators of development, I think maybe the most useful thing we can do is to create the right conditions for teachers to develop: the space, the time, the right questions and the right support, and trust that what they do benefits them. I actually read that teachers often value their colleagues' views over the views of teacher trainers (Sandholtz, 2000).

Matt: That's interesting. So, how does it affect our approach if teachers are more heavily influenced by the discussions they have with their fellow teachers than by a faculty development session that we run?

Peter: I think that means we don't have to overthink things and just ensure teachers are provided with sufficient opportunities to communicate with each other. But I also wonder if just sitting and talking is enough to count as teacher reflection. Do we need to train them in certain skills, or does reflection emerge through discussion by itself? I mean, I think the questions that we ask are deliberately reflective in nature. A lot of research (e.g. Edge, 2002; Diaz Maggioli, 2018; Wenger, 1998) places communication amongst teachers at the center of professional development, even if reflection is not actually explicit as a goal. Yet, while teachers obviously need opportunities to communicate with each other, I wonder how much reflection is done and how much time spent with other teachers is actually looking forward to future lessons and planning for them, rather than looking back and reflecting on lessons past. When the focus is on reflection, I would hope that teachers look at the bigger picture, and focus on regularly emerging themes where they feel that they can improve overall, rather than on what happens in just one lesson.

Matt: I think contemporary notions of teacher training have shifted away from a model that tries to result in quantifiable improvement (Kumaravadivelu, 2012). Nobody really expects that kind of outcome from a professional development session. But if the purpose of development is reflection, I think that through experience and through reflecting on what we do, we can reach a point where we're better at responding to changes within the classroom. And then perhaps the next stage is being able to push students a little bit further in terms of what you think they can achieve. So I think there might be an aspect of improvement, although it's obviously not a straight line and we can never know all the factors that affect it.

Peter: I think you're right that reflection should play a central role in teacher development; it helps ensure that it's teacher-centered and can be tailored to each teacher's individual needs. That's important for all teachers, whatever their background, their experience and their qualifications.

Matt: All of this talk about reflection reminded me of an article that I read a few years ago in the *New Yorker* about a surgeon (Gawande, 2011). He was at the top of his profession, his operation results were much higher than the national average, and he had basically reached a point where he couldn't see how he could get any better at what he did. But then one day he was watching Rafael Nadal playing tennis on TV and the camera cut to Nadal's coach sitting in the stands. This made him realize that even the best athletes in the world need to have people who observe them and give them feedback on how they are doing. So he asked a former professor of his to come in to his operating room and act as a coach. The coach obviously didn't intervene during any operations, but afterwards he would give notes to the surgeon, small things that only an outside observer would notice. And eventually the surgeon felt himself starting to improve again.

Peter: That reminds me of what Fanselow (1977) said about teachers not always being conscious of, or being able to accurately recall, their own practices, and also how the perceptions of what actually happens in the classroom can be extremely surprising (Richards & Farrell, 2005).

Matt: Right. We can't always notice what we're doing while we're doing it. But I think the article was also about the importance of realizing that no matter how good you think you are at something, there's always room for improvement. And the surgeon identified this kind of coaching as a way to continue to develop. But I think it's also connected to the idea that development doesn't equal just getting better, it suggests some kind of evolution. And perhaps it has value even if it's just a way to stave off staleness or to increase motivation. I wanted to give that article to our more experienced teachers to explain why we still want them to continue with their professional development.

Peter: Maybe one of the biggest mistakes any experienced teacher can make is thinking that they've learned it all. Being an effective teacher can boil down to many things, but I don't think experience is necessarily always one of them. It could be instinct, making the right decisions in the classroom, being able to read students' needs and plan clear goals; it could be creativity, or it could be motivation too. But I think a large part of it is down to reflection.

Matt: What's interesting is the attitude of experienced teachers towards their own development. A few years ago I spent a semester reading about peer observations, including Steve Walsh's SETT framework – the self-evaluation of teacher talk (Walsh, 2013) – in order to create a new peer observation system for our more experienced teachers. It included focusing on critical incidents and transcribing samples of teacher talk. It was a disaster! Teachers basically said, 'We already know how to teach this course, so why are we being forced to reflect on it in this specific way?' I think I tried to impose too much structure on the whole thing. At the extreme end, some teachers reacted by questioning whether or not we trusted them to do their jobs. At the time, I found it hard to connect that criticism with what we were asking them to do.

Peter: The most effective professional development focuses on classroom practices (Walter & Briggs, 2012), and given that the aim of observations is to focus on classroom practices, it's interesting that they reacted like that. I've actually seen some research that suggests that receptiveness to professional development tends to decrease with experience (Gallup Rodriguez & McKay, 2010). Do you think that's true in our context?

Matt: Perhaps, but I think if it's presented in the right way, most experienced teachers understand the need for professional development. It may be a case that, in our center, where some teachers have been teaching the same course repeatedly for five years, they may just be tired of it and feel they'd be happy to develop professionally in any other aspect of teaching, just not about this course.

Peter: From a management perspective, we have an obligation to provide a good professional development program due to the benefits derived by the institution. It seems clear that good professional development helps ensure high levels of motivation in teachers and, by extension, in students (Dörnyei & Ushioda, 2011), as well as playing a role in teacher retention (Lavania *et al.*, 2011). Do you think teachers would be disappointed if there were no opportunities for development on offer?

Matt: That's a really good question. I think for our experienced teachers it becomes very autonomous. But imagine if we said, 'From now on, your professional development is entirely self-directed. All we ask is that once a month you give us an update on what you're doing, and we'll give you some advice if you want it. Other than that, you do whatever you want.' And if they don't end up doing something, then that's okay.

Peter: Yeah, you can't force people to develop. It has to come from within. We have a responsibility to train them to be able to carry out the duties of the role and deliver the course in a way that we expect. But it's hard to force development or reflection; there's even a risk that if reflection is imposed on people, then they just decide to make something up. I sometimes struggle to understand why some teachers don't want to engage in reflection. It's partly because, since I decided that this was what I was going to be doing as a profession, I decided to commit to it and felt a certain obligation to learn more about the trade that I'm doing. When people who have made the same decision aren't interested in learning about things, I find it hard to understand. But to be honest I don't understand why I find it hard to understand! Teaching seems to be fairly unique in that you're expected to think about it a lot, and to constantly try to improve what you're doing. If you've worked in an office job for 20 years, I don't imagine the same expectation exists to continue your own professional development.

Matt: I wonder if one reason is the central issue of language teaching, which is that nobody really knows...

Peter: ...how languages are learnt.

Matt: Right. So, if that's the starting point, maybe it's not surprising that we end up spending so much time thinking about it.

Peter: And given that the central issue is so unclear, I think it's important our reflection focuses on things that are tangible and that we can do something about. One thing I think our program is particularly effective at doing is encouraging teachers to reflect on their actual classroom practices. For example, I think we've both noticed that when teachers join our program, they can be quite wary of lesson observations; it seems that many of them have experience of observations being used for evaluative rather than formative measures in previous contexts, which can be a major source of anxiety (Copland, 2010; Cornford, 2002). However, I think we do a lot to convince them that this needn't be the case, and that observations can be a really powerful developmental tool.

Matt: By coincidence, the two of us shared the same Director of Studies at International House Lacunza in San Sebastián, albeit a few years apart. He was the first manager I had who observed me and I remember having a couple of really horrific lesson observations. But he conducted the post-lesson conferences well in that he was very diplomatic and helpful. I mean, he didn't have to point out how terrible the lessons were because I would always start the conferences by acknowledging that.

Peter: Looking back, he must have had a lot of experience of dealing with fairly novice teachers, seeing all these first-year teachers coming into the school and being fully aware that, in all likelihood, they wouldn't be around much longer than a year. I can imagine that might have been frustrating for him, but the fact that we're sitting here talking about him now is quite a nice testament to the impact he had on us.

Matt: I guess his viewpoint about us teachers might have been 'There's no reason to come down hard on them. They don't have much experience, they probably haven't been challenged or been asked to think about their teaching much, so I'll just plant a few seeds for them to think about.'

Peter: That's a very good point and I think we were lucky to have someone so supportive at such an early stage of our careers. I've been observed countless times since then and the most disappointing conferences have been the ones where I've just been told that everything was fine. My quickest post-observation conference took place during an elevator ride; once we reached the ground floor it was done. The best approach is definitely one where those seeds are planted, as I've come away really considering my own practices and wanting to change; it's clear that that approach ultimately leads to more teacher autonomy and reflection. We could spend a lot of time discussing observations as they're so focused on reflecting on actual classroom practices.

Matt: In our course we do video observations. Do you think this means that, when our teachers write up their reflections on the lesson, they're doing it from too objective a point of view? In other words, because they're watching a video recording of their lesson, are they reflecting on what they can see from the camera's perspective rather than remembering how they actually felt during the lesson itself?

Peter: Not necessarily. I think there are a lot of benefits of video observation and one of them is that teachers have that chance to reflect on action after the lesson rather than relying on their reflections in action, which might be more subjective and perhaps less well-informed. In previous jobs where I've observed others, sometimes you realize that any attempt that you make to encourage teachers to reflect on something is not going to be successful. So, then it becomes a case of getting across the main points of your feedback of the lesson, but in a way where you're judging who you're talking to and considering how defensive they might be.

Matt: That's a good example of when you go to an observation and think, 'This person isn't going to listen to me. If I try to tell them that what I think they're doing is not the best approach to take, I know they're going to be resistant to it, so that's not going to get me the result I want.' So why not skip doing that and just have a chat about the lesson instead? That seems like the easy approach to take, but I also wonder if there are some ways of communicating your points without coming across as too negatively critical.

Peter: The balance of power in an observation conference tends to be tipped in favor of the observer. And even though we encourage the teacher to lead the conference, it doesn't always happen. Arguably it's better for reflection if you say. 'Talk me through the lesson and

I'm going to ask you some questions.' You sort of play the role of a less-experienced teacher and ask the teacher what they did and why they did it. And if that's more reflective than us leading a reflection as managers, it might end up being more genuine. But that's not an atmosphere or dynamic that you can easily create. It seems that our beliefs about encouraging reflection have converged in a few key areas. We both believe that reflection can be encouraged, but not forced, and we share a conviction that feedback from trainers is most effective when planting seeds, rather than giving prescriptions. This discussion has hinted at experiences which have led us to these beliefs, but as we said at the outset, we have not received any formal guidance in this role. Perhaps we should explore the question of how we developed our identities as reflective teachers and teacher trainers.

Dialogue 3: Identity and Development as Teachers and as Teacher Trainers

In this final dialogue, we explore our developing identities as teachers and teacher trainers, looking to our past experiences and charting how those early influences led us to our current beliefs and practices.

Matt: One question I often ask when I meet other teacher trainers is 'How did you develop as a teacher trainer?' They usually answer that it was only through experience or by having someone mentor them. And thinking about it, I guess there have been those people – CELTA trainers, Delta trainers, directors of study and other senior teachers I've worked with – who, in theory, have been a model for me as teacher trainers. But when I think about how I developed as a teacher trainer, I rarely think about those people.

Peter: Yeah, that's the same for me.

Matt: And then I wonder if I *should* think about those people and appreciate more how they've influenced me. But then, at the same time, I think that they were teacher trainers, but they weren't teacher trainer trainers. And the job of teacher trainer trainers doesn't really seem to exist.

Peter: You're absolutely right, I've had a couple of really important trainers and managers in my time and, although I learned a lot from them, I've never styled my own approach on theirs. Having said that, I'm not sure I really analyzed how trainers approached their role in my time as a novice teacher. I was much more concerned with teaching practices and developing as a teacher back then. Do you think there are many differences between our roles as teachers and as academic managers?

Matt: I was thinking about the difference between how comfortable I feel as a teacher and as a teacher trainer, and how reflection-in-action is something I can point to that I do as a teacher which makes me feel more confident. But my reflection-in-action as a teacher trainer is perhaps less developed.

Peter: Why do you think that is?

Matt: I think it's mainly from having spent enough hours in the classroom that I feel confident making adjustments or organizing activities in a way that I hadn't previously planned. But with observation conferences, for example, I just don't have as many hours under my belt, which is why I still feel like I have so much to learn.

Peter: That's interesting. I agree that teaching is the easier aspect of the job we do. It's certainly the most familiar aspect; we've been teaching a lot longer than we've been managers. Maybe another reason that we're more comfortable in the classroom than in the training room is that the feeling that you're more of an authority and you're less likely to have people challenging you in the classroom means it feels like a safer environment.

Matt: That's a very interesting point. You do get big differences in the types of students you encounter, but you get just as big a range with the approaches that teachers take when they sit down for an observation conference, in terms of how defensive they're going to be about the lesson, or how well they're going to reflect. Thinking about this reminds me that, while we have a very structured professional development program for our teachers, we don't have anything similar for ourselves. We've talked about putting something like that together and I can't really see a good argument for us not having more formalized professional development.

Peter: Perhaps the assumption is that, as someone who's responsible for other people's development or other people's training, you're also able to analyze your own needs and take steps to meet those needs; you can set yourself learning goals, assess your progress regularly, and you change them and adapt as needed when new needs emerge. This current role is the first time that my own professional development has been entirely self-directed. It was slightly hard to choose a focus for myself at first, and I spent a fair bit of time wondering what possible paths my own development could take. At your suggestion, I kept a reflective journal which focused on the learning curve of coming into a context from the outside and managing and training people who knew the course much better than I did (Brereton, 2018). None of the duties were new to me, as such, so I ended up focusing a lot more on my identity and my development as a manager, and the challenges I faced. Generally speaking, the difficulty is that the lack of oversight makes it necessary for our own professional development to be self-directed. When I came into the role, I remember thinking I was responsible for the development of 42 teachers, but that my own development seemed secondary to that. As managers, we spend a lot of time developing the course, and in doing so, we develop professionally ourselves.

Matt: Which is a good thing given the absence of anyone in the structure of our center who might be able to oversee or train us.

Peter: Plus, our development often fits around what emerges from the course development. For example, you probably learned a lot about strategic competencies and communication skills last year when you analyzed that for the program (Schaefer, 2018a), but I don't imagine you planned to include that as part of your professional development that year.

Matt: No, maybe not. It was just reacting to what I thought was a need for the course. In that sense, our professional development is not only self-directed, but also peer-directed by our fellow managers, and directed by the specific demands of the role. Another interesting question to ask is, 'What are the differences and similarities between teacher reflection and teacher trainer reflection in terms of the actual process?' I mean, it's possible that there aren't any differences and that we should just be applying all the same principles. Perhaps one good way to frame a discussion on reflection is to look at Farrell's five different levels of reflection (Farrell, 2018). My understanding is that the levels he refers to are not levels of progression, but rather different categories. He acknowledges that it's fine to focus on just one of the levels if that's the area of reflection that interests you. He also says that one should never tell anyone else how to reflect, and that reflection should never become a tick-box exercise. The first level is what he calls 'philosophy', which refers to acknowledging the fact that a teacher is a person with their own background and values, not necessarily teaching values but personal values, that influence how they teach.

Peter: I think that's perhaps easier to do if you're comparing yourself to someone else's teaching approach. This is probably also true as trainers and as managers as well. I mean, there are four of us doing the same job but I think we have quite different approaches to it. In teaching, even if you haven't seen another person's lesson, you can often understand their approach by seeing the materials they use. At other times you might overhear other people teaching and you think, 'I wouldn't be doing it that way myself' but then they're probably listening to my class thinking. 'I wouldn't be doing that either'. And so maybe it's easier to recognize what kind of teacher you are through recognizing what kind of teacher you *aren't*. However, I think as trainers, we have to be careful that we don't impose our own ideals or ideas about teaching on to the people we're supporting. In observations too, we have to be very objective and look at things in terms of whether or not the teacher you are observing has achieved certain aims, even if you are thinking to yourself, 'That's not how I would have done it at all'.

Matt: That's a really interesting point. We could also look at it in terms of how we compare ourselves as teacher trainers. We see each other deliver faculty development sessions much more often than we see each other teach, so we should have a much better sense of how we carry out our jobs as trainers. It's not something we talk about that much, but I'm sure it's something we all think about. At the same time, I think the different approaches that the four of us take are probably a benefit to the center. We try to keep things as standardized as possible, but I'm sure that our instructors are aware of, and appreciate, the ways in which we differ.

Peter: We do have a desire to personalize even small things, however. For example, even though we have email templates that we can use when we contact teachers about certain things, we all tweak them slightly to make the emails sound like they came from us as individuals. Why do you think we need to do that?

Matt: It's probably a basic human need to be recognized as a person and as an individual. I think it's another case of where the similarities between being a teacher and a teacher trainer are fairly clear. Of course, who you are is how you teach, that's sort of indisputable. But at the same time, you're being a version of who you are. And I think that's true of who you are as a manager. It's a version of who I am, but it's not necessarily the entirety of who I am.

Peter: That's really interesting and kind of brings me to my next point. The transcription of our last discussion that I was working on recently made me think. You said that sometimes in training sessions you might hear an idea which you try out and which doesn't work, and it's worth considering why something would work for one teacher but not for another. I mean, in theory, and all other things being equal, everything should work for everyone, or not work for everyone. There shouldn't necessarily be things that work for some but not for others, but there clearly are.

Matt: That's true. When teachers find an activity they like that was created by another teacher, I hope they don't just print it off and take it straight into the classroom. I can't imagine any experienced teacher using another teacher's materials in that way. Hopefully, if you've had any experience at all, you know it's impossible to take another teacher's materials and expect them to work for you. Even if the other teacher who created it says that they've just had the best lesson ever with it and suggests you use it. It may work to an extent, obviously, but you have to make it your own in some way.

Peter: I couldn't agree more. Everything needs a certain amount of personalization, if only to help you familiarize yourself with the materials and work out how you're going to approach the activity.

Matt: That actually brings me to another point that I wanted to discuss. There's a podcast that I started listening to recently hosted by a chef called David Chang, in which he talks to other chefs and various creative types. There were two things that struck me in a recent episode I heard (Chang, 2018). One was when he was explaining how, as the head chef, he has a small team of other chefs, and when they start a new restaurant they create the 20 or so recipes they need and then they train the various station chefs to cook those recipes. So when an order comes in, there's someone whose job it is to make the chicken dish, and someone else whose job it is to make the sauce, and so on. And that's all the station chefs do, they just follow the recipes. So, I started thinking of this as an analogy for a unified syllabus in a language course such as ours, particularly in the way that we aim to provide a fairly standardized product, if that's the right word, for our students. But then the next thing that Chang discussed was how limiting it can be for the station chefs, from a creativity point of view. So to battle this, he gets their feedback. He asks them, for example, 'You make this dish night after night, over and over again – is there any way that we can make it better?' Which is something we also do, so I thought that maybe there's a very clear analogy emerging from this.

Peter: That's a really good analogy.

Matt: And then he started talking more about being a manager. He was reflecting on the challenge of getting the people who you manage to do the best that they can do without telling them explicitly how to do it. He was also trying to figure how you can get them to a point where they care enough about what they're doing that they want to improve themselves.

Peter: Which is difficult, because that has to come from within.

Matt: Exactly. Chang said that what he used to do if he tasted a dish in his restaurant that didn't meet his standards, was to find the station chef who had made the dish and tell them directly, 'You're doing this wrong.' Now, he thinks he gets better results if he asks, 'What do you think about this dish?' and enters into a dialogue with the person who has probably made the dish more times than anyone else. What's also interesting to consider is that, in three-star Michelin restaurants, not all the dishes are being prepared by the creative genius head chef who designed them. They're being made by station chefs who've been trained how to make the dishes, and they understand that it's important that each time they make the dish, it has to be more or less the same. But I'm sure for the really good ones, even when they're making exactly the same dish, each particular piece of celery that's put in front of them will be slightly different so they still have to make some decisions about how to cook it. However, their aim is always to provide each customer with the same high-quality product each time. If they came in to work one day and thought to themselves, 'Today, I feel like cooking a completely different sauce' they may be satisfying their creative urges…

Peter: …but they'd be sacked the next day.

Matt: Absolutely! It would be interesting to know how long a station chef can stay in the same kitchen. I wouldn't be surprised if it was something like five years before they decide they have to go and open their own restaurant or work somewhere else making different recipes.

Peter: Yeah, I really like that analogy; it's very appropriate. And it might be that not every chef can work in that system, but most of them must have to at least train in that system. It must be very rare to have a chef who can look at a bunch of ingredients and create something without having trained under the guidance of someone else.

Matt: Right. And if we think about it in terms of initial teacher training, teaching the person to make the sauce in the first place means that in the end they're better at making that sauce. But then to keep them engaged with making that sauce on a long-term basis, you would need to sit down with them and discuss the elements of making it.

Peter: Or offer them the opportunity to experiment with making different types of sauce. That really helps to increase the sense of ownership of the dish. If you feel like you own the sauce, there's a better chance you're going to work hard to perfect it.

Matt: So, hopefully we can instil some sense of ownership in our teachers if they feel like they've somehow contributed to the program, and that it reflects who they are as a person or as a teacher. The more invested they are, the more ownership they feel they have of the course, which may mean that they stay engaged with how they teach it for longer. I think this discussion has highlighted our role and identities as teacher trainers. We aim to give ownership of the course to the teachers, while still providing a certain standard to the students. In the same way, we have each been able to incorporate our own identities and interests into our training, while still being able to maintain a standard in our training approach.

Conclusion

Matt: Before we started this project, I think I had the impression that doing a duoethnography was basically just talking a lot. But now that we've been doing it for a while, I think I see that the value is that it's not just talking – the transcribing and the compiling of the relevant points provide further opportunities for reflection.

Peter: I've really enjoyed the process; it's been very rewarding to reflect in a more formalized way. I don't imagine that sitting down and just talking for extended periods is something that many people would do just for the sake of talking, but the whole process has really proved to be a very reflective tool for me. I saw a quote from E.M. Forster once, asking, 'How do I know what I think until I hear what I say?' That's something that struck a chord with me, particularly when it comes to reflection; I'm certainly at my most reflective when I have the opportunity to actually discuss teaching with others. Despite that, I've been surprised at how reflective I've been when listening and transcribing our conversations. At the end of the first 90-minute discussion, the idea of listening back to the recordings and having to write it all out seemed fairly mind-numbing. However, actually having to concentrate on what we said when listening back gave me a perfect opportunity to consolidate and reflect on our ideas from previous sessions and inform my thoughts for the next one.

Matt: Looking back at what we wanted to explore when we started this project, specifically our first research question, I think we've discovered that we share a lot of beliefs about reflective practice. It's also interesting that the way we arrived at those beliefs was similar for both of us. I'm not sure what that tells us, except that I suppose it helps to know that we have this shared understanding when we get into discussions about how to develop the course we both work on.

Peter: Through this duoethnography, I've realized that I hadn't truly reflected on our roles as teacher trainers to the same depth as I feel like we have now. I've been thinking a lot about this project, about our roles as teacher trainers, how we can best develop as professionals ourselves, and how we can support the teachers whose development we're responsible for. It has been especially interesting to see the parallels between the two roles, and the areas where they converge. I think this was particularly evident to me in our beliefs about our roles as facilitators of reflective practice and how we work towards providing the optimal environment for teacher reflection and supporting teachers' own reflections through tools like developmental lesson observations, which touches on both our first and second research questions.

Matt: One of the concerns I had at the beginning of this project was how we would balance the two main focuses of teacher training and reflective practice. But throughout the whole transcribing process, it was clear that both of them were interwoven into everything we talked about. This was partly because the project itself is a form of reflection but also because we were always speaking about how we reflect and how we encourage teachers to reflect. Through our transcribing of the discussions we've had, a lot of themes have emerged that we weren't aware of, and a lot of questions also went unanswered. For example, one of our initial aims was to uncover differences in how we approach the same job. We might not actually have reached that point this time around, but being aware of what those differences are could help us to know ourselves better and enable us to consider how we could better carry out our roles.

Peter: That's a good idea. We work in a very unique context, and collaboration really is key to its success. As I think we've learned, that's also very true of a duoethnography.

References

Brereton, P. and Kita, S. (2019, May) A creative look at creativity: Discussion and duoethnography. Paper presented at *excitELT* 2019.

Brereton, P. (2018) One year in: Reflections of a new academic manager. *New Directions in Teaching and Learning English Discussion* 6, 231–235.

Burns, A., Westmacott, A. and Ferrer Hidalgo, A. (2016) Initiating an action research programme for university EFL teachers: Early experiences and responses. *Iranian Journal of Language Teaching Research* 4 (3), 55–73.

Copland, F. (2010) Causes of tension in post-observation feedback in pre-service teacher training: An alternative view. *Teaching and Teacher Education* 26, 466–472.

Cornford, I. (2002) Reflective teaching: Empirical research findings and some implications for teacher education. *Journal of Vocational Education and Training* 54 (2), 219–225.

Chang, D. (2018) The Dave Chang show, audio podcast, August 16 (accessed 19 November 2018). Retrieved from https://www.theringer.com/

Diaz Maggioli, G. (2018) Empowering teachers through continuous professional development: Frameworks, practices and promises. *IATEFL 2017: Glasgow Conference Selections*, pp. 3–30.

Dörnyei, Z. and Ushioda, E. (2011) *Teaching and Researching Motivation* (2nd edn). Harlow, UK: Longman.

Edge, J. (2002) *Continuing Cooperative Development: A Discourse Framework for Individuals as Colleagues*. Ann Arbor, MI: Michigan University Press.

Fanselow, J.F. (1977) Beyond *Rashomon*: Conceptualizing and describing the teaching act. *TESOL Quarterly* 11 (1), 17–40.

Farrell, T.S.C. (2008) *Reflective Practice in the Professional Development of Teachers of Adult English Language Learners*. Washington, DC: Center for Applied Linguistics.

Farrell, T.S.C. (2016) The practices of encouraging TESOL teachers to engage in reflective practice: An appraisal of recent research contributions. *Language Teaching Research* 20 (2), 223–247.

Farrell, T.S.C. (2018) *Research on Reflective Practice in TESOL*. New York, NY: Routledge.

Gallup Rodriguez, A. and McKay, S. (2010) Professional development for experienced teachers working with adult English language learners. *CAELA Network Brief*.

Gawande, A. (2011) Personal best. *The New Yorker*. Available at: https://www.newyorker.com/magazine/2011/10/03/personal-best

Killion, J.P. and Todnem, G.R. (1991) A process for personal theory building. *Educational Leadership* 46 (6), 14–16.

Kumaravadivelu, B. (2012) *Language Teacher Education for a Global Society*. New York, NY: Routledge.

Lavania, D., Sharma, H. and Gupta, N. (2011) Faculty recruitment and retention: A key for managing talent in higher education. *International Journal of Enterprise Computing and Business Systems* 1 (2), 1–14.

Lawrence, L. and Nagashima, Y. (2019) The intersectionality of gender, sexuality and native-speakerness: Investigating ELT teacher identity through duoethnography. *Journal of Language, Identity and Education*.

Lowe, R. and Kiczkowiak, M. (2016) Native-speakerism and the complexity of personal experience: A duoethnographic study. *Cogent Education* 3 (1).

Mann, S. (2005) The language teacher's development. *Language Teaching* 38 (3), 103–118

Richards, J.C. and Farrell, T.S.C. (2005) *Professional Development for Language Teachers*. New York, NY: Cambridge University Press.

Rose, H. and Montakantiwong, A. (2018) A tale of two teachers: A duoethnography of the realistic and idealistic successes and failures of teaching English as an international language. *RELC Journal* 49 (1), 88–101.

Ross, J. and Bruce, C. (2007) Professional development effects on teacher efficacy: Results of randomized field trial. *The Journal of Educational Research* 101 (1), 50–60.

Sandholtz, J.H. (2000) Interdisciplinary team teaching as a form of professional development. *Teacher Education Quarterly* 27 (3), 39–54.

Schaefer, M.Y. (2018a) Communication skills for strategic competence. *New Directions in Teaching and Learning English Discussion* 6, 273–279.

Schaefer, M.Y. (2018b) How to implement a successful equal opportunities policy, blog post, 13 June (accessed 19 November 2018). teflequityadvocates.com/2018/06/13/how-to-implement-a-successful-equal-opportunities-policy-by-matt-schaefer/

Schaefer, M.Y., Lesley, J., Livingston, M. and Young, D. (2016, November) *Ongoing program evaluation of a unified curriculum.* Research-Oriented Long Presentation presented at the JALT2016: Transformation in Language Education conference, Nagoya, Japan.

Schön, D.A. (1983) *The Reflective Practitioner.* London: Temple Smith.

Walsh, S. (2013) *Classroom Discourse and Teacher Development.* Edinburgh: Edinburgh University Press.

Walter, C. and Briggs, J. (2012) *What Professional Development Makes the Most Difference to Teachers?* Oxford: University of Oxford.

Wenger, E. (1998) *Communities of Practice: Learning, Meaning and Identity.* New York, NY: Cambridge University Press.

Part 3

Duoethnography for Language Teaching

Part 3: Duoethnography for Language Teaching

The previous two sections focused on the uses of duoethnography from the perspectives of researchers and of teachers. These two focuses reflect the ways the method has been used outside the field of English language teaching, especially in the area of mainstream education. However, in this section we will shift focus somewhat to explore an ELT-specific use of duoethnography. The chapters in this section will suggest ways in which the duoethnographic research process could be adapted and used as a form of project-based learning in the language classroom which develops all four skills, facilitates language development and promotes positive group dynamics within the class.

In Chapter 8, Robert J. Lowe and Luke Lawrence give a full practical guide to implementing duoethnographic projects, including stages that can be followed by teachers hoping to engage in this kind of teaching approach. Following this, the authors provide an argument in favour of using duoethnography as a classroom project, drawing on second language acquisition theory in order to show the benefits such a project may have in terms of language development, and also exploring the psychological literature regarding the effects of group dynamics on language learning which may be affected by students engaging in duoethnographic projects. An example is also included of a complete student duoethnography in the appendix to this chapter in order to give an idea of what a student-produced duoethnography might look like.

In Chapter 9, Robert J. Lowe explores the benefits of duoethnographic projects for language learning in greater depth. Based on data collected from students engaged in this kind of project over a four-week period, examples are given of how the extensive peer interaction and the opportunities for collaborative writing in the project led to situations in which students were able to experiment with language and scaffold each other's utterances in order to achieve higher levels of linguistic performance than they may have been able to achieve had they been working on their own.

In Chapter 10, Luke Lawrence discusses the implications for utilising the intimate and trust-building nature of duoethnography in order to strengthen relationships between students in the class, bolster engagement in the language learning process and inspire motivation in the dynamics of the group as a whole. Data highlighting students' feelings and perceptions of carrying out a duoethnographic project is used to show the key strengths and weaknesses of using the method in the classroom.

The chapters in this section should provide practitioners with a clear guide and rationale for introducing duoethnographic projects into their own classroom, both from the perspective of language development among their students, and in terms of the positive group dynamics that may be fostered through such a project. These chapters are intended to make a cumulative case for the benefits of duoethnographic projects in the language class.

8 Duoethnography in the Language Class

Robert J. Lowe and Luke Lawrence

Introduction

This chapter provides a rationale and guide for using duoethnographic projects as a form of project-based learning in the language class. This chapter is based on the theoretical account provided by Lowe (2018), which put forward the idea of adapting the process for language teaching on the basis of initial tentative classroom experimentation. This account is supported by research in second language acquisition from a sociocultural theory (SCT) perspective, and is further informed by two years of experimentation in implementing duoethnographic projects by the authors. This chapter will begin by giving a practical account of how to implement a duoethnographic project in a language class, giving a step-by-step guide for teachers to follow. It will go on to outline the ways in which the extensive peer interaction and the opportunities for collaborative writing afforded by the duoethnographic process may help students in terms of their language development. Finally, a further theoretical account will be given of how duoethnographic projects may help students to develop stronger interpersonal relationships and bonds, promoting positive group dynamics in the class.

Implementing a Duoethnographic Project in the Language Classroom

The method of implementing a duoethnographic project in the language classroom is, in large part, drawn from the process of carrying out a duoethnography for the purposes of research or teacher reflection. In a duoethnographic project, the learners first choose (or are provided with) a topic. They then engage in multiple recorded discussions on the topic, and finally write up a fictionalised report based on their discussions. However, in order to make this process suitable for language learning, a few more steps need to be included. A duoethnographic project can perhaps most easily be carried out by following the stages below (adapted from Lowe, 2018):

Stage 1: Setting up the project

- The teacher first provides an explanation of what the students will be doing, providing reasons for why and how they will be doing this project. Following this, the teacher can put the class into pairs, or the class can put themselves into pairs. These pairs should not change during the project.
- The teacher will either provide the students directly with a topic to discuss, offer a list of topics to choose from, or leave the topic completely open to the students. This topic will be the focus of the duoethnographic project. It is best if this topic is one of personal relevance to the students. The freedom the teacher gives both in terms of the topic itself (dictated by the teacher, or chosen by the students), and the scope of the topic (a general topic such as 'school pressure', or specific questions such as 'did you feel pressure from your family to work hard in school?') should be based on the level of the class and the teacher's judgment. It may also be the case that the topics covered reflect what has been studied in previous lessons so that the students have a base to work from. If the teacher feels it is necessary, they may also like to pre-teach topic-relevant vocabulary or allow time for the students to do this by themselves before the first discussion. Other skills such as active listening and asking follow-up questions could also be introduced as a precursor to the first session.
- The students carry out their first recorded discussion. The mode of recording could be through IC recorders provided by the teacher, or through the use of students' smartphones. Each student should have a recording of the discussion to take home. The length of the discussion should again be based on the level of the class, but we have found that 10–15 minutes is enough time to generate sufficient data.

At home: Reflecting and notetaking

- The students should be given some reflection questions such as 'what did you learn about your partner?', 'what did you share about yourself?' and 'what would you like to ask your partner more about?' These questions are intended to help the students reflect on the topics which came up in the discussion, start considering the emerging themes, and focus in on the topics they would like to pursue in the next stage.
- The students listen to the recording at home and make some notes based on their reflection questions. Using these notes, they put together some questions that they would like to ask in the second discussion.

Stage 2: Digging deeper

- Using their homework notes, the students take part in a second recorded discussion (of the same length as the first discussion) with their partner, hopefully delving more deeply into the topic and their personal experiences.
- During this discussion the teacher should monitor the pairs and be available to students as a support and resource to help them express their ideas clearly and concisely. It may also help to keep the pairs as physically distant as possible, if space is available, in order to allow maximum intimacy between students. Luke found that putting pairs in separate classrooms helped the students feel a sense of privacy and may have helped them to give a greater amount of disclosure in their conversations. However, it should be noted that this did make it more difficult for him to monitor and be available for support.

At home: Finding similarities and differences

- Once again, the students listen back to their discussion recording, and think about the same reflection questions.
- The students should make notes about the similarities and differences between their experiences and those of their partner. These will help them to identify themes in stage 3 of the project.

(Although we suggest two stages here, teachers may choose to ask the students to engage in a third discussion, or even more. There is also the flexibility for motivated students to carry out extra dialogues and gain more data if they wish to do so, which can even be done outside of class time. For example, in one class that Luke taught one pair of students was absent for the Stage 2 class, but they decided to carry out the dialogue in their own time in order not to fall behind with the research procedure.)

Stage 3: Identifying themes and writing dialogues

- Students should bring their notes to the lesson, and together with their partner try to find the main themes that arose from their discussions. These should be connected to the similarities and differences they identified while listening to the discussions at home.
- With their partner, students should write up a fictional dialogue based on these themes and on the experiences they shared in their discussions. The teacher can help the students to edit and write their dialogues. This could take more than one lesson, depending on the proficiency of the class. Alternatively, it could be set for homework using Google Docs or a similar document sharing website.

Stage 4: Sharing with the class

- Students should share their dialogues with the rest of the class, either through a traditional presentation format, performance of the dialogues, or through other students reading the dialogues. This can be followed by a question and answer session.
- Students could follow up on the project by writing a reflective account about what they learned from the experience.

Extensions and adaptations

- For advanced classes students could submit a full academic report including a literature review on the relevant topic, data presentation, discussion of findings and full reference list.
- For lower level classes a short summary of the main points and what they learned may be sufficient.

The role of explicit teaching

The duoethnographic project, as outlined above, does not include much in the way of explicit language teaching; rather, it provides opportunities for other effective language learning processes such as scaffolding and languaging to take place. However, this does not necessarily mean that explicit teaching has no role in the duoethnographic process. For example, this process could be coupled with the teaching of discussion skills and functional language, or with useful communication strategies such as negotiation of meaning. A duoethnographic project could be the capstone to a course focusing on these skills, or alternatively these skills could be introduced gradually throughout the project (e.g. a set of functional language could be taught before each of the recorded in-class discussions), thus integrating the skills with the duoethnographic process. While explicit teaching of language is not the key focus of carrying out duoethnographic projects, this certainly does not mean it need be excluded entirely, and there are many points at which teachers could creatively integrate explicit teaching into the process.

The Benefits of Duoethnographic Projects for Language Learning

Duoethnographic projects have a number of potential benefits for language learning, which we will attempt to give a theoretical account of in this section. Primarily, we would like to focus on the benefits of duoethnographic projects concerning the following major points:

- language development through high levels of peer interaction both during dialogue and collaborative writing;
- the development of motivation, relationship building and whole-class group dynamics.

We will provide a discussion of each of these points below, outlining what the current literature in each area states, and showing how duoethnographic projects provide opportunities and contexts for these to take place.

Language development through peer interaction

In discussing the benefits of duoethnographic projects for language development, we take as our starting point the sociocultural theory (SCT) approach to second language acquisition (SLA), which has been popular among applied linguistic researchers for several decades. Beginning with the work of Vygotsky (1978), sociocultural researchers in psychology have sought to understand how the relationship between the human mind and the physical world is mediated and organised through 'culturally constructed artifacts' (Lantolf, 2000: 1), including symbolic tools such as numbers, musical notation and language. When applied to language learning, SCT researchers seek to 'maintain the richness and complexity of "living reality", rather than distilling it "into its elementary components"' (Lantolf, 2000: 18; citing Luria, 1979). In other words, they attempt to understand the process of language learning not only in terms of the cognitive processes through which language is acquired, but also the social circumstances, relationships and resources available to the learner which impact and mediate those processes. It seems natural therefore that interaction between learners should be an area of primary interest for those working in second language learning from a SCT perspective.

The role of interaction in second language learning has a long history, principally within what has come to be called the 'Interaction Approach' to SLA (Gass & Mackey, 2007). Belief regarding the positive benefits of interaction for language learning has its genesis in the interaction hypothesis (Long, 1981, 1983), which Long (1996: 451–452) sums up as 'negotiation work that triggers interactional adjustments by the NS or more competent interlocutor,' and which 'facilitates acquisition because it connects input, internal learner capacities, particularly, selective attention, and output in productive ways'. Long's hypothesis rests on the belief that negotiation of meaning influences and assists language acquisition by simplifying input to make it more comprehensible, providing feedback to learners on their utterances, and pointing them towards more target-like uses of the language. As Ellis (2008: 254–255) notes:

> Interactionally modified output works for acquisition when (1) it assists learners to notice linguistic forms in the input and (2) the forms that are noticed lie within the learner's 'processing capacity'.

In short, through interaction learners are presented with both positive and negative evidence of what works and what does not work in their utterances, in a way which they can recognise and which helps them to appropriately modify their utterances in response. Pica (1994: 495) supports this view, arguing that 'modification and restructuring of interaction...occurs when learners and their interlocutors anticipate, perceive, or experience difficulties in message comprehensibility'. This focus on the benefits of interaction for language development in SLA led to much work on the role of negotiation in second language learning.

Research into the interaction hypothesis 'was initially proposed based on interaction between native speakers and learners' and was 'generally conducted under laboratory conditions, rather than by using naturalistic classroom data' (Philp *et al.*, 2014: 41), however scholars working from an SCT perspective have sought to take a different approach to this research in two key ways. First, there has been an increasing interest in the role that peer (that is, student-to-student) interaction may play in language learning, rather than focusing on teacher/student or more competent/less competent speaker interactions. Secondly, these researchers have attempted to move away from experimentally collected data and have focused instead on the analysis of naturally occurring classroom data, reflecting the sociocultural belief in investigating the complexity of reality as a whole, rather than splitting it into its component parts. Ellis (2018: 128–129) notes that 'SCT, like the Interaction Approach, views language learning as dialogically based', however SCT differs in a key way: 'whereas the Interaction Approach considers that interaction prompts the internal mechanisms responsible for learning, SCT sees acquisition occurring within interaction when learners act collaboratively to produce linguistic forms that they are not capable of producing independently'.

SCT theorists such as van Lier (2000) argue that interaction is useful for more than simply comprehensible input and feedback, which is considered to be its main role in the Interaction Approach. Writers adopting an SCT perspective claim that interaction should also be acknowledged for the opportunities it provides to *use* the target language in the form of 'output'. Swain (2000: 99) suggests that output 'pushes learners to process language more deeply – with more mental effort – than does input', and that as a result language development occurs when learners push themselves to meet their communicative needs, something that can only be achieved through output. Output, when occurring in interaction, is the basis of the construct of 'languaging' (Swain, 1998). This can be defined as 'talk about language', which allows linguistic thought to be concretely externalised, and thus available for reflection and reformulation (Ellis, 2018: 129). As Storch (2013: 16) neatly summarises it, languaging is 'the articulation of thinking'. Through a process of languaging, students are able to articulate their internal linguistic processes, and thus reflect on them and reformulate them into more target-like utterances. Languaging can be either monologic, in which a learner talks through an element of language out loud to themselves, but is more commonly dialogic, as learners work together to co-construct language. Swain (2000: 102) argues that in this way SLA can be influenced by what she termed 'collaborative dialogue', or dialogue in which 'speakers are engaged in problem solving and knowledge building'. According to Swain (2000: 112), in such dialogues, language (particularly in the form of output) acts as a mediating tool, one which 'serves second language learning by mediating its own construction'. In other words, the language used in collaborative dialogue makes internal language external, and therefore available for reflection and reformulation; the very act of using the language in dialogue makes reflection on the language being used inevitable and thus leads to second language development on the part of learners.

Scholars working in SLA from an SCT perspective attempt to investigate the reality of language use, rather than the kinds of language use occurring under experimental conditions. As such, these researchers rely largely on the analysis of language-related episodes (LREs). These are defined as instances of languaging 'where learners address the linguistic forms needed to express specific meanings' which 'arise in interaction, but can also involve self-repair in monologic language use' (Ellis, 2018: 136). Languaging can take place during many kinds of dialogue or task. Previous studies have involved tasks such as dictogloss, jigsaw tasks and tasks which require the construction of a narrative text (Fortune, 2005; Kim, 2008; Swain & Lapkin, 2002). An example of this is a study by Swain and Lapkin (1998) in which two learners of French worked together to make a story based on pictures they had been given. At several points, the learners negotiated towards more accurate forms of the language, eventually attaining a higher level of accuracy than either may have reached on their own. Additional work has been conducted more recently on the LREs that occur between students engaged in collaborative writing. Storch (2013) notes that during collaborative writing students engage in languaging as they co-construct a text and work together to produce the most suitable linguistic forms. There is a growing body of evidence which demonstrates that languaging in dialogue between peers leads to opportunities for, and incidents of, language learning and development among second language learners.

For a more concrete framework in which to analyse language development through peer interaction, we turn to recent work by Philp *et al.* (2014: 17). These authors have investigated the concept of peer interaction in language learning in great depth, noting three main contexts in which peer interaction may influence the language learning process: *experimenting*, *correcting* and *polishing*. Firstly, they note that peer interaction provides a context in which learners may *experiment* with language. During peer interaction, learners 'may collaboratively revise words and phrases' in response to peer feedback, 'may draw from explicit knowledge' of the language to 'try out new possibilities by trial and error', and thus work collaboratively to deal with linguistic problems that they may face. This can be seen most explicitly through examples of LREs drawn from naturalistic classroom data, in which students engage in metalinguistic discussion of the language they are using, prompting conscious attention to form, and thus promoting language learning. Secondly, the authors note that peer interaction may function as a context for *correcting* language. This can occur in three main ways; through feedback, through modified output and through 'learners' own reflections and revisions of language use' (Philp *et al.*, 2014: 37). This correction may take the form of recasts, in which one learner provides a more accurate form of their classmate's utterance, or through more explicit and overt correction of a grammatical or lexical feature. Finally, Philp *et al.* (2014) note that peer interaction provides opportunities for *polishing* language, particularly with a focus on the benefits this kind of interaction may have for developing automaticity in speech through the repetition of language, and the further opportunity this affords for breaking down language into chunks and recognisable common patterns.

So, where does this leave us with regard to duoethnography? As argued above, from an SCT perspective, dialogue and peer interaction are central components of language learning, and it is in this area that the duoethnographic process has the most obvious benefits in terms of language development. These projects contain extensive opportunities for peer interaction in the forms of both oral discussion and collaborative writing, and the dialogic mode in which these projects are carried out has a great potential for helping students develop their language skills while engaging in discussion and collaborative writing with their classmates; in other words, through forms of peer interaction. When engaging in a duoethnographic project, learners are exposed to large amounts of peer interaction, and thus all three of these contexts (experimenting, correcting and polishing) are made available to them for improving their language skills. These contexts exist in the two main stages of the process: firstly, the discussion students engage in during the early stages of the project, and secondly the collaborative writing through which students construct the final dialogue. During the discussion at the outset of the project, students engage in lengthy interaction in which they may test tentative hypotheses, correct each other's production and support and scaffold their partner's language use. During the construction of the final written dialogue, learners engage in similar processes with their partner through collaborative writing. Storch (2013: 156) has noted how during the process of collaborative writing, learners 'verbalise gaps in their interlanguage, formulate and test hypotheses, assess alternatives, self-and other-correct', and otherwise engage in many of the same processes in order to develop linguistically through interaction with their classmates. In short, during both the initial discussions and the writing of the final fictional dialogue in a duoethnographic project, learners are afforded many opportunities to experiment with language, engage in peer-correction, and work towards polishing their language in terms of both automaticity and accuracy.

An SCT perspective on SLA sees dialogue and interaction as of central importance in language learning, and duoethnographic projects provide ample opportunities for such dialogic peer interaction to take place. As such, we believe that implementing duoethnographic projects in the classroom is likely to be an effective way to help students improve their linguistic skills and proficiency. Chapter 9 in this book provides a more focused study exploring LREs that occurred during a duoethnographic project.

The benefits of duoethnography for individual motivation, emotional and social development, and whole-class group dynamics

As well as the practical language benefits of using duoethnography as a pedagogical tool, as outlined above, there are also several social benefits. On an individual level, it can provide intrinsic motivation to successfully complete a medium-term project. On the level of pair work it can aid in deepening relationships between classmates and emotional development, and on the level of the whole group, a duoethnographic project can improve overall group dynamics and increase class cohesion.

Individual motivation

Research on student motivation in ELT has enjoyed an unprecedented level of interest and popularity over the last few decades (Boo *et al.*, 2015) and gone through a number of iterations, from social psychological, to cognitive, to complex and dynamic as new theories emerged and were blended with previous concepts (Swain, 2000). In terms of motivation theory that focuses on the individual learner, Ushioda's (2009) 'person-in-context relational view' of motivation provides a useful conceptual framework within which to examine the benefits of duoethnography in the language classroom.

Within this framework, 'person' is distinguished from 'student' or 'learner' in that being a student or learner is only one of the multitude of identities that each person brings into the classroom and as such 'are necessarily located in particular cultural and historical contexts' (Ushioda, 2009: 216). However, these cultural and historical contexts should not be seen as external fixed entities that are the objects of our perceptions or the sole determinants of who we are and what we do. Instead, by focusing on the 'person-in context', the relationship between persons and the context they are in are 'mutually constitutive...dynamic, complex and non-linear' (Ushioda, 2009: 218). This 'non-linear' aspect recognises the complex, idiosyncratic and unpredictable nature of individual motivation as it reacts and relates to events and experiences. In this sense, an individual's motivation cannot be neatly explained by cause and effect theory and anticipated commonalities and is more of an organic process that emerges from the individual identity of each student/person as they relate to the contexts, situations and people around them as an active agent in the learning process.

If we follow this ontological framework, the obvious question is how we can best organise our classroom and design activities that allows room for students to be 'people' in relational context to others. Duoethnography has an emphasis on individual lived experience wherein differences and contrasts are seen as strengths rather than obstacles to overcome. It is committed to following emergent rather than prescribed themes and has a poststructuralist approach that that views self as 'layered, nonlinear, contradictory, emergent, and always open to uncertainty and change' (Sawyer & Norris, 2013: 23). It thus offers an ideal platform for positive individual student motivations.

In practical terms, based on the outline of the stages of implementation detailed above, the transition from learner or student to 'person' is initiated in Stage 1 as the students choose the topics that best reflect their own lived identities, both in their personal histories and in the here and now, and begin the first dialogues. This allows students to bring in aspects of their identities that may be hidden in the course of usual classroom discourse and unearth parts of the self that may no longer exist or even still be in the process of emerging – in this way, they can truly be 'persons'. The final part of Stage 1, in which students reflect on their dialogues and look for emergent patterns, and the final part of Stage 2 when students reflect again to identify similarities and differences creates the context of the 'person-in-context'. By placing their individual identities into the past and the present (and sometimes future), while comparing and contrasting with a classmate, the complex, dynamic self is encouraged to emerge. The final aspect of Ushioda's framework comes into being as students engage in Stage 3 and 4 of the process. As they enter the writing up and presentation phase of the research project, they become an active agent, interpreting the data and (in the case of advanced learners carrying out a duoethnographic project) relating it to others and the wider social world through a literature review.

In short, utilising duoethnography in an ELT class can be a strong motivating force for students, putting a focus on:

> the agency of the individual person as a thinking, feeling human being, with an identity, a personality, a unique history and background, a person with goals, motives and intentions; a focus on the interaction between this self-reflective intentional agent, and the fluid and complex system of social relations, activities, experiences and multiple micro- and macro-contexts in which the person is embedded, moves, and is inherently part of. (Ushioda, 2009: 220)

Building relationships through collaboration

Although implementing duoethnography in a language class can help to facilitate individual motivation along the lines of Ushioda's (2009) 'person-in-context relational view', at the heart of the methodology of duoethnography is its collaborative nature. In the language classroom, the personal and intimate disclosures that often result from duoethnographic enquiry and the shared journey of reflecting, identifying themes and working as a unit to produce a final document can provide substantial benefits in terms of relationship building. This can lead to discursively produced 'emotional intersubjectivity' (Denzin, 1984) that can help to assuage language anxiety and lack of confidence, while facilitating cognition and mediating emotional development (Imai, 2010) as well as creating, building and cementing friendships in the classroom.

The concept of emotional intersubjectivity refers to 'an interactional process that joins two or more persons into a common, or shared, emotional field of experience' (Denzin, 1984: 130). This emotional field of experience is in constant flux according to time, place and interlocutor and should be viewed as a social phenomenon, rather than a purely cognitive or psychological experience. This idea is also linked to Vygotsky's (1978) social theory of mind, mentioned above, that posits that learning and development, or in this case emotional learning, take place through social interaction. Therefore, as well as aiding development of learning content, this same thinking can be applied to emotional development and learning.

The implications for this in the language classroom are that by interacting on an emotional level with a classmate, students can help to overcome some of the barriers to classroom communication and participation, such as language anxiety (Gkonou *et al.*, 2017; MacIntyre, 1995; Scovel, 1978) and willingness to communicate (Yashima, 2002) as well as increasing student autonomy (Chang, 2007). A study by Imai (2010) which investigated the emotional intersubjectivity of a collaborative project involving three female students at a university in Japan found that through dialogue the students were able to intersubjectively verbalise their emotions in a manner that emerged discursively. This led to the participants exercising their autonomy and agency in a prescribed project and setting new goals. Duoethnography in a language class provides just such a collaborative opportunity and actively encourages students to verbalise their thoughts, feelings and emotions in order to interpret a selected topic or phenomenon.

The second social aspect of close pair work is that of relationship and friendship building. By engaging in a difficult project with the same partner over a number of weeks learners can often transition from classmates to friends and in doing so can shed some of the inhibitions that cause anxiety and feelings of discomfort in the language classroom.

Whole-class group dynamics

Group dynamics has also been identified as a key factor in motivation, not only for individual students or small groups, but for each class as a whole, cohesive unit (Dörnyei & Murphey, 2003; Hadfield, 1992). The benefits for students of a cohesively bonded class may be a greater investment in the class, with stronger engagement and a sense of responsibility to their classmates (Dörnyei & Murphey, 2003; Lawrence, 2017) combined with an absence of fear to communicate and a sense of warmth and camaraderie in the classroom (Senior, 1997). From the point of view of the teacher, Senior (1997: 3) found that any group that was seen to have a 'positive whole-group atmosphere' was perceived as being 'good', while any group that failed to display this cohesion was seen by the teacher as 'bad', irrespective of target language achievement or test scores reached. Despite its potential importance to the day-to-day lives of teachers and learners, group dynamics is a surprisingly under-researched field in ELT. In this section I will draw on selected literature on group dynamics, focusing on four identified aspects of successfully bonded groups: trust, listening with empathy and interest, sharing personal information and creating a shared group history. I will then outline how initiating a duoethnographic project in a language class can help to support these aspects.

According to Hadfield (1992: 8), reasons given by teachers for why their classes 'did not gel' included: 'students don't listen to each other', 'they are teacher dependent', and 'there is no trust' (Hadfield, 1992: 8). Conversely, factors that contribute to a successful group may include: 'Group members are interested in each other and feel they have something in common', 'Members co-operate in the performing of tasks and are able to work together productively' and 'The members of the group trust each other' (Hadfield, 1992: 12). Setting a duoethnography project in a language class may be a way to avoid the pitfalls that can cause a lack of gelling and promote the factors that can help make a successful group.

As outlined in the introduction to this volume, trust between participants is one of the key requirements for duoethnography. For students, this willingness to open themselves up to the class and divulge their personal experiences and opinions can sometimes, understandably, present some difficulties. A duoethnography project allows this to be built up in stages. In Stage 1 and 2 they are afforded the privacy of a two-person conversation and encouraged by their partner's own divulgences. The writing stage (Stage 3) prepares the student to share the information that they are willing to with an agent outside of the research pair (the teacher), which requires trust in an empathetic and non-judgemental response from the teacher. It is not until Stage 4, after discussion, reflecting and writing for the teacher that the information is shared with the whole class. This final act of sharing, either through performance or presentation, can help to promote trust between all group members and cement the group as a bonded entity.

Additionally, the close intimacy of the pair dialogues and the subsequent listening back to the recordings for close analysis ensure that students listen to each other closely (multiple times). Again, this is extended to the whole group through performance of dialogues. Unlike a general presentation of abstract ideas and opinions, by performing dialogues out loud (or having other students perform the dialogues of a different group) the audience (the rest of the class) is invited into the conversation and 'recognized as active coparticipants and meaning makers in the emergent process' (Sawyer & Norris, 2013: 24), listening closely to one another as each class member joins the communal conversation.

As a logical extension of his work on motivation, Dörnyei, along with a series of collaborators (Clement *et al.*, 1994; Dörnyei, 1997, 2005; Dörnyei & Malderez, 1997; Dörnyei & Murphey, 2003; Ehrman & Dörnyei, 1998; Ushioda & Dörnyei, 2012) helped to establish the study of Group Dynamics as a focused discipline in the ELT field. Building on the earlier work of Hadfield (1992) and Senior (1997), indicators of a successfully bonded group put forward by Dörnyei and Murphey (2003) included: learning about each other by sharing personal information, cooperation between members to achieve common goals, overcoming joint hardship, and having a shared group history.

Sharing personal information between students is a common aspect of many communication-focused language classes. However, these are often reduced to surface recounts of weekend activities or simple likes and dislikes. A duoethnography gives students the opportunity to go much deeper into sharing personal information, not only simple day-to-day activities, but past experiences, present dilemmas, future dreams, trials, tribulations, thoughts, feelings and anxieties. By participating in the level of personal disclosure that a duoethnography can often produce, students are creating a bond that extends beyond the individual pairs to the group as a whole, as an entity that is trusting and trusted.

Similarly, the cooperation required to complete a challenging project such as a duoethnography offers a common goal and presents joint hardships for students to overcome. From the dialogues to the analysis to the collaborative writing, completing a duoethnography requires students to cooperate at every stage of the process. This involves compromises, negotiation of role, joint responsibility and constant communication between partners over a number of lessons. These all help to bring about 'an enhanced sense of community, access to opportunities for face-to-face interaction, and peer support' which 'strengthen our capacity to learn course content and approach our work as more confident learners and scholars' (Diaz & Grain, 2017: 132).

From the individual to the pair/small group to the whole class, by implementing a class duoethnographic project, as outlined in the stages above, we can offer our students individual agency, but also a chance for 'human connection and a sense of care for the other' (Lund *et al.*, 2017: 116), with mutual support and a sense of community and group belonging.

Conclusion

In this chapter we have laid out an approach to implementing duoethnographic projects as a form of group learning in the language class. We have argued that these projects are beneficial for students in a number of ways. As well as providing ample amounts of practice in the four skills of speaking, listening, writing and reading, the approach has the potential for more specific benefits in terms of language development and the development of motivation and positive group dynamics. Through large amounts of peer interaction, learners have extensive opportunities to experiment with their language, engage in self- and peer-correction, and polish their language to a level of improved automaticity. In terms of student-to-student relationships and whole class group dynamics, a duoethnography project provides a wealth of opportunities for relationship building and class cohesion.

References

Boo, Z., Dörnyei, Z. and Ryan, S. (2015) L2 motivation research 2005–2014: Understanding a publication surge and a changing landscape. *System* 55, 145–157. https://doi.org/10.1016/j.system.2015.10.006

Chang, L.Y.-H. (2007) The influences of group processes on learners' autonomous beliefs and behaviors. *System* 35 (3), 322–337. https://doi.org/10.1016/j.system.2007.03.001

Clement, R., Dörnyei, Z. and Noels, K.A. (1994) Motivation, self-confidence, and group cohesion in the foreign language classroom. *Language Learning* 44 (3), 417–448.

Denzin, N.K. (1984) *On Understanding Emotion*. New Brunswick, NJ: Transaction Publishers.

Diaz, C. and Grain, K. (2017) Community, identity, and graduate education: Using Duoethnography as a mechanism for forging connections in academia. In J. Norris and R.D. Sawyer (eds) *Theorizing Curriculum Studies, Teacher Education, and Research through Duoethnographic Pedagogy* (pp. 131–152). New York: Palgrave Macmillan US. https://doi.org/10.1057/978-1-137-51745-6_7

Dörnyei, Z. (1997) Psychological processes in cooperative language learning: Group dynamics and motivation. *The Modern Language Journal* 81 (4), 482–493.

Dörnyei, Z. (2005) *The Psychology of the Language Learner: Individual Differences in Second Language Acquisition*. Mahwah, NJ: Erlbaum.

Dörnyei, Z. and Malderez, A. (1997) Group dynamics and foreign language teaching. *System* 25 (1), 65–81.

Dörnyei, Z. and Murphey, T. (2003) *Group Dynamics in the Language Classroom*. Cambridge: Cambridge University Press.

Ehrman, M.E. and Dörnyei, Z. (1998) *Interpersonal Dynamics in Second Language Education: The Visible and Invisible Classroom*. Thousand Oaks, CA: Sage Publications.

Ellis, R. (2008) *The Study of Second Language Acquisition* (2nd edn). Oxford: Oxford University Press.

Ellis, R. (2018) *Reflections on Task-based Language Teaching*. Bristol: Multilingual Matters.

Fortune, A. (2005) Learners' use of metalanguage in collaborative form-focused L2 output tasks. *Language Awareness* 14 (1), 21–38. https://doi.org/10.1080/09658410508668818

Gass, S.M. and Mackey, A. (2007) Input, interactions, and output in second language acquisition. In B. VanPatten and J. Williams (eds) *Theories in Second Language Acquisition: An Introduction* (pp. 175–200). Mahwah, NJ: Lawrence Erlbaum.

Gkonou, C., Daubney, M. and Dewaele, J.-M. (eds) (2017) *New Insights into Language Anxiety: Theory, Research and Educational Implications.* Bristol: Multilingual Matters.

Hadfield, J. (1992) *Classroom Dynamics.* Oxford: Oxford University Press.

Imai, Y. (2010) New insights from collaborative learning for an EFL classroom. *The Modern Language Journal* 94 (2), 278–292.

Kim, Y. (2008) The contribution of collaborative and individual tasks to the acquisition of L2 vocabulary. *The Modern Language Journal* 92 (1), 114–130. https://doi.org/10.1111/j.1540-4781.2008.00690.x

Lantolf, J.P. (2000) Introducing sociocultural theory. In J.P. Lantolf (ed.) *Sociocultural Theory and Second Language Learning* (pp. 1–26). Oxford: Oxford University Press.

Lawrence, L. (2017) The role of student-led social media use in group dynamics. *The Language Teacher* 41 (5), 17–22.

Long, M. (1981) Input, interaction and second language acquisition. *Annals of the New York Academy of Sciences* 379, 259–278. https://doi.org/10.1111/j.1749-6632.1981.tb42014.x

Long, M. (1983) Native speaker/non-native speaker conversation and the negotiation of comprehensible input. *Applied Linguistics* 4 (2), 126–141. https://doi.org/10.1093/applin/4.2.126

Long, M. (1996) The role of the linguistic environment in second language acquisition. In W. Ritchie and T. Bhatia (eds) *Handbook of Second Language Acquisition* (pp. 413–468). New York, NY: Academic Press.

Lowe, R.J. (2018) Duoethnographic projects in the language class. *Modern English Teacher* 27 (1), 74–77.

Lund, D.E., Holmes, K., Hanson, A., Sitter, K., Scott, D. and Grain, K. (2017) Exploring duoethnography in graduate research courses. In J. Norris and R.D. Sawyer (eds) *Theorizing Curriculum Studies, Teacher Education, and Research through Duoethnographic Pedagogy* (pp. 111–129). New York: Palgrave Macmillan US. https://doi.org/10.1057/978-1-137-51745-6_6

Luria, A.R. (1979) *The Making of Mind: A Personal Account of Soviet Psychology.* Cambridge, Mass: Harvard University Press.

MacIntyre, P.D. (1995) How does anxiety affect second language learning? A reply to Sparks and Ganschow. *The Modern Language Journal* 79 (1), 90–99.

Philp, J., Adams, R.J. and Iwashita, N. (2014) *Peer Interaction and Second Language Learning.* New York, NY: Routledge, Taylor & Francis Group.

Pica, T. (1994) Research on negotiation: What does it reveal about second-language learning conditions, processes, and outcomes? *Language Learning* 44 (3), 493–527. https://doi.org/10.1111/j.1467-1770.1994.tb01115.x

Sawyer, R.D. and Norris, J. (2013) *Duoethnography.* New York: Oxford University Press.

Scovel, T. (1978) The effect of affect on foreign language learning: A review of the anxiety research. *Language Learning* 28 (1), 129–142.

Senior. (1997) Transforming language classes into bonded groups. *ELT Journal* 51 (1), 3–11.

Storch, N. (2013) *Collaborative Writing in L2 Classrooms.* Bristol: Multilingual Matters.

Swain, M. (1998) Focus on form through conscious reflection. In C. Doughty and J. Williams (eds) *Focus on Form in Classroom Second Language Acquisition* (pp. 64–82). Cambridge: Cambridge University Press.

Swain, M. (2000) The output hypothesis and beyond: Mediating acquisition through collaborative dialogue. In J.P. Lantolf (ed.) *Sociocultural Theory and Second Language Learning* (pp. 97–114). Oxford: Oxford University Press.

Swain, M. and Lapkin, S. (1998) Interaction and second language learning: Two adolescent French immersion students working together. *The Modern Language Journal* 82 (3), 320. https://doi.org/10.2307/329959

Swain, M. and Lapkin, S. (2002) Talking it through: two French immersion learners' response to reformulation. *International Journal of Educational Research* 37 (3–4), 285–304. https://doi.org/10.1016/S0883-0355(03)00006-5

Ushioda, E. (2009) A person-in-context relational view of emergent motivation, self and identity. In Z. Dörnyei and E. Ushioda (eds) *Motivation, Language Identity and the L2 Self* (pp. 215–228). Bristol: Multilingual Matters.

Ushioda, E. and Dörnyei, Z. (2012) Motivation. In S.M. Gass and A. Mackey (eds) *The Routledge Handbook of Second Language Acquisition* (pp. 396–409). New York: Routledge.

van Lier, L. (2000) From input to affordance: Social-interactive learning from an ecological perspective. In J.P. Lantolf (ed.) *Sociocultural Theory and Second Language Learning* (pp. 245–260). Oxford: Oxford University Press.

Vygotsky, L.S. (1978) *Mind in Society: The Development of Higher Psychological Processes*. Cambridge, MA: Harvard University Press.

Yashima, T. (2002) Willingness to communicate in a second language: The Japanese EFL context. *The Modern Language Journal* 86 (1), 54–66.

Appendix

In this student-produced duoethnography, taught using the framework outlined above, the researchers present a reflective critique of the mandatory English program that is in place at the university. Throughout the paper, the pseudonym XYU is used for the university and the pseudonym Real English (RE) is used to refer to the mandatory English program. At this particular institution students are required to pass this course in order to graduate. The passing requirements involve attendance in the minimum required number of lessons and achieving either a TOEFL score of 500 or a TOEIC score of 600. If students surpass this score in the initial placement test, they are exempt from attending the classes.

More Productive English Education Style in XYU

Shotaro Uehara & Akira Kobayashi

Introduction and Literature Review

In this paper, we are going to talk about the English education at X Y University. English education, especially Real English (RE), we discussed the negative points of it and how it should change in the future education style. Since we have two different types of educational backgrounds in learning English in our group, we think that it would be great to share our thoughts and think about the best way of learning English. Akira was taking RE when he was in the first year of university, and now he goes to the English cram school for TOEIC. On the other hand, Shotaro had already passed RE at the beginning of the university entrance, and has an experience of studying abroad and English communication lessons on Skype.

Higher education in Japan, educational systems used to focus on grammatical sides. 'Junior- and high-school teachers focus on grammar and writing skills that are needed for exams such as EIKEN. So, for most Japanese students, English learning is usually a requirement to achieve high grades and pass admission exams, rather than a skill for personal enrichment or future career prospects' (Gabriel, 2016). We think almost all of the recent news about Japanese English education is saying that we have to focus on the communication skills (Gabriel, 2016; JIJI, 2016; Kodera & Kameda, 2013). Even though we understand what Gabriel says, he does not mean learning grammar is not useless. At some points of view, university students need to write more reports compared with high school English education, so including grammatical lessons, it is also required to teach how to write reports and papers. We discussed a decent balance of lessons between the fundamental and communication skills.

In addition to the critical point above, we also discussed the students' motivation. 'In some instances, extrinsic motivation – perhaps in the form of extrinsic reinforcers for academic achievement or productive behavior – may be the only thing that can get students on the road to successful classroom learning and productive behavior' (Ormrod, 2014). As you read this article, it is clear that motivation has the huge rule on students' behavior and studying, so we think how teachers and educational systems can give them motivation in RE class.

Dialogue 1

The central theme of the first dialogue is 'Change of the RE Class.' We talked about the negative points, and then discussed what we might need to change.

Shotaro: How was it like in RE class?

Akira: I felt it was okay because I could make friends in RE class, but I have to say it was not the best environment for studying English. It was no different from the English education in high school.

Shotaro: I heard so many things like that. I think RE class needs to change a lot. My opinion is that dividing the students based on the individual score is not good. Since they are at the almost same level of English, I think they have fewer chances to improve or get motivated by other members. When I was in high school, some students can speak English more fluently than me, and who can get higher scores on TOEIC, right? When the class has a lot of different type of students, you have more chances to know how to study English in the better way and learn how to speak English well.

Akira: By that, we can have a lot of chances to have more information from other members, right?

Shotaro: Exactly! I have one more thing I want to say. I think the RE class needs to have the different style of English education from high school. For example, English presentation, speech, discussion and more oral communication in English. To do that, I guess the RE class needs to be randomly selected and more diverse. One of my ideas, in that case, RE can be mandatory for freshmen students.

In this dialogue, we talked about the diversity in RE class. If the current RE class is not divided by the specific scores and becomes mandatory, it would be more diverse. That 'diversity' is necessary to increase the average of English level in XYU.

Dialogue 2

The theme of the second dialogue is 'Two Different Types of English Improvement.' We would like to know what the best way of learning English is. Akira goes to the English cram school for TOEIC, so he learns English as a reading base, on the other hand, Shotaro learns English as a communication base.

Akira: What's the best way to improve your English skills?

Shotaro: I think speaking. In this university, so many students want to be able to speak English, but not many of them can do that. For me, to improve speaking skills, we have no way of studying it except actually speaking English with others. Not just only talk about 'how was your week?' or kind of easy question.

Akira: I agree with you. Also, I want to add, in this university, we have medical and science course, so these students need to write a lot of papers and reports. In that case maybe for them, they need to learn proper grammar and technical terms.

Shotaro: Right. I think so too. At that point, I believe it is essential to keep all the students' motivation; for the students who want to improve their speaking skills and the others who want to learn grammar and vocabularies.

Akira: And RE class needs to integrate the education style. Currently, some teachers are focusing on reports and reading, but others are working on communication. It is not good.

Shotaro: Good point!

We talked about the best ways of learning English. Shotaro thought that it is more important to speak in English, but Akira pointed out that medical students and students in the science course, they need to learn grammatically correct English and know about the particular terms used in their field when they write papers and reports. We concluded this second dialogue that both types of English education are necessary, and more importantly, keeping a decent balance of learning fundamental English skills and communication skills is essential.

Since every student has different kinds of incentives towards learning English, it is challenging, but essential to keep them motivated, so teachers and educational systems need to find some ways of giving them motivation. In addition to the dialogue, we hypothesized that oversea fieldwork and short-term studying abroad can be the proper incentives too.

Conclusion

XYU is advertising as an 'international university' to every high school student, and it is introducing 'Real English' as if it is 'the best' way of studying English. However, even from the students' view, there are still so many points that are needed to change and improve. As we introduced at the beginning, the diversity in RE class and making it mandatory are some of the critical points of improving RE class.

In the second dialogue, we understand there are different kinds of incentives towards learning English, so it is necessary to keep a decent balance of studying for TOEFL and TOEIC and improving communication skills. The more presentation and discussion we do, the more essential grammar and vocabularies become. RE should help to meet the demands of students' incentives.

Also, we talked about motivation. Giving students' motivation has a big rule in education. Oversea fieldwork and short-term of studying abroad can be a good motivation for students. Like some other universities, we can make overseas experience mandatory for graduation. That is the actual 'real English' as it should be. It is very difficult to create the real place in XYU as long as we do not have an interaction with foreign exchange students, so we think that this proposal should be ideal.

We do not say that the current RE class is useless nor meaningless, but it is not the best way of learning English. Certainly, there might not be the best way of studying English. However, we think it is more important to try to become and get closer to the best education.

References

Gabriel, J. (2016) *English Education in Japan; Challenges and Changes* Retrieved from https://blog.gengo.com/english-education-japan-challenges-changes/

JIJI. (2016) *Let's discuss English language education in Japan* Retrieved from https://www.japantimes.co.jp/life/2016/02/15/language/lets-discuss-english-language-education-japan/#.Wz2qe6BUs0M) 1st July 2018.

Kodera, A. and Kameda, M. (2013) *English Education Set to Get Serious* Retrieved from https://www.japantimes.co.jp/news/2013/12/13/national/english-education-set-to-get-serious/#.W0NmRsaB28o

Ormrod, J.E. (2014) *How Motivation Affects Learning and Behavior.* Retrieved from https://www.education.com/reference/article/motivation-affects-learning-behavior/

9 Language Development Through Duoethnographic Peer Interaction

Robert J. Lowe

Introduction

This chapter will report on preliminary results from an ongoing classroom investigation in which duoethnographic projects were used as part of a CLIL-style class at a Japanese university. The class was focused on the teaching of various issues in sociolinguistics and applied linguistics through the medium of English, and the duoethnographic project was used as the final piece of assessed work in the course. As argued in Chapter 8 of this book, duoethnographic projects have the potential to help learners in their language development due to the extensive opportunities such projects provide for peer interaction both in terms of extended oral discussions and collaborative writing. This chapter aims to provide some empirical backing for these claims through an analysis of language-related episodes (LREs) in which learners showed evidence of language development in accordance with a theoretical framework laid out by Philp *et al.* (2014). Firstly, the chapter will briefly review the theoretical literature on peer interaction in language learning, and will set out the theoretical framework used to analyse the results of the research. Secondly, the background of the course will be given, followed by an overview of the methods of data collection and the approach taken in analysing the data. Finally, the chapter will present examples of LREs which provide evidence of language development among learners during the discussion and collaborative writing portions of the duoethnographic process.

Theoretical Background

The theoretical justification for engaging in duoethnographic projects for the purposes of language development was laid out in some detail in the previous chapter (Lowe & Lawrence, this volume). As a result, in order to avoid undue repetition, I will only briefly review the main points here in order to concretely establish the theoretical framework used to analyse the data in this chapter.

From a sociocultural theory (SCT) perspective, dialogue and peer interaction are seen as central to second language learning. SCT theorists are interested in how the relationship between the human mind and the external world are mediated by cultural artifacts, one of the most important of which is language (Lantolf, 2000). As learners engage in peer interaction during tasks and activities, they use their language collaboratively to reach levels of linguistic performance that they would not have been able to attain had they been working alone. Peer interaction allows for large amounts of 'output' on the part of learners, which externalizes their language, making it available for discussion and reflection. This discussion and reflection, or 'talk about language' is known as 'languaging' (Swain, 1998), and is a key mechanism through which learners can develop their linguistic competence. Through languaging (either individual, or more commonly, collaborative), learners can attain higher levels of language performance and competence.

While there is much written on the role of peer interaction for second language learning, for the data analysis in this chapter I have adopted a theoretical framework based on the work of Philp *et al.* (2014), whose research into peer interaction and second language learning suggests three key contexts for language development to take place in during peer interaction. This framework was selected because it is based on a comprehensive review of the peer interaction literature and clearly lays out a usable system for classifying episodes of language development.

Firstly, learners may use peer interaction as a context for *experimenting* with language (see Philp & Tognini, 2009). This experimentation may be in the form of:

- joint construction, in which the learner's utterances act as stimulus for their partner in an ongoing attempt to express their ideas;
- feedback followed by reformulation, in which the feedback from a partner triggers a reconsideration and linguistic modification of an utterance;
- the pooling of their collective knowledge to solve linguistic problems, a process which requires some metalinguistic awareness in order for the learners to effectively move towards a more target-like form of the language;
- the practicing of formulaic language used in the class by trying the formula out in a variety of similar but distinct constructions (see Philp *et al.*, 2014: 19).

Secondly, peer interaction may act as a context for *correcting* language. Philp *et al.* (2014) describe three ways in which correction may take place in the context of peer interaction. Correction may take place through:

- feedback (such as recasts, explicit correction, etc.);
- modified output (in which the listener may prompt a reformulation of language into something more target-like);
- reflection (in which the speaker may reformulate their utterance based on self-reflection).

Finally, peer interaction may be used as a context for *polishing* language, defined by Philp *et al.* as (2014: 57) 'increasing automaticity in production'. This may be more familiar to most readers as the concept of fluency, which is defined through a trio of attributes: speed, fluidity and accuracy (Segalowitz, 2000). Referring to Ellis (2005), Philp *et al.* (2014: 60) argue that 'by repeating the same sequence, learners become a little more skillful and a little faster in producing target language forms and sentences'.

The framework proposed by Philp *et al.* (2014) applies not only to spoken interactions, but also to instances of collaborative writing. Storch (2013), through an examination of LREs (defined as examples of languaging in which learners either individually or in groups engage in metalinguistic discussion of target language), found evidence of languaging between learners, which she describes as 'the process of using language in an attempt to make sense of complex information or when confronting a difficult task' (Storch, 2013: 16), neatly summarizing it as 'the articulation of thinking'. Through a process of languaging, learners not only come to resolve the issue they are discussing, but are also able to develop new insights into the language they are using to discuss it. Languaging engaged in by an individual is a largely 'inside-the-head' activity, which is rather difficult to access. However, when occurring between peers, it is possible for researchers to not only identify incidents of languaging, but also to analyse the types of new knowledge constructed through these episodes. Collaborative writing engaged in by learners provides many opportunities for collective languaging, as learners use their metalinguistic knowledge to discuss the correct forms of the target language to use in their writing. In addition to spoken interaction, collaborative writing provides further opportunities for peer interaction among learners, and through this peer interaction further opportunities for language development are made available to the learners.

In short, peer interaction, both in terms of oral discussion and collaborative writing provides opportunities for learners to experiment with language, correct language and polish language. This may be accomplished through feedback, self-correction, languaging and a number of other processes. The data presented in this chapter will provide examples of several of these processes at work during a duoethnographic project, showing that duoethnographic projects can benefit learners by providing opportunities and incentives for this language development to take place. This report does not aim to show that duoethnographic projects are necessarily superior to other activities with regards to encouraging peer interaction. Rather, it forms part of a cumulative case (along with the other chapters in Part 3 of this book) for using duoethnographic projects in the classroom.

The Study

Course background

The course on which the data for this chapter was gathered took place over a period of fifteen weeks in 2018, meeting once a week for a period of 90 minutes. The class was elective and was fairly small, with 11 learners of roughly upper-intermediate proficiency in English (one student dropped out midway through the course, bringing the number participating in the project to an even 10), all of whom had joined the course in order to learn more about sociolinguistics and critical issues in applied linguistics. The learners were all English majors at a private women's university in Japan, and the majority of the learners had studied abroad in Canada, the UK, Australia or New Zealand for a period of between one and six months. The initial plan in teaching the course was to introduce and critically examine three key concepts in sociolinguistics: language and gender, the concept of the 'native speaker', and World Englishes. The course began with a lesson introducing sociolinguistics as a concept, before spending three weeks per unit studying each of the key themes. In each unit, the learners were first introduced to the core idea, they then moved on to read extracts from key literature, and finally engaged in a variety of tasks such as examining profiles of different speakers of English to decide who they believed to be a 'native speaker', or analysing gendered depictions of characters in English language coursebooks. The goal was to give them both background knowledge of the three key concepts, and also to provide them with tools for carrying out sociolinguistic analysis.

During the first iteration of the course in 2017, the final assessment was intended to comprise a short presentation by the learners based on a piece of research they had done, as was fairly common in many other classes the learners were taking at the time. However, as the author had been experimenting with duoethnography as a researcher, and was reading some of the recently published literature around the use of the method for research and reflection, they began to consider the possibility of the final project taking the form of a learner-produced duoethnography. The rationale for this was that such a project would allow the learners to engage in a deeper and more personal exploration of the issues they had been discussing in class; experiencing them as more immediate and personal than as the abstract concepts discussed during lessons. However, it became evident during the course of the 2017 project that the learners were benefitting from the classroom discussions not only in terms of their understanding and connection to the issues, but also in terms of their language development, which was evident in the amount of metalinguistic discussion and linguistic experimentation and adjustment occurring around the class. This led to the writing of a speculative paper about the use of duoethnography as a language teaching tool (Lowe, 2018), and after making some adjustments on the basis of discussions with colleagues, a second attempt was made at the project in 2018. It is the 2018 course from which the data in this chapter was drawn.

The project

The project was implemented over the final four weeks of the class, and adhered to the following schedule (for a more detailed proposed timetable for the implementation of a duoethnographic project, see the previous chapter):

- *Week 1:* The project was explained to the learners, and they were provided with some useful discussion-based language to help them carry out the task. The learners were then put into pairs and asked to choose one of the three concepts from the course to research. Finally, they engaged in a 20-minute recorded discussion with their partner. For homework they listened back to their recording with reflection questions in mind and made notes to prepare for the secondary discussion.
- *Week 2:* The learners shared what they had thought about at home, and then worked together to write discussion questions that they could use to spur on the second discussion. They engaged in the second discussion, also lasting 20 minutes, and then reflected once more at home, this time attempting to identify the key themes that had arisen from their discussions, and the key points of similarity and difference between their experiences.
- *Week 3:* The learners brought their reflections to class and shared them with their partner. Following this, they engaged in collaborative writing to produce a polished dialogue, which the teacher helped them with. They completed this at home.
- *Week 4:* The learners took it in turns to perform their duoethnographies in front of the class, with the other learners asking questions once the performance was finished, followed by small-group discussions.

This project contained extensive opportunities for peer interaction, both in the form of the extended discussions learners engaged in with their research partner, and also in the collaborative writing required to produce the final written report for submission and presentation to the class. This means that the learners were spending a large amount of time in the Zone of Proximal Development (ZPD) (Vygotsky, 1978), which

Lantolf (2000) defines broadly as 'the collaborative construction of opportunities for individuals to develop their mental abilities' (p. 17), and as such had multiple ongoing occasions to co-construct and develop their language knowledge and skill.

Data collection and analysis

The data for this study was drawn from a series of recordings taken from the class described earlier while they were engaging in their projects. Data was collected from two different stages of the project: the learner to learner discussions in weeks one and two, and the in-class section of the collaborative writing of the final report in week three. As part of the duoethnographic process, learners were engaged in discussions which were recorded on their smartphones, and these were then sent to the researcher. These recordings were then analysed for examples of LREs which exemplified the contexts for language development outlined earlier in the chapter, related to *experimenting* with language, *correcting* language and *polishing* language. During the collaborative writing section of the project in Week 3, the learners were observed by the teacher, and observation notes of LREs related to the writing process were kept by the researcher, including short transcripts made while the learners were talking. While it would have been preferable to make recordings of these interactions, the learners were not comfortable with the idea of being recorded while writing, and felt it would be overly stressful for them. This was identified as what Kubanyiova (2008: 516) refers to as an 'ethically significant moment', and it was felt that within the framework of an ethics of care, in which the potential harm to individuals (in this case the potential damage to their language learning) outweighs 'any generally defined "greater good"' (Kubanyiova, 2008: 515). Nevertheless, enough examples were noted to provide compelling evidence of the effectiveness of this approach for language development among learners.

Language Development through Examination of LREs

Following sociocultural approaches to researching language development such as Swain and Lapkin (1998) and Storch (2013), the data collected was examined based on a qualitative analysis of LREs that occurred during the discussion and collaborative writing sections of the duoethnographic project outlined above. As noted earlier, the data collection was somewhat inconsistent due to the fact that, while students were happy to have their recordings analysed for this project, they did not allow for their collaborative writing sessions to be audio recorded. This means that an attempt at quantitative analysis would be partial and unrepresentative. However, while Ellis (2018: 139) notes that 'LREs lend themselves to quantification', he also writes that they do not 'lend themselves to experimental manipulation', and that as such 'the main strength of the research lies in the qualitative analysis of specific LREs aimed at demonstrating how learning can take place on the fly'. This analysis is therefore not focused on a quantitative account of the amount of different kinds of LREs that occurred during the interaction between the students, but rather on a qualitative analysis of what kinds of interaction occurred, and how these indicate language development among the students as a result of peer interaction during the duoethnographic process. The examples have been selected to represent each context of language development (experimenting with, correcting and polishing language). In the first two contexts, the LREs have been further subcategorized. In terms of experimenting with language the LREs have been categorized as either form-based (focused on morphology or syntax), lexical-based (focused on vocabulary or word choice), or mechanical (focused on spelling or pronunciation). In the context of correcting language, LREs have been categorized based on the form of correction strategy the learners used; as feedback, modified output, or examples of self-reflection. In the final context of polishing language, an example is given of learners engaging in repetition leading gradually towards automaticity. See Figure 9.1 for a breakdown of the LRE categorization.

Each example will be presented as a short transcript, and followed by a discussion surrounding what form of language development it represents. Different SLA researchers have chosen to present LRE transcripts with varying levels of detail, from the very complex to the very simple. In this chapter I have chosen to follow researchers such as Storch (2008) in making the transcriptions very simple with little use of coding. This has been done both to eliminate unnecessary detail, and also to follow the spirit of duoethnography in making the work accessible to the non-specialist reader. All of these examples are taken from discussions conducted by only one class in which duoethnographic projects were trialled, and as such these results cannot be generalized beyond those borders, nor are they fully representative of the language use in the class. Rather, they are intended to be suggestive and to provide supporting evidence that duoethnographic projects may lead to language development among learners. The examples given serve to put some meat on the theoretical bones outlined in the previous chapter and in previously published work (Lowe, 2018).

Experimenting	Correcting	Polishing
Form-based LREs	Feedback	Repetition leading to automaticity
Lexical-based LREs	Modified output	
Mechanical LREs	Self-reflection	

Figure 9.1 Categorization of LREs by context

1: Experimenting with language

During peer interaction learners have many opportunities for experimenting with language. As Philp *et al.* (2014: 36) note, 'a primary strength of peer interaction is that it allows learners the space to experiment with language, to try out language forms without being corrected, to struggle a little and discover the limitations of their knowledge, and to confirm or query the way they express things'. In this section several examples will be presented of students engaging in peer interaction during the discussion portions of the project. One example will be given of a form-based LRE, a lexical-based LRE and a mechanical LRE.

Form-based LREs

The first type of LRE presented here will be those focused on form. That is, on instances of peer interaction where students were engaged in discussion of, or featuring a focus on, morphology and syntax. The first example, given below, is taken from the second discussion period in week 2 of the project, between two students discussing language and gender.

A: Have you ever experienced that you talk more than men?
B: I...
A: Have you ever been to experience that you talk more than men?
B: (repeating) have you ever been to experience that you...
A: In your life?
B: Ahhh, my life, ね *(ne – right?)*? Experienced a time?
A: Have you ever experienced a time when you talked more than men?
B: I don't know, but I ... I don't like talking. I always listen, so I don't have experience, do you have experience?

In this extract, we can see some form-based experimentation on the part of learner A, leading to a joint construction between the two learners. First, Learner A asks 'have you ever experienced that you talk more than men?', using imperfect but understandable grammar. When this question is not answered by her partner, A modifies the question to 'have you ever been to experience that you talk more than men?' Here, A appears to be experimenting with a previously learned language chunk ('have you ever been...'), in an effort to make her utterance more understandable. Ironically, this actually renders her question less grammatical than it had been. B attempts to understand this by repeating the question, which A then modifies with 'in your life?' This addition of another chunk at the end of the question seems to spark understanding in B, who supplies an additional piece of language in the form of 'experienced a time?', which leads A to formulate the full and accurate question 'have you ever experienced a time when you talked more than men?', which B is then able to answer. While the two learners do not explicitly engage in any metalinguistic discussion, the communication difficulty that arises in this interaction allows them to notice a gap in their linguistic knowledge, and reformulate their language together until they have co-constructed a correct utterance. This is an example of a joint construction occurring through experimentation during duoethnographic peer interaction.

In the second extract, taken from the first discussion period in week 1 of the project, we can see an example of a second form-based LRE. In this instance, the learners were discussing the difference between the ways in which men and women speak, based on their own experiences with their family members.

E: I always talk with my mom *(pause)*
F: About
E: About *(pause)*
F: Your
E: My...university's life.

In this dialogue the two learners are engaged in an explicit co-construction of an utterance. Learner E begins to make her statement, but then pauses, seemingly lost for how to continue the sentence. Learner F, anticipating perhaps the intended meaning, suggests the word 'about' as a possible continuation. This is taken up by Learner E, who again pauses, apparently unsure of how to continue. Once again, Learner F suggests the word 'your', which learner E alters into 'my' and then completes the sentence with 'university's life'. It is apparent from this interaction that without the peer interaction and the contributions made towards the utterance by Learner F, Learner E would likely have been unable to complete her idea. However, this was not simply a case of Learner F correcting or providing the answer for Learner E. Rather, the two work together, using guesswork and suggestions in order to come to a complete sentence. In other words, through peer interaction the learners were able to co-construct this utterance, which one (and possibly neither) would have been able to do by themselves.

These two examples provide evidence that the duoethnographic project the learners were participating in provided opportunities for experimenting with language during peer interaction, and that this experimentation led to language development. The act of externalizing the language allowed the learners to reflect on the form of the language used and negotiate towards a more acceptable level of linguistic performance.

Lexical-based LREs

The second type of LRE presented here focuses on lexis. Lexis here refers to both individual words as well as phrases and prefabricated chunks of language. Once again, two examples from the data recordings will be provided and analysed in order to show how the students experimented with lexis, eventually arriving at higher levels of lexical performance through peer interaction. The following extract is taken from the first discussion period in week 1 of the project, and occurred as two learners began their first discussion.

C: *何と言えばいいの？ (nan to iebaiino? – What's a good thing to say?)*
D: Maybe, Can I start?
C: Ah…Can I start?
D: Ok.
C: So…what do you think difference between British and Canadian English?

The learners here seem unsure of a natural way to begin their discussion. They begin by whispering Japanese (perhaps in the hope it would not be picked up by the recorder), with learner C asking what would be a suitable phrase for them to use to begin their discussion. Learner D replies by supplying the phrase 'can I start' (with a rising intonation, indicating she herself is unsure of this) which, while being a somewhat stilted phrase, accomplishes the communicative purpose for which it is employed. Learner C then gives a sign of acknowledgement ('ah') and repeats the phrase. Learner D then signals permission for Learner C to begin speaking, and Learner C asks the first question which launches the discussion. This extract shows the two learners experimenting with a piece of lexis that is foundational to their discussion, and while the language they decide upon may sound somewhat stilted it is perfectly acceptable grammatically, and allows them to start their discussion, thus acting as a communicatively useful piece of language.

The second example once again shows the learners employing their first language skills while experimenting with lexis. In this case, the learners are discussing the issue of world Englishes, and considering the ways in which this may relate to their own experiences.

G: Because in my… in my… in my…in my town? In my country? *自分の住んでいる場所 (jibun no sundeiru basho – the place where I live)*
H: Town, town.
G: In my town many Philippines people live there.

In this extract we see learner G is confused as to which word to use to describe the place in which they live. They try out both 'town' and 'country', before clarifying in Japanese 'the place where I live'. Her partner, learner H, selects the correct word for learner G to use, saying 'town, town', which learner H is then able to build into her utterance in order to produce the correct sentence. This extract again shows an example of two learners engaging in peer interaction in order to find the correct piece of lexis to express their meaning. By experimenting with two different possibilities, and then clarifying the meaning through use of their first language, the learners are together able to find the correct word to suit the situation.

Mechanical LRE

Finally, we will look at 'mechanical' LREs, that is, focused on spelling or pronunciation. Two of these LREs will be presented, one focusing on spelling, and one on pronunciation. The first extract is taken from the first discussion period in week 1 of the project, in which two learners were discussing their experiences with World Englishes. In this extract, learner A is describing an experience she had while studying in New Zealand, when a friend attempted to teach her about Maori Culture:

I: He said 'do you know mari greeting?'
J: Sorry?
I: Mari greetings? He said.
J: Mari greetings?
I: Like Kiwi, mari.
J: You mean Maori?
I: Yes! He said, 'do you know Maori greetings?'

Learner I initially pronounces the word as 'mari', rather than 'maori', a slight change in pronunciation, but one which renders Learner J unable to understand. This is surprising, as in Japanese the pronunciation of this word is close to the English 'Maori'. This may have been due to the learner attempting to mimic the pronunciation of the word she encountered while studying abroad, perhaps trying to pronounce it at a 'natural' speed so the longer vowel sound was reduced. Learner J signals her lack of understanding by exclaiming 'sorry?' Learner I repeats her main idea in a simple form, while retaining all the relevant information, perhaps unclear on what the issue was. Learner J, still unable to understand, provides more focused feedback by repeating the phrase 'mari greetings?' with emphasis on the word 'mari'. Learner I, having understood which word was causing problems, provides a contextually related word in the form of 'Kiwi', at which point Learner J asks 'you mean Maori?', thus providing the correct pronunciation. This pronunciation is then picked up by Learner I, who continues to use this pronunciation form for the rest of the discussion. This example shows how by externalising the word 'Maori', Learner I was able to spot an issue with her pronunciation and use feedback from her partner to come to the correct pronunciation of the word.

The second example comes from the collaborative writing of the final project in week 3. In this extract, the same two learners are engaged in writing up a section of their dialogue and are writing a sentence which eventually became: 'I had one experience when I was in New Zealand':

I: Is this is correct? 'new Zealand'?
J: I think so.
I: Should 'new' have capital letter?
J: I…is it adjective? Or name?
I: I think part of name.

J: So capital is best here?
I: I think yes.

In this extract the students have become confused about whether or not the 'New' in 'New Zealand' is a modifying adjective or a part of the name of the country itself, and therefore whether it should be capitalized or not. After a brief discussion, they come to the decision that it is in fact a part of the country's name, and so should therefore receive capitalization. This LRE shows how the peer interaction during the collaborative writing stage of the project allowed the students to engage in repair of a mechanical feature of their written language.

This section has provided several examples demonstrating the ways in which students engaged in duoethnographic projects were able to take advantage of the extensive peer interaction of the approach for the purpose of language development. These are only a few short examples of the many LREs which occurred during the class. The majority of the LREs did not feature metalinguistic talk (though some did), and most focused on form and lexis, rather than mechanical issues.

2: Correcting language

The second context in Philp *et al.*'s (2014) framework is that of 'correcting' language, which may take the form of peer feedback, modified output, or self-reflection. As with the previous section, examples will be given of each of these processes taking place within the class. The analysis will again be qualitative rather than quantitative, with the aim of showing how the extensive peer interaction in duoethnographic projects can lead to the production of LREs and thus to language development.

Feedback

The first example given in this section focuses on an LRE in which direct feedback from one learner led to another correcting their language in a productive way. This LRE occurred in the first discussion in week 1 of the project, during which the two learners were discussing the topic of language and gender.

E: You speak more brother than father?
F: You want to say, do I speak more than my brother or father?
E: Yes, that's right. Do you speak more than your brother or father?
F: Ummm, I don't think so

In this extract, Learner E asks a somewhat incomprehensible question with an unclear grammatical structure. Learner F, attempting to understand what was asked of them, provides direct feedback, first by marking their feedback as such ('you want to say'), and then by providing a more grammatically accurate recast of the question. Learner E, confirms the intended meaning, and then repeats the question, this time utilising the correct grammatical structure, and also modifying the pronouns to turn it into a more appropriate question. Here the direct feedback and reformulation of Learner F allowed Learner E to notice a gap in their knowledge and react to it accordingly. This can be seen by the fact that they both acknowledge and confirm the suggested meaning by Learner F, thus indicating they understood the question to be a form of feedback. They then repeat and modify the new form of the question provided by Learner E. Learner E is not simply parroting the phrase spoken by learner F, but is instead modifying it grammatically, indicating a level of understanding. This example of explicit feedback from Learner E is one of many that occurred during the recordings in which feedback was provided, thus creating opportunities for language development during the discussion and collaborative writing portions of the project.

Modified output

The second example given is an instance of modified output, in which recasting of a grammatical form by one learner led to uptake from another. The following exchange took place during the second discussion in week 2 of the project, once again on the topic of language and gender.

A: My mother is more...kind?
B: Kinder?
A: Yes, kinder than my father. So, she lets him speak.

In this extract, learner A attempts to make a comparative using 'more' to modify 'kind', to make 'more kind'. However, she also shows some hesitation, as indicated by the pause between these two words. Seeming to notice that her partner is unsure of the correct grammatical form to use, learner B supplies the correct comparative form of the adjective 'kinder', which learner A then acknowledges and uses correctly. This is a short, but very clear example of an LRE in which modified output from a partner led to a reformulation of the initial utterance, and thus towards language development. Learner A, by externalizing her language was able to find a grammatical form she was unsure about, and the act of externalizing the language allowed learner B to suggest the correct form, which was then picked up on by learner A. Again, this exchange did not feature any use of metalanguage in the L2, but shows how the learners were experimenting with language, and were thus able to develop their language knowledge through interaction with their peer.

The second example is taken from the collaborative writing portion of the project, in which two learners are constructing their dialogue on the topic of World Englishes. In the following extract, Learner A is suggesting sentences for the dialogue based on their notes of what was shared during the discussions.

C: My home family wasn't non-native speakers
D: Your home family was non-native speaker?

C: Yes yes, non-native speakers. So I was worried I would learn bad English. I'll write.

In this extract, Learner C first creates a double negative sentence, which would hold the opposite of her intended meaning. Learner D then provides a modified version of the sentence, changing the word 'wasn't' to 'was', and thus rendering the meaning clear. Learner C confirms this meaning verbally ('yes yes, non-native speakers') and continues the sentence to its conclusion. She then indicates that she will write down the corrected sentence to form part of the dialogue. Here we see another example where the modified output of learner D helped learner C to notice their mistake, correct their mistake, and then record it as part of their writing. Once again, this example shows how peer interaction during collaborative writing led to modified output on the part of the learner, and then correction of errant language.

Self-reflection

The final form of correction shown here is that of self-correction, in which the externalising of language leads learners to reflect on and reconsider their choices of language, thus leading to self-correction. Two short examples will be presented in which a learner can be seen to reconsider their utterance and self-correct. The first example was taken from the beginning of the first discussion in week 1 of the project.

B: Why don't we discuss this one or you...er, no...yours?

In this extract, the learner is asking their partner which of their discussion questions they should discuss. After initially producing the erroneous form 'this one or you', she seems to notice that she has made an error, signaling this awareness with 'er, no', spoken to herself rather than her partner. She then corrects this to 'yours'. Here the act of verbalizing the sentence gave the learner an opportunity to reflect on her construction, and even engage in some personal languaging, in which she refutes her own utterance before making a correction. This is a clear example of self-reflection leading to correction in the context of peer interaction. The second example follows a similar pattern, and is also taken from the discussion in week 1, in which two students were discussing world Englishes.

D: Do you...did you have a problem when pronounce is difference? I mean, when pronounce is different?

Here, the student quickly reformulates their utterance twice. Initially, they ask 'do you...', before immediately correcting this to 'did you...' More interestingly, once the learner has completed the sentence, she goes back and reformulates the final word, signalling this reformulation to her partner with the phrase 'I mean...'. The fact she uses this phrase to indicate to her partner that she has modified her utterance demonstrates the degree to which the considerations of her partner's understanding are influencing her need to self-reflect and self-correct. This highlights the role that peer interaction plays in self-reflection and self-correction.

This section has shown how the duoethnographic interaction became a context in which language could be corrected through the processes of explicit feedback, modified output and self-reflection. By verbalizing and making their language available for reflection and reconsideration, the learners were able to develop their language in ways which they may not have been able to had they been working alone. These examples show the benefits of the peer-interactions necessitated by the duoethnographic process for correcting and thus developing language.

3: Polishing language

The final context suggested by Philp *et al.* (2014) is that of polishing language, in which language use becomes automatized (or 'polished') though repetition. One example of this from the project will be presented here which occurred during the collaborative writing of the final dialogue on the topic of native-speakerism. At the start of the lesson, one pair became rather confused about the order of adjectives in the phrase 'white native English speaker', suggested variously 'native white English speaker' and 'native English white speaker'. As they could not decide on the correct form to use, they consulted the teacher who suggested they could use 'white native English speaker' (the only unambiguously correct option in the context of their dialogue). This phrase came up several times in their dialogue and was something they repeated numerous times during the collaborative writing portion of the project. During the final class discussion, the two students were using the phrase accurately and smoothly in discussing their project with others, and maintaining the correct order of adjectives in each case. This is a simple example, but shows how the students in the projects were polishing their language through repetitive use of a phase with a set word order which had earlier been very difficult for them to decide on.

Conclusion

This chapter has focused on the benefits of duoethnography for language learning through an analysis of LREs which occurred during the project, leading towards language development. These LREs occurred as a result of peer interaction during both the discussion and collaborative writing portions of the project, and show the learners experimenting with language (in terms of form, lexis, pronunciation and spelling), correcting language (through feedback, modified output and self-reflection) and polishing language (in which language became automatized through repetition). This chapter has not (and is not intended to) show that duoethnographic projects are superior to other forms of tasks which aim to promote peer interaction. Rather, the purpose here has been to demonstrate empirical evidence for the claim that the extensive peer interaction provided by the duoethnographic process allows learners to develop their language through both discussion and collaborative writing. The extensive opportunities for this kind of peer interaction provided by the duoethnographic project allowed for large amounts of experimentation, correction and polishing of language by the learners. The relatively non-interventionist stance taken by the teacher in the process encouraged learners to express what they could as best they could, and created space for this kind of interaction to occur. Therefore, while duoethnography may not be unique in encouraging peer interaction, it is an approach in which large amounts of effective peer interaction are generated, as evidenced by the data in this chapter.

This data was taken from a pilot study of just one group and has been presented in the form of a qualitative analysis of representative examples, and therefore cannot be taken to demonstrate the wider effectiveness of the method. However, these results are suggestive of the kinds of benefits students may get in terms of language development through peer interaction during a duoethnographic project, due to the extended amount of time learners spend in the ZPD, both in terms of the in-class discussion and collaborative writing portions of the project, and also the time spent on collaborative study outside of class. The primary element which recommends duoethnographic projects as language learning tasks is the space such projects provide for both discussion and collaborative writing, and the language development which occurs through this peer interaction. However, these benefits should be considered in the larger context of the project and the other potentially positive aspects of the process, such as the promotion of positive group dynamics in class, which will be the subject of the next chapter.

References

Ellis, N.C. (2005) At the interface: Dynamic interactions of explicit and implicit language knowledge. *Studies in Second Language Acquisition* 27 (2), 304–352. https://doi.org/10.1017/S027226310505014X

Ellis, R. (2018) *Reflections on Task-based Language Teaching*. Bristol: Multilingual Matters.

Kubanyiova, M. (2008) Rethinking research ethics in contemporary applied linguistics: The tension between macroethical and microethical perspectives in situated research. *The Modern Language Journal* 92 (4), 503–518.

Lantolf, J.P. (2000) Introducing sociocultural theory. In J.P. Lantolf (ed.) *Sociocultural Theory and Second Language Learning* (pp. 1–26). Oxford: Oxford University Press.

Lowe, R.J. (2018) Duoethnographic projects in the language class. *Modern English Teacher* 27 (1), 74–77.

Philp, J., Adams, R.J. and Iwashita, N. (2014) *Peer Interaction and Second Language Learning*. New York, NY: Routledge.

Philp, J. and Tognini, R. (2009) Language acquisition in foreign language contexts and the differential benefits of interaction. *IRAL – International Review of Applied Linguistics in Language Teaching* 47 (3–4), 245–266. https://doi.org/10.1515/iral.2009.011

Segalowitz, N. (2000) Automaticity and attentional skill in fluency performance. In H. Riggenbach (ed.) *Perspectives on Fluency*. Ann Arbor, MI: University of Michigan Press.

Storch, N. (2008) Metatalk in a pair work activity: Level of engagement and implications for language development. *Language Awareness* 17 (2), 95–114.

Storch, N. (2013) *Collaborative Writing in L2 Classrooms*. Bristol: Multilingual Matters.

Swain, M. (1998) Focus on form through conscious reflection. In C. Doughty and J. Williams (eds) *Focus on Form in Classroom Second Language Acquisition* (pp. 64–82). Cambridge: Cambridge University Press.

Swain, M. and Lapkin, S. (1998) Interaction and second language learning: Two adolescent French immersion students working together. *The Modern Language Journal* 82 (3), 320. https://doi.org/10.2307/329959

Vygotsky, L.S. (1978) *Mind in Society: The Development of Higher Psychological Processes*. Cambridge, MA: Harvard University Press.

10 Collaboration and Cohesion: Using Duoethnography to Enhance Group Dynamics and Pair Relationship Building in a University Speaking Class

Luke Lawrence

Introduction

The core aspect of duoethnography that sets it apart from other research methods is the 'duo' element. Most research, especially that which contains an ethnographic approach, is either carried out by a single 'lone wolf' (Mitteness & Barker, 2004) researcher or by two or more researchers researching a site or a population. In multi-authored research projects, each contributor brings a unique set of skills, knowledge and way of viewing the data (see Copland & Creese, 2015 for a clear guide to team working in an ethnographic study). In autoethnography, duoethnography's closest comparison, the researcher acts as the site of research, but the solitary nature of the research can often be singularly focused. In contrast, one of the key aspects of duoethnography is the relationship between researchers that requires initial trust to begin the project and builds on this as personal and sometimes never before discussed experiences are revealed, 'disrupting the metanarrative' (Sawyer & Norris, 2013) of solitary research.

Peer collaboration between students in the classroom can also be an effective way for language learners to build relationships, both with individual partners (in a two- or three-person group) and also with the class as a whole. This chapter will present and analyse responses from a post-project questionnaire given to students after completing an in-class duoethnographic project (as outlined in Chapter 8 of this volume) in order to establish how the learners perceived the project in terms of enjoyment, difficulty, usefulness, relationship-building with a partner and relationship-building with the class as a whole.

Pair Collaboration and Emotional Intersubjectivity

Pair and small group collaboration has long been identified as a key component of second language acquisition (SLA) (see Lowe, this volume for an overview of SLA and the benefits of duoethnography for language acquisition), but the emotional and social aspect of collaborative learning remains under-researched. As Pavlenko (2013) points out, much of the research into emotions and affect in SLA and language learning has focused on negative emotions such as anxiety, lacks a solid theoretical framework within which research can be framed and relies on simplistic, linear models of acquisition. Pavlenko argues that this line of enquiry is 'ultimately doomed to failure because anxiety, attitudes and motivation are dynamic and social phenomena and the relationship between these phenomena and levels of achievement is reciprocal rather than unidirectional' (Pavlenko, 2013: 8). Thus, in what has been termed the 'Affective Turn' in SLA, researchers have recently begun to combine psychological and cognitive theories with poststructuralist ideas around the discursive construction of social interactions to create new theories with which to approach research into language learning (Pavlenko, 2013). In this chapter I will draw on Denzin's (1984) framework of emotional intersubjectivity in order to highlight the social and emotional benefits of pair collaboration and show how using duoethnography as a pedagogical tool can fit into this framework. This framework was chosen due to its flexibility and equal attention to the psychological, cognitive and social.

Denzin's (1984) framework of emotional intersubjectivity follows Vygotsky's (1978) social theory of the mind that situates learning and development not as simple cognitive or psychological activities, but as something that takes place through social interaction with others. Our emotional experiences are in constant flux and change according to time, place and interlocutor, which may be heightened in a language classroom by anxiety and fear (Horwitz *et al.*, 1986). If we understand 'subjectivity' to be the knowledge we have of our own mental states, and 'intersubjectivity' to be the shared knowledge of mental states shared by two or more persons, the concept of emotional intersubjectivity refers to 'an interactional process that joins two or more persons into a common, or shared, emotional field of experience' in which 'one feels one's way into the feelings and intentional feeling states of the other' (Denzin, 1984: 130) and leads to a 'reflective intertwining of rays of emotionality from one person to another and back again' (Denzin, 1984: 131).

Denzin outlines six categories of emotional subjectivity: feelings in common, fellow-feeling, emotional infection, emotional identification, shared emotionality and spurious emotionality. Feelings in common are an everyday experience and occur when two people share the same or a similar emotion about a subject or an experience. In contrast, fellow-feeling refers to a situation in which we acknowledge the feelings of others, but do not necessarily share the emotional meaning that they attach to it. Thirdly, emotional infection refers to the unintentional contagion of our own emotional mental state to others. This can be positive or negative and is often seen in a classroom where one student may be identified as the mood maker that elevates the other students or drags the class down (Dörnyei & Murphey, 2003; Hadfield, 1992). Similarly unintentional, or involuntary, is emotional identification. This is 'the act of identifying one's self with, or through, the self of another person' (Denzin, 1984: 151) that often involves surrendering our own emotional selves to the emotional state of our partner. The fifth category identified by Denzin is shared emotionality or 'emotional embracement'. Unlike the one-sided nature of emotional identification, shared emotionality is a deep and mutual emotional bonding that can only be brought about through sharing and intimacy with a partner. Finally, spurious emotionality on the other hand is a form of egocentrism whereby we mistake and misinterpret our own feelings for the feelings that the other experiences. This can result in a lack of empathy and an inability to put ourselves in the other's shoes, although we may think we understand. In this situation we may confuse and conflate our own experiences and memories with that of our partner's.

When we implement a duoethnographic project as a pedagogical tool in the classroom, students are put into pairs, either by the teacher or through self-selection. In this situation the students may already be friends or acquaintances, either from a relationship formed outside of the language class or from previous lessons and activities shared in the class. Conversely, they may be relative strangers and have had minimal interaction prior to beginning the project. In both scenarios Denzin's framework can be useful in understanding the interpersonal emotional relationship that may be unfolding as the project progresses. Although duoethnography emphasises differences between participants (Sawyer & Norris, 2013), it is often the case in the initial stage of data collection that commonalities are identified, which can lead to Denzin's first category of 'feelings in common'. Next, as differences begin to emerge and as students become more comfortable in admitting to and sharing juxtapositions, Denzin's concept of 'fellow-feeling' comes into play. This ability to empathise with a classmate, without necessarily sharing the same emotion can be an important factor in building friendship and understanding, which recognises that 'engaging in dialogic forms of research offers human connection and a sense of care for the other that too often seems missing in the scholarly world, and many would argue, in the world at large' (Lund *et al.*, 2017: 116). Finally, perhaps the most pertinent of Denzin's categories is that of 'emotional embracement'. The step-by-step process of a duoethnographic project requires emotional vulnerability and openness in the data collection and analysis stages and trust and cooperation in the writing up and presentation stages. Banting and De Loof (2017) describe their experience of engaging in duoethnography with a relatively unknown partner as part of a graduate studies course, with one half of the duo remarking that they 'had no idea that I would become so open with Stephan throughout this course through this vehicle of duoethnography' (Banting & De Loof, 2017: 41) and both reported that they emerged from the process 'knowing one another deeply' (Banting & De Loof, 2017: 60). This emotional embracement thus acts to establish an intimate emotional bond that may be considered a form of friendship (Rankie Shelton & McDermott, 2015).

By encouraging the positive aspects of emotional intersubjectivity in the classroom and strengthening the relationship between student pairs and small groups, duoethnography can help to reduce stress and anxiety in the language classroom and facilitate communication.

Whole Class Group Dynamics

In addition to acting as a bond and facilitator between pairs and small groups in the classroom, the social benefits of using duoethnography as a pedagogical tool can also radiate out to promote whole class group cohesion.

From the point of view of the teacher, a study by Senior (1997: 3) found that any class that was sensed to have a 'positive whole-group atmosphere' was judged to be 'good', while a class that did not have this cohesion was deemed to be 'bad'. This supports Stevick's (1980: 4) statement that 'success depends less on materials, techniques and linguistic analyses, and more on what goes on inside and between the people in the classroom'. Despite the potential significance that this suggests, and Dörnyei and Murphey's (2003: 19, italics in original) assertion that 'peer affiliation does *not* necessarily occur automatically', group dynamics remains an underexplored area of research in ELT. In this section I will highlight identifiers of a successfully bonded group, as suggested by the literature, and show how use of duoethnography in the classroom can help to bring these about.

Hadfield (1992: 12) lists a number of factors that identify a successfully bonded group, which include:

- the members of the group trust each other;
- group members are interested in each other and feel they have something in common;

- group members are able to empathise with each other and understand each other's point of view even if they do not share them;
- there is a positive, supportive atmosphere: members have a positive self-image which is reinforced by the group, so that they feel secure enough to express their individuality;
- the group has a sense of fun.

Implementing a duoethnography in the classroom can help to facilitate a number of these criteria. For example, the final stages of the project involve students sharing their projects with the teacher and with the whole class. This gives the students an opportunity to extend the individual trust they have built up over the previous several lessons to the rest of the class. It also gives a supportive space for each student and each small group to express their ideas and findings in a secure and empathetic atmosphere, with all students participating equally and sharing in a similar manner.

Respondents in Senior's (1997: 3) study added to Hadfield's (1992) list of factors, describing the properties of a 'good' language class as including:

- a feeling of warmth;
- mutual support;
- a feeling of cooperation;
- rapport between class members;
- the class came together.

Again, the use of duoethnography as pedagogical tool can help to achieve these indicators. The very act of carrying out a new, and potentially difficult – both mentally and linguistically – medium-term project can bring a number of challenges. In this situation, mutual support and co-operation between the whole class in checking and confirming the requirements of the project and the progress of other groups can be important. This communication may occur through social media outside of the classroom (see Lawrence, 2017a on the use of social media in building group cohesion) and helps to build support and rapport between all students in the class.

Finally, Dörnyei and Murphey (2003: 19) expand the list of factors that enhance intermember acceptance to include:

- learning about each other;
- proximity, contact and interaction;
- extracurricular activities;
- joint hardship.

As Dörnyei and Murphey (2003) note, lack of acceptance or understanding between all kinds of people or member states often stems from a lack of information or knowledge about the 'other'. Thus they consider the first point, learning about each other, to be the most crucial factor in promoting relationships in the class. Duoethnography offers a two-step process to help to facilitate this by allowing students to share information in the safety of a closed pair before opening up to the group. It also requires sustained contact and interaction over a number of weeks on a joint project wherein the behaviour of each person influences the others, which can act as a 'powerful gelling agent' (Dörnyei & Murphey, 2003: 21). Similarly, the emotional labour and commitment to a new form of studying that all students are equally required to bring to the project can represent a joint hardship and a feeling of all-in-it-togetherness, which can be beneficial in terms of group bonding. Additionally, the fact that a great deal of the actual work, for example listening to dialogues and writing the paper, were required to be completed outside of class time, could be considered extracurricular activities.

As these examples illustrate, and as has been noted by graduate students engaging in duoethnographies as part of their graduate course, implementing a duoethnographic project in a second language classroom can 'develop a sense of community and alleviate some of the issues of isolation' (Diaz & Grain, 2017: 150) which are often found in ELT classes.

Background to the Study

A duoethnographic project was introduced as part of an elected course for advanced (a minimum TOEFL-ITP score of 520 is required to join the course) learners in a public university in Japan. The course consisted of two consecutive 90-minute lessons per week over a single 15-week semester. The focus of the course was developing speaking skills (discussion, short presentations, formal debates etc.) and was based on critical issues in contemporary society such as gender issues, the ownership of the English language, corporate ethics, poverty, LGBTQ rights, othering, immigration, English education in Japan, terrorism and English as a Lingua Franca. The duoethnography project, which occupied one lesson per week, began in Week 8 and continued to Week 12. This consisted of three lessons of language input and data collection (with homework assigned each week) and one lesson of presentations, with a break in Week 11 to allow time for the writing of a final report paper.

My initial purpose when designing the study was to get feedback on the students' reaction to the project in order to help me adapt and improve my teaching of duoethnography for future classes. Due to my research interest in group dynamics (see Lawrence, 2017a, 2017b) I was also keen to evaluate the students' perception of how (or if at all) the project helped to strengthen the relationship between themselves and other group members.

Participants

The class consisted of 12 students that were all either first- or second-year students. Despite the official minimum exam score required to join the course there was a range of ability and language experience in the class. Several students had spent time abroad and were fairly fluent and comfortable using English, while for others it was their first time in a communicatively-focused English learning class. At the time of data collection for this study one of the students was absent, therefore the data set contains responses from 11 participants.

Data Collection

In order to investigate the participants' perceptions of their experiences of the duoethnography project, I issued a questionnaire immediately after the completion of the project. This was distributed in class and collected in the same lesson. The survey consisted of six 'attitudinal questions' (Dörnyei, 2007: 102) with an answer choice of either 'Yes', 'No' and 'A little' or 'Yes', 'No', 'Not sure' with free space below each question to write details, which was required. A seventh question offered a larger free space for participants to write about their feelings regarding their experience of conducting the project. This simple multi-item scale was chosen in order to get a broad overview of the participants' feelings towards the project and the compulsory free spaces were included in order to gain depth and richness with the hope that they would yield 'graphic examples, illustrative quotes' and lead me to 'identify issues not previously anticipated' (Dörnyei, 2007: 107). The questions in the survey included: enjoyment of the project, difficulty of the project, usefulness of the project, the relationship with their partner, the relationship with the whole class and whether or not they would recommend a similar project to other students.

Results

Duoethnography as enjoyable

As identified by Hadfield (1992), the group having a sense of fun is a key component of group dynamics and an important factor in facilitating shared emotionality. With this in mind, the first question in the survey relates to the enjoyability of the project.

Did you find the experience of collaborating with your partner to carry out and write a duoethnography enjoyable?

Yes	No	A little
11	0	0
100%	0%	0%

As the results clearly indicate, students overwhelmingly found the experience an enjoyable exercise. Comments that accompanied this question focused on the novelty of the experience: 'Usually, I don't have the chance to talk about each other's experience, opinion and feeling, so it was fresh', 'Recording our voice was fresh for me because I have never done it'; the building of relationships: 'Both of us had the same kind of experiences, which made it fun to share', 'We can find a lot of similarity and differences and getting to know new opinions is really interesting'; the pure enjoyability: 'I don't feel that report is studying'; and enjoyment of the process: 'It was so interesting to build a logical theory by finding hints from our dialogue'. However, one comment also highlighted the possible negative side of a duoethnographic project when a pair is composed of students with perceived language level differences: 'I enjoyed collaborating with my partner to learn new thoughts about our topic. But I was afraid that I might make my partner do a lot of work because my English skills is very low. I was concern about that'. This final comment points to a potential area for classroom management when considering how to match students when selecting pairs.

Duoethnography as difficult

One concern that teachers may have when considering whether or not to implement duoethnography in their own classes is that it may be beyond the capability of their students, in terms of the language ability required. However, as Dörnyei and Murphey (2003) assert, the joint hardship of difficulty can help to bring students together and enhance overall group dynamics.

Did you find the experience of collaborating with your partner to carry out and write a duoethnography difficult?

Yes	No	A little
3	2	6
27.3%	18.2%	54.5%

The results here provide more nuance than the previous question, with more than three quarters of respondents stating that they found the project difficult or a little difficult, and only 2 out of 11 replying that it was not difficult. Again, a look at the comments will provide us with more insight into the students' thoughts. Most comments centred on the difficulties they faced with producing an academic document, which may have been the first time for most students, either in English or in their own language. For example, one student commented that 'it was difficult to connect our experiences to articles', while another said that it was 'difficult to write a polite sentences and reference rightly'. Of the students that replied 'No', the comments pointed to the power of mutual support in overcoming any potential difficulties: 'We can help each other and think how we make paper better together so it's not so difficult'.

Duoethnography as useful

Although being enjoyable is important for relationship building and indeed for learning, if an activity is not perceived as useful by the students, it may lead to demotivation and seen as lacking pedagogical value.

Did you find the experience of collaborating with your partner to carry out and write a duoethnography useful?

Yes	No	A little
8	0	3
72.7%	0%	27.3%

The more positive comments referred to both practical skill acquisition as well as the social, relationship-building element. Comments that looked to how skills learned in the project may be useful in the future included: 'I learned how to write academically which might be useful in the future', 'I think answering, gathering, and writing skill can be used for the group work or assignment in the future', and 'It's not just because we can better understand the topic but also we can learn how to cooperate with others and it's so important if we work'. Other comments focused on the broadening of experience that duoethnography engendered: 'Through duoethnography, I realized various ways of thinking and dealing with problems', 'We can find other new perspectives and experiences and that is useful for us'. One comment simply stated: 'improve my English, understand people, team'. Of the slightly negative responses, the focus was on the unfamiliarity of the methodology: 'It was my first time to do "duoethnography" so I am not sure how to make use of it'.

Duoethnography for relationship building with a partner

As indicated above, pair collaboration can act as a key factor in facilitating peer support to set a positive social and emotional state of mind that can be conducive to learning.

Do you feel that the experience of doing a duoethnography helped to strengthen the relationship between you and your partner?

Yes	No	A little
10	0	1
90.9%	0%	9.1%

As the stark numbers indicate, the response to this question was extremely positive, with only one respondent stating that it helped to strengthen the relationship 'a little'. The less positive response came from the same student who lacked confidence in their ability compared to their partner in the first question above. The same lack of confidence was displayed in the accompanying comment: 'Because I'm afraid that I might make him do a lot works', which again indicates a potential pitfall of using duoethnography in a mixed-ability class. Interestingly, although the emphasis in the duoethnographic method is on finding differences (Sawyer & Norris, 2013), the similarities and shared experiences appeared to be the points that brought students closer together, which can be seen as a manifestation of emotional intersubjectivity, especially 'feelings in common' (Denzin, 1984). For example: 'In my case, my partner and I had the same experience, so duoethnography helped to strengthen our relationship', and 'When we talk about a lot of experiences and especially when we found that we had same experiences, we became closer'. Others talked about the positive experience of simply sharing: 'We can share a lot of things that we didn't know before, so I think our relationship got deeper through the research', 'It's rare experience for me to listen to one person's opinion about one topic. I think it's helpful'. In addition, one comment pointed to the usefulness of extending the collaboration time outside of the parameters of set class time (Dörnyei & Murphey, 2003), stating that: 'Except the time on the lesson, we also work together for this assignment. Then we can know each other more'. Others mentioned the positive aspect of sharing the workload: 'When I was busy, my partner helped me. For example, she looked for references and wrote introduction. I'm so greatful to her'.

Duoethnography for whole class group dynamics

As discussed above, enhancing group cohesion can be an important aspect of the overall learning experience that can have a wide range of beneficial effects. This includes learning more efficiently if they feel relaxed and feeling less nervous and vulnerable about practising language (Senior, 1997). Compared to the perception of the role of the project in strengthening pair relationships, the results for the success of duoethnography in promoting whole group relationships was less positive.

Do you feel that the experience of doing a duoethnography helped to strengthen the relationship between you and all of the other students in the group?

Yes	No	A little
3	1	7
27.3%	9.1%	63.6%

Only three participants felt that it definitely did strengthen the relationship for the whole group. One comment implicitly referred to the usefulness of the final presentation when each group shared their projects with the whole class: 'It was interesting to share the each pare's dialogue', while another pointed to the usefulness of group communication outside of lesson time and the role of the joint hardship of completing an unfamiliar assignment: 'We helped each other in writing duoethnography and share information a lot as we didn't really know about duoethnography'. For the students that circled 'A little' the comments ranged from the reasonably positive; 'I learned other students experiences which strengthen the relationship', to the more nuanced; 'I sometimes consulted with other students about the contents of duoethnography essay', 'Talking about each other's topic made a little bit closer each other', to the more direct; 'I think there was not enough opportunities to communicate with other students through the research'. For the respondent that answered 'No', this was justified by the comment that '...if we try to make relationship with other students in the group, we have to set more opportunity of announcement and exchanging the opinions'.

The data from this question points to a deficiency in the usefulness of the project (in its current form) for whole class group dynamics and offers ideas for adjustments that can be made when teaching future classes.

Duoethnography as a recommended project for others

In the social media-directed environment which we all now inhibit, none more so than university students, where whole businesses and careers can be decided by the number of 'Likes' received, the willingness to recommend to others can be seen to have real value and meaning.

Would you recommend a duoethnography project for other groups that want to improve relationship between students?

Yes	No	Not sure
11	0	0
100%	0%	0%

Most of the comments accompanying the question were as positive as the simple numbers suggest, however there were some qualifications: 'Once you get how to do it, it is fun!', and 'But students should choose the topic together! If one students decide a topic and the other just agrees with that their duoethnography wouldn't go well'. Of the purely positive comments, some focused exclusively, as the question directed, on the relationship-building aspect: 'Some people think it's difficult to speak up in a group, especially in English. So, this might be helpful', 'Group work can make a good relationship. It's the chance to talk with more students', 'The duoethnography project will be a chance for them to get to know each other'. Despite not explicitly asking about the language acquisition aspect, other comments mentioned it along with the social element: '… a duoethnography project is good way to improve not only relationship but also English skill', and 'Duoethnography can not only help us improve English skills but also deepen the relationship between students by talking about a specific topic'.

Duoethnography as an experience

The final question in the survey left a blank space and asked students to record their feelings about the experience of undertaking a duoethnographic project, paying particular attention to the relationship-building aspect.

> *Please use the space below to write about your feelings regarding the experience of conducting a duoethnography project (they can be positive, negative or neutral), particularly in relation to inter-group relationships with other students and the teacher.*

The comments here were longer than previous answers and contained a variety of views. Although the over-riding view was very positive, some of the qualifications proved effective in revealing the potential negative effect of the project for some students and questioned the usefulness of the project for promoting whole group dynamics.

For example, some comments touched on the difficulty of tackling a new kind of studying and suggested deficiencies in the way the project was presented to the students by the teacher:

- 'At first, everyone was not sure what to do'
- 'It is not usual assignment so it took time to get the concept of "duoethnography". I wanted to read a model paper before start the project to grasp what it is going to be'.

Other comments alluded to fact that it may not be a useful form of promoting whole group interaction:

- 'Overall it was a rare opportunity for me to write a English essay (?) with a partner. It helped me a lot to know more about my partner and myself. Yet, I'm a little bit worried about some feel it difficult to talk with just one person'
- 'However, I feel that we couldn't get enough communications with other students in different groups'
- 'I think this project will help strengthen the relationship between the partner because we talk about ourselves and take time to write a report. But I think it's not as useful for relationships between the teacher or the other students because we don't communicate during this project'.

Although, this assertion that there was little communication with the teacher was disputed by other comments:

- '... also with the teacher, there are many times that we got advicese'
- 'We can communicate with the teacher a lot and get some good advices'.

Additionally, the potential problem associated with difference in ability between partners identified earlier was seen here as a positive aspect of the project by some students:

- 'Fortunately, my partner was very good English speaker, so I was helped by her and works went smoothly'
- 'Also it was good experience of doing the same project with people whose English proficiency is a bit different from mine'

The most positive comments were reserved for the improvement of English skills:

- 'It was very good opportunity in that I can not only improve my English speaking, listening and writing skills but also understand each other'
- 'I think consequently the duoethnography has positive point and negative point. But finally the project made me improve my English skill or motivation and so on'

as well as promoting and strengthening the relationship between partners:

- 'Making a thing together also strengthen our relationship'
- 'Especially with my partner, it was a nice experience to make relationship'
- 'This was really interesting project. Especially with partner, we could talk about a lot of experiences and find a new perspective was good. Also, writing a paper together was interesting because we can help each other'

Discussion

As the figures and the accompanying comments suggest, the experience of undertaking a duoethnographic project in a university English class was seen as a largely positive one, with some qualifications given for uncertainties caused by engaging in a new and unknown methodology and for a lack of confidence brought about by perceived inequality in the language level of partners.

In terms of the benefits of duoethnography to the building and strengthening of relationships in pairs and small groups, with reference to Denzin's (1984) framework of emotional intersubjectivity, it can be said to be very successful. Comments from students explicitly recognised the value of the project in this regard, using language like 'we became closer' and 'our relationship got deeper', which directly allude to Denzin's (1984) concept of 'emotional embracement'. Additionally, statements like '... my partner and I had the same experience, so duoethnography helped to strengthen our relationship' point to Denzin's (1984) 'feelings in common' category.

However, with regard to the usefulness of the project for the promotion of whole group cohesion, the data suggests that it was less successful. The majority of respondents thought that the relationship between all students was strengthened only a little, with the project offering few opportunities to interact outside of the pair relationship. However, one respondent recognised the value of the sharing the final group presentations allowed and another indicated that whole group discussions had taken place outside the classroom in response to uncertainties regarding the methodology.

In summary, the respondents in this study perceived that carrying out duoethnographic project was very useful for building pair relationships, but less so for the purpose of fostering whole group dynamics. As one comment on the survey succinctly summarised: 'The relationship between me and my partner was strengthened very much, but other student's relationship making was not enough. So it is good way to strengthen relationship between two people'.

Limitations and Implications for Future Projects

This study only included data from one small group of students in the particular context of an advanced, non-compulsory EFL class in a university in Japan. However, I believe that the conclusions reached can suggest certain general truths for other teachers looking for opportunities to create a level of emotional intersubjectivity between students and, to a lesser extent, to promote whole-class group dynamics.

Additionally, the feedback provided by the survey comments offer advice for teachers (myself included) on how the implementation of a project could be improved. Firstly, providing more opportunities for each student to share their progress and ideas with the rest of the class at every stage of the project, not only at the end. This could be done by setting up a class social media group (Lawrence, 2017a) or by allowing time at the start of each class for students to share their preliminary ideas and findings with others. Secondly, teacher awareness of different ability levels between partners. While some students welcomed the opportunity to work with someone with higher or lower ability, for others it caused a lack of confidence and sense of guilt. Teachers should monitor these potential problems closely and intervene if necessary to settle any concerns before they become larger problems. Finally, a clear explanation of the methodology of duoethnography, along with a model paper should be provided in order to resolve uncertainties about a completely new way to study English. This should be checked and re-iterated in every lesson by the teacher and students allowed a safe space to ask questions or voice any concerns.

I hope that if these suggestions are taken on board that the insights gleaned from this study will be beneficial for teachers interested in new and innovative classroom pedagogies.

References

Banting, N. and De Loof, S. (2017) Right and wrong (and good enough): A duoethnography within a graduate curriculum studies course. In J. Norris and R.D. Sawyer (eds) *Theorizing Curriculum Studies, Teacher Education, and Research through Duoethnographic Pedagogy* (pp. 39–62). New York: Palgrave Macmillan US. https://doi.org/10.1057/978-1-137-51745-6_3

Copland, F. and Creese, A. (2015) *Linguistic Ethnography: Collecting, Analysing and Presenting Data.* Los Angeles: SAGE.

Denzin, N.K. (1984) *On Understanding Emotion.* New Brunswick, NJ: Transaction Publishers.

Diaz, C. and Grain, K. (2017) Community, identity, and graduate education: Using duoethnography as a mechanism for forging connections in academia. In J. Norris and R.D. Sawyer (eds) *Theorizing Curriculum Studies, Teacher Education, and Research through Duoethnographic Pedagogy* (pp. 131–152). New York: Palgrave Macmillan US. https://doi.org/10.1057/978-1-137-51745-6_7

Dörnyei, Z. (2007) *Research Methods in Applied Linguistics.* Oxford: Oxford University Press.

Dörnyei, Z. and Murphey, T. (2003) *Group Dynamics in the Language Classroom.* Cambridge: Cambridge University Press.

Hadfield, J. (1992) *Classroom Dynamics.* Oxford: Oxford University Press.

Horwitz, E.K., Horwitz, M.B. and Cope, J. (1986) Foreign language classroom anxiety. *The Modern Language Journal* 70 (2), 125–132.

Lawrence, L. (2017a) The role of student-led social media use in group dynamics. *The Language Teacher* 41 (5), 17–22.

Lawrence, L. (2017b) Transforming classes through group dynamics: From theory to practice. In P. Clements, A. Krause and E. Brown (eds) *Transformation in Language Education.* Tokyo: JALT.

Lund, D.E., Holmes, K., Hanson, A., Sitter, K., Scott, D. and Grain, K. (2017) Exploring duoethnography in graduate research courses. In J. Norris and R.D. Sawyer (eds) *Theorizing Curriculum Studies, Teacher Education, and Research through Duoethnographic Pedagogy* (pp. 111–129). New York: Palgrave Macmillan US. https://doi.org/10.1057/978-1-137-51745-6_6

Mitteness, L.S. and Barker, J.C. (2004) Collaborative and team research. In C. Seale, G. Gobo, J.F. Gubrium and D. Silverman (eds) *Qualitative Research Practice* (pp. 276–294). London: SAGE Publications.

Pavlenko, A. (2013) The affective turn in SLA: From 'Affective Factors' to 'Language Desire' and 'Commodification of Affect'. In D. Gabrys-Barker and J. Bielska (eds) *The Affective Dimension in Second Language Acquisition.* Bristol: Multilingual Matters.

Rankie Shelton, N.R. and McDermott, M. (2015) Duoethnography on friendship: Continue to breathe normally. *International Review of Qualitative Research* 8 (1), 68–89. https://doi.org/10.1525/irqr.2015.8.1.68

Sawyer, R.D. and Norris, J. (2013) *Duoethnography.* New York: Oxford University Press.

Senior. (1997) Transforming language classes into bonded groups. *ELT Journal* 51 (1), 3–11.

Stevick, E.W. (1980) *Teaching Languages: A Way and Ways.* Rowley, MA: Newbury House Publishers.

Vygotsky, L.S. (1978) *Mind in Society: The Development of Higher Psychological Processes.* Cambridge, MA: Harvard University Press.

Epilogue: New Directions for Duoethnography in ELT

Luke Lawrence and Robert J. Lowe

Introduction

This book is intended to introduce duoethnography to the field of English language teaching as an approach to conducting research, engaging in professional reflection and as a potentially beneficial class project focused on dialogue and the sharing of personal experience. Due to the personally and contextually specific nature of duoethnography, the chapters presented here obviously cannot explore all of the potential areas of enquiry that researchers and teachers may wish to investigate using this method, nor have we yet discussed any serious limitations of the method that could be addressed by future work. As such, in this epilogue we hope to point towards some new and future directions for duoethnography in ELT. These new directions include potential research topics, different research contexts, new theoretical orientations and possible aspects of professional practice or experience that duoethnography could fruitfully be used to investigate. It is our hope that readers who have been inspired to engage in duoethnographic research or reflection of their own may find in this short discussion some possible directions for their own enquiry to take.

Limitations of Duoethnography: Process and Application

In this book, we have argued that duoethnography, as a method both of research and of engaging in reflective practice, has the potential to contribute greatly to our field. The chapters have, we hope, given strong support to this claim. However, this is not to say that duoethnography is beyond criticism, either in terms of the ways in which it is carried out, or of the fields in which it is applied. One concern that has been raised regarding the method is the way in which the dialogues are constructed. Indeed, this is a question that contributors of this book have run into when submitting duoethnographic work for peer review. While duoethnography is generally based on the collection of naturalistic data in the form of recorded conversations (either spoken or written), this data is usually presented as semi-fictionalised dialogues, in which the data is thematised and presented as a coherent whole. Concerns have been raised that this leaves the method open to potential manipulation of data, as researchers may tweak their statements to present a more favourable picture of themselves or their life history. This is particularly troublesome in cases when it is not stated clearly to the reader whether the dialogues are naturalistic or artificial. We believe that this is a valid criticism (though one that could perhaps also be made of other forms of qualitative research), and in recent work efforts have been made to minimise bias by introducing elements of triangulation and member checking to the process (see Lowe & Lawrence, 2018) that are used in more traditional ethnography to overcome this problem. Co-researchers must also take responsibility for ensuring that their partner is not biasing the dialogues as they are constructed. Connected to this are concerns around the ways in which data are selected for inclusion in the final study; there is little in the way of developed guidelines or criteria regarding this point. These are both important questions, and ones that must be considered carefully by researchers using the method.

Alongside this is the role that duoethnography has for wider research. As stated in Chapter 1, duoethnographic research serves the principle aim of deconstructing and problematizing grand narratives, as well as providing personal accounts illustrating the effects of larger, more structural phenomena. We believe that these are important and valuable contributions that duoethnography can make to research in ELT and applied linguistics. However, there is a danger that use of the method can become self-indulgent; serving more a therapeutic end for the researcher than providing useful insights for the field more broadly. This would not necessarily be negative in and of itself, but if we intend to produce serious work of wider interest to the field it is vital that researchers keep in mind the goals of their duoethnographic work, and guard against the method becoming an exercise in navel-gazing.

An additional aspect is the potential for unequal power hierarchies between researchers. Due to the fact that in duoethnography the participants are both researchers, there may be a tendency to assume that the power dynamics are more egalitarian than in traditional researcher/participant research. However, it should be borne in mind that unequal power relations also exist between researchers. This can affect the direction and content of the narratives, the selection process of relevant excerpts and the overall presentation of the final work. It is important for duoethnographers to acknowledge this unequal dynamic when it does occur and to make it explicit in the duoethnography itself (see Smart & Cook, this volume, for an example of this reflexivity).

These are challenges for practioners of the duoethnographic method to bear in mind, and to be aware of. However, such challenges also present opportunities, as they open the possibility that the method can be refined, developed and moulded in various ways so that it may become more robust, rigorous and acceptable to the wider academic community, while retaining its roots in the personal, the dialogic and the polyvocal.

New Directions

Theoretical orientations

As mentioned in Chapter 1 of this volume, duoethnography as a research method has been associated with a broadly postmodern approach to inquiry. This requires adopting a relativist position both in terms of ontology and epistemology – in other words, an assumption that not only is our understanding of social reality partially subjective, but that social reality itself is not an objective or measurable thing; that it is instead an understanding that is discursively and socially constructed. While we have found this approach to be very useful, particularly in the opportunities it affords for critical deconstruction of limiting grand narratives, we would like to suggest here that it is not necessary to adopt a postmodernist orientation in order to engage in duoethnographic research. Those who are more sympathetic to the idea of an objective grounding to reality may also be able to use duoethnography to their advantage.

Critical realism

Davies (2008) has argued that within ethnography, researchers can link positivist and interpretivist approaches to research through adopting a perspective known as critical realism. Critical realism is a philosophy associated with the work of Roy Bhaskar and assumes a realist ontology in which the existence of a social world outside our perception is granted, and a relativist epistemology in which it is accepted that our knowledge of the social world lies in a subjective interpretation of data (Collier, 1994). It can therefore be read as a form of weak constructionism which accepts that although the social world exists outside our perceptions, our accounts of that world are socially constructed (Elder-Vass, 2012). According to this view, qualitative study of the particular can tell us something about the universal, at least as far as that universal applies to the specific case in question. From a critical realist view, qualitative studies can point us towards mechanisms and tendencies in society, but only as they manifest in one historically, geographically and socially specified setting. As Davies (2008: 21–22) puts it, 'we can ask of ethnographic research that it provide explanations, but not strictly causal statements', arguing that critical realism 'promotes a creative tension between the empirical, the actual and the real' which forces ethnographic researchers to 'rework theoretical abstraction in the face of concrete experience'. With a format which is designed to foreground difference and juxtapose distinct life experiences, it seems that duoethnography is a research method to which critical realism could fruitfully be applied.

Under critical realism 'both human actors and social structure are accorded ontological reality' (Davies, 2008: 22) and so researchers working from this perspective assume that humans can interpret and build understandings of the social world and that these can affect the social world, but not that these make up the social world itself. Human agency and social structure can interact and be mutually influential, but they are separate entities. For ethnographers (and duoethnographers) this means that while we must be aware of our influence on society, objects and so on, we must not assume that our influence is the only or primary element in the creation of these objects and structure. In other words, we must be reflexive while maintaining a certain ontological humility.

On a practical level, for duoethnographers this may require a more thorough attention to the validity of recollection regarding personal experiences. Lowe and Lawrence (2018) adopted a broadly critical realist approach to their duoethnographic study of native-speakerism in ELT training by using elements of triangulation in their data collection. This included the collection of documentary evidence from their training courses, and the validation of their accounts by colleagues and fellow students. Duoethnography, while built on a broadly postmodern foundation, may be adopted by those from other theoretical orientations as well. Critical realism seems to be well placed as a philosophical foundation for future duoethnographic work.

Intersectionality

As outlined in the introduction chapter and mentioned above, and as exemplified by the nuance and complexity of the chapters, a key aspect of current duoethnographic theoretical underpinnings is a commitment to a poststructuralist, postmodern approach that recognises the diversity of experience and the context-bound discursive construction of identity. As an alternative to critical realism, another way to take this framework one step further would be for future duoethnographies in ELT to take intersectionality as a more explicit theoretical base (see Lawrence & Nagashima, 2019).

Within intersectionality, as with a poststructuralist framework, hierarchies of power dynamics are seen as the key element against which ALL facets of identity and experience are examined. The chapters in this book touch on a number of these aspects. In Chapter 2 Hooper, Oka and Yamazawa examined the complex and nuanced elements associated with 'native' and 'non-native' speaker status alongside how these categories are also intermingled with notions of race. Additionally, Nagashima and Hunter foregrounded their juxtaposed gender and sexual identities in order to examine how their identities and life histories contributed to their roles as critical language teachers. In Chapter 4 Pinner and Ushioda candidly examined the relationship between supervisor and student to provide a dissection of hierarchical power structures across time and (digital) space. Although, all of these took a broadly poststructuralist approach and at points there were allusions to critical points where two or more identity aspects intersected (for example Hooper, Oka and Yamazawa with linguistic status and race) these could not be considered to be truly intersectional.

Intersectionality is both a theoretical concept and an analytical framework that posits that 'when it comes to social inequality, people's lives and the organization of power in a given society are better understood as being shaped not by a single axis of social division, be it race or gender or class, but by many axes that work together and influence each other' (Collins & Bilge, 2016: 2). The term itself was coined by US civil rights lawyer Kimberlé Crenshaw (1989, 1991) in order to draw attention to the marginalisation of women in the antiracist movement and the marginalisation of black women in the feminist movement.

One example of how this can be applied to the ELT field is with regard to gender, race and the native-speakerism debate. It could be argued that the current debate in around native-speakerism has tended to treat all 'native' and 'non-native' English speakers as monolithic entities that fails to take into account the diversity of identities each individual contains. The result of this has been to push for equity and justice for some idealised 'non-native speaker' at the expense of other categories that an individual teacher may identify as, leading to the marginalisation of the most vulnerable, i.e. female 'non-native' speaker teachers from Outer Circle countries.

A research methodology such as duoethnography, in which 'two or more researchers of difference juxtapose their life histories to provide multiple understandings of the world' (Norris & Sawyer, 2012: 9) fits well with the stated aims of intersectionality that '(r)ather than downplaying or dismissing differences, an intersectional methodology requires *negotiating* differences that exist within discrete scholarly and political traditions of race, class, gender, sexuality, ability, nationality, ethnicity, colonialism, religion, and immigration' (Collins & Bilge, 2016: 168, italics in original). The dialogic nature of duoethnography provides just such a negotiating space for researchers to explore the complexity and nuance that an intersectional approach requires.

Research topics

As explained in Chapter 1 and exemplified by the chapters in Part 1 of this book, duoethnographic research generally focuses on critical issues; that is to say, issues in which power imbalances in society play an important role. Within ELT, these may include discrimination against so called 'non-native speaker' teachers, as well as issues of gender and race. While this book has explored some critical issues, there are many more topics which could fruitfully by explored through a duoethnographic lens.

For example, Block (2014: 19) notes that **social class** has been somewhat neglected in applied linguistics research and argues that its inclusion is long overdue as class is 'a key construct in discussions of inequality'. Block suggests that social class could be explored in terms of second language acquisition research, particularly from a sociocultural perspective in which second language identities (see Block, 2003, 2007) are a central topic. We further suggest that social class could also form a part of other research agendas such as attitudes towards teachers on the basis of their social class, and of any identifying linguistic markers that may be perceived as negative by students, employers, or coworkers. Through duoethnography, teachers and researchers could explore some of the ways in which social class has affected their lives within the profession, and lead us towards a more nuanced understanding of the ways in which different facets of our identity intermingle and influence our experiences as professionals within applied linguistics and ELT.

Political economy is another area which has recently begun to gain the attention of researchers. For example, a recent issue of the journal *Language Sciences* (Jones, 2018) was devoted to Marxist analysis and influence in applied linguistics (along with related fields such as semiotics and communication), and more scholars have recently been turning their attention to this topic (see Block, 2018). As a highly influential concept with an increasingly influential role in the world today, explorations of **neoliberalism** in ELT are long overdue. Block *et al.* (2012) discuss a number of topics related to neoliberalism in applied linguistics, focusing on issues such as the use of 'aspirational content' in language teaching textbooks, and the ways in which language teacher education has been 'marketized'. What is missing from these analyses, however, is a human lens through which to understand the influence of this neoliberal ideology. While these questions have been explored through some limited interview data (Gray, 2012) and ethnographic work (Gray & Block, 2012), these lack the emic perspective provided by a duoethnographic discussion of life history. For example, it would be valuable to see how the aspirational content of coursebooks impacts on teachers and learners in terms of their self-identity, their orientation to the language, and how their self-image may have been influenced by this content. Duoethnography would be a productive approach for researchers to take in exploring the ways in which neoliberalism has affected the field not only from a macro view, but also from a more personal perspective.

In addition to the critical issues outlined above, we believe there are some aspects of the teaching and learning process which could be explored through duoethnography, and which would not necessarily require a critical orientation to carry out. One example of such an issue is **motivation**, which is seen to be a key factor in the success of language learning. Recent work has attempted to explore motivation through autoethnographic research approaches (Pinner, 2019), and a duoethnographic tracing of life histories could be a valuable addition to the motivation literature, exploring how motivations change, and both increase and decrease in intensity. Recent work on motivational currents, that is, long-term periods of motivation that are superior to the student's regular motivational drive (Dörnyei *et al.*, 2016), has examined the ways in which periods of motivational focus may be structured and could be facilitated by teachers in the classroom. Duoethnography could be used to examine and retrace these currents in order to better understand and encourage them.

These are just three examples of topics which we believe could be explored through duoethnographic research. We do not claim that this is exhaustive, and we strongly suspect that readers will be able to think of more areas. However, these suggestions can be seen as starting points for further research, and areas that are potentially open to duoethnographic exploration.

Research contexts and purposes

In addition to research topics, use of duoethnography in a wide range of contexts, for a variety of purposes could be explored in further research. The flexible and evolving nature of the duoethnographic method means that it can easily be adapted to any context, by any type of researcher (or learner), for a number of purposes.

Until now, while the topics of research have been varied, duoethnographic research has stayed largely within the North American context. This volume expands on this somewhat by focusing on EFL in the Japanese educational context, although with the exception of Chapter 2 these are situated in the tertiary education sector. Further applied linguistics-focused research would benefit from expanding on this into other geographical and situational areas.

For instance, Kabel (2016) has called for a decentering of ELT and applied linguistics research away from the core inner circle of dominant Western countries. By doing so, he argues that perceived truths and authenticities that surround English and its teaching can start to be questioned and ultimately dismantled. By leveraging the lived experience of the researcher or learner, duoethnography could provide a platform to give voice to the voiceless that have hitherto been marginalised from wider ELT discourse or have had their experiences filtered through the gaze of Western researchers, rather than telling their own stories on their own terms and investigating the topics that matter to them.

Similarly, further research into different areas of education using duoethnography could also shine a light on less examined contexts. Mann and Walsh (2017) highlight the disconnect between teaching and research, lamenting that school teachers are often busy and lack the time or inclination (and sometimes the skills) to engage in academic research. At the same time, research that is often carried out in the name of teachers often bears little relevance to the needs and realities of the classroom. The accessible nature of the reconstructed dialogues and the intuitiveness of the narrative, conversational approach positions duoethnography as a useful methodology for primary and secondary school teachers to carry out research and to shift the emphasis of academia away from the university. Additionally, as shown by the investigation into native-speakerism in eikaiwa in Chapter 2, private language schools and other institutions that can often be closed to researchers, may also benefit as duoethnography is able to circumvent this problem by dint of the fact that the teachers that work there are the site of the research.

In this volume, duoethnography has been used to expose inequalities and investigate critical issues, as well as for reflective practice and as an aid to professional development. In terms of potential further research to attend to a wider variety of purposes, we would like to suggest three possibilities: as a problem-solving tool, as a means of intercultural communication, and as a tool of interdisciplinary research and integration.

Firstly, although duoethnographers often avoid direct conclusions (Sawyer & Norris, 2013), the commitment to challenging grand narratives and established truths position duoethnography as an ideal methodology for solving some of the current issues in applied linguistics and the ELT field. At the same time, the intimate and personal nature of duoethnography also make it a useful tool for solving small-scale context-derived day-to-day problems. For example, on the macro scale, issues such as those related to discrimination in the ELT industry such as gender, race, sexuality, class and native-speakerness may be served well by further research using duoethnography. By exposing these inequities by pairing researchers of juxtaposed positionalities, further research may help to go some way towards changing the discourse of acceptability to these major structural inequalities. In terms of micro-level problem-solving, as indicated in Section 2, by using duoethnography as a form of reflective practice teachers and researchers may be able to pinpoint particular issues that they want to address and engage in dialogue in order to explore them in detail and find solutions.

Secondly, and related to this, is the potential for use of duoethnography as a means of exploring intercultural communication. Intercultural communication has long been established as a site of education and research, although as Piller (2017: ix) notes, 'the main challenges of intercultural communication are the linguistic challenges of language learning, the discursive challenges of stereotyping, and the social challenges of inclusion and justice'. These are all aspects that we hope the contributions in this volume have gone some way towards investigating. Further exploration of these issues, especially with regard to new forms of communication, world Englishes and cultural identities could be potential sites of further research for duoethnographers.

Finally, as related methodological frameworks such as Linguistic Ethnography (Copland & Creese , 2015) that also employ a poststructuralist approach and a commitment to micro/macro, emic/etic discourse move towards a fully interdisciplinary approach (Snell *et al.*, 2015), a possible future direction for duoethnography may also be to reach out across fields in order to pair up researchers of different expertise and interests in order to address larger global issues that affect all of us, regardless of language, nationality, race, gender, class or status.

Reflection and professional practice

As well as being a method of research, Part 2 of this book provided three examples of the ways in which duoethnography could be used as an approach to reflective practice in ELT, highlighting how life histories influenced both the understandings of teachers towards their students, and their relationships with each other.

The three chapters presented earlier explored some key issues for teachers, however they clearly do not represent every issue a teacher may face (which given the differences in working contexts, professional situations and personal relationships, could potentially be infinite). As such, there is a great scope for the use of duoethnography as a form of reflective practice between **teachers and other teachers** as a way of exploring their personal relationships, their orientations towards their subjects and their beliefs about teaching and learning (see Nagashima & Lawrence, 2019).

In addition, duoethnography could further be used to explore professional relationships which have not been touched on in this book. One area which might benefit from this kind of dialogic exploration might be the relationships between **teachers and administrators**. The different roles, concerns and priorities between these groups makes it likely that duoethnographic interaction would lead to more mutual understanding and a reduction of the kinds of stress and unease that can arise when these different concerns come into conflict.

Finally, the duoethnographic process could be used as a way of exploring the classroom experiences of **teachers and students** together. While this differs somewhat from usual approaches to reflective practice, in that the student acts as an active and critical participant in the process, it could lead to valuable insights that can only be accessed through allowing the voices of the teacher and student to meet on an equal footing. In some contexts (for example, elementary schools) this could pose both ethical and practical difficulties, and many teachers may be uncomfortable in engaging with their students in this way due to the effect it would have on the teacher/student dynamic. However, for those who attempt this kind of dialogue, important insights could arise concerning how both the teacher and the students view the lesson content, the efficacy of materials and teaching approaches, and the management of the classroom.

Conclusion

We hope that the ideas presented in this short epilogue will point the way forward for those considering using duoethnography as either part of their research, their professional reflection, or even in their classroom teaching. More broadly, it is our hope that this book has highlighted and demonstrated some of the strengths that duoethnography could bring to the field of English language teaching, and applied linguistics more broadly. In a field such as ELT, which is spread over the entire world, and in which collaboration and international cooperation plays such a central role, the importance of dialogue cannot be understated. We believe that duoethnography can contribute to three major and ongoing forms of dialogue in ELT. First, the method itself can facilitate dialogue between professionals and researchers working in ELT, who may gain valuable knowledge and insights from engaging with each other using this methodology. Secondly, the accessible nature of duoethnography has the potential for opening up the often arcane and rarefied world of academic discourse to the wider teaching community, creating a channel for dialogue between teachers and researchers, the lack of which has often been lamented. Finally, the personal reflections and findings that emerge from duoethnographic interaction can contribute to the ongoing dialogues surrounding critical issues in the field of ELT. It can also help professionals find their place within these discussions and add their voice to these important and evolving debates.

References

Block, D. (2003) *The Social Turn in Second Language Acquisition*. Washington, DC: Georgetown University Press.

Block, D. (2007) *Second Language Identities*. London: Bloomsbury Academic. https://doi.org/10.5040/9781474212342

Block, D. (2014) *Social Class in Applied Linguistics*. London; New York: Routledge.

Block, D. (2018) *Political Economy and Sociolinguistics: Neoliberalism, Inequality and Social Class*. London: Bloomsbury Academic.

Block, D., Gray, J. and Holborow, M. (2012) *Neoliberalism and Applied Linguistics*. London; New York: Routledge.

Collier, A. (1994) *Critical Realism: An Introduction to Roy Bhaskar's Philosophy*. London: Verso.

Collins, P.H. and Bilge, S. (2016) *Intersectionality*. Cambridge: Polity Press.

Copland, F. and Creese, A. (2015) *Linguistic Ethnography: Collecting, Analysing and Presenting Data*. Los Angeles: SAGE.

Crenshaw, K. (1989) Demarginalizing the intersection of race and sex: A black feminist critique of antidiscrimination doctrine, feminist theory and antiracist politics. *University of Chicago Legal Forum 1989* (1), 139–167.

Crenshaw, K. (1991) Mapping the margins: Intersectionality, identity politics, and violent against women of color. *Stanford Law Review* 43 (6), 1241–1299. doi: 10.2307/1229039

Davies, C.A. (2008) *Reflexive Ethnography: A Guide for Researching Selves and Others* (2nd edn). London: Routledge.

Dörnyei, Z., Henry, A. and Muir, C. (2016) *Motivational Currents in Language Learning: Frameworks for Focused Interventions*. New York; London: Routledge.

Elder-Vass, D. (2012) *The Reality of Social Construction*. Cambridge: Cambridge University Press.

Gray, J. (2012) Neoliberalism, celebrity and 'aspirational content' in English langauge teaching textbooks for the global market. In D. Block, J. Gray and M. Holborow (eds) *Neoliberlaism and Applied Linguistics* (pp. 86–113). London: Routledge.

Gray, J. and Block, D. (2012) The marketisation of langauge teacher education and neoliberlism: Characteristics, consequences, and future prospects. In D. Block, J. Gray and M. Holborow (eds) *Neoliberalism and Applied Linguistics* (pp. 114–153). London: Routledge.

Jones, P. (ed.) (2018) Karl Marx and the language sciences – critical encounters. *Special Issue: Language Sciences* 70, 1–204.

Kabel, A. (2016) Afterword: Decentring the Hydra: Towards a more equitable linguistic order. In P. Bunce, R. Phillipson, V. Rapatahana and R. Tupas (eds) *Why English? Confronting the Hydra* (pp. 269–284). Bristol: Multilingual Matters.

Lawrence, L. and Nagashima, Y. (2019) The intersectionality of gender, sexuality, ace and native-speakerness: Investigating ELT teacher identity through duoethnography. *Journal of Language, Identity & Education*.

Lowe, R.J. and Lawrence, L. (2018) Native-speakerism and 'hidden curricula' in ELT: A duoethnography. *Journal of Language and Discrimination* 2 (2), 162–187.

Mann, S. and Walsh, S. (2017) *Reflective Practice in English Language Teaching: Research-based Principles and Practices*. New York: Routledge.

Nagashima, Y. and Lawrence, L. (2019) Reflective practice through duoethnography. *Pan Sig Journal 2018*, 167–173.

Norris, J. and Sawyer, R. (2012) Toward a dialogic methodology. In J. Norris, R. Sawyer and D.E. Lund (eds) *Duoethnography: Dialogic Methods for Social, Health, and Educational Research*. (pp. 9–40). Walnut Creek, CA: Left Coast Press.

Piller, I. (2017) *Intercultural Communication: A Critical Introduction* (2nd edn). Edinburgh: Edinburgh University Press.

Pinner, R.S. (2019) *Social Authentication and Teacher–Student Motivational Synergy: A Narrative of Language Teaching*. London: Routledge.

Sawyer, R.D. and Norris, J. (2013) *Duoethnography*. New York: Oxford University Press.

Snell, J., Shaw, S. and Copland, F. (eds) (2015) *Linguistic Ethnography: Interdisciplinary Explorations*. Houndmills: Palgrave Macmillan.

Index